FIFTY YEARS OF ASSOCIATION WORK AMONG YOUNG WOMEN

1866—1916

A History of Young Women's Christian Associations in the United States of America

BY
ELIZABETH WILSON
Executive of the Secretarial Department
of the National Board

National Board
of the Young Women's Christian Associations
of the United States of America
600 Lexington Avenue
New York

DEDICATED

TO THE WOMEN AND GIRLS WHO IN ANY PLACE
AND IN ANY TIME HAVE COMBINED THEIR
EFFORTS TO BRING IN THE KINGDOM
OF GOD AMONG YOUNG WOMEN

PREFACE

The purpose of this historical account is to show why and how Young Women's Christian Associations came into being and to indicate that the first half century is but the beginning of the movement.

In order to represent the conditions which called out certain features, the language of old reports, circulars, addresses and correspondence has been freely used; while there has been a wealth of these original sources, in some instances it is undated, or annual and biennial reports have not stated the calendar month or year in which a measure was passed or new ventures undertaken. Some of the attempts to determine these dates through comparison of material will probably prove faulty. I wish to thank all the friends who have assisted in collecting and comparing data and who have described historic work in which they had a part.

It has been impossible to mention as many individual Associations as might have been desired. Emphasis has been laid on the recognition of unusual needs and the invention of successful means of meeting them and upon the development of phases of work rather than upon the consecutive events in given localities.

ELIZABETH WILSON.

New York City, 1916.

TABLE OF CONTENTS

PART I—BEFORE 1866

PRELIMINARY ORGANIZATIONS IN GREAT BRITAIN AND AMERICA

CHAPTER PAGE

I INTRODUCTION 3

Status of young women in the United States before the Christian Association. Their work in relation to the home. Higher education.

II UNITED PRAYER IN THE UNITED KINGDOM . . 7

George Williams and the Association idea (1844). Miss Robarts and other early members (1855). Prayer Union Branches (1859). First use of the name Young Women's Christian Association.

III AN OPEN DOOR IN LONDON 13

Women's occupations in Great Britain (1851). The Knight of Womanhood, Lord Shaftesbury. The Nurses' Home. The Honorable Mrs. Kinnaird and the North London Home (1855). The Pall Mall Institute (1861).

IV FEDERATION LOOKING TOWARD THE FUTURE . . 19

The Prayer Union and the Home and Institute Branch united (1877). The United Central Council (1884) leading to founding of the World's Association (1894).

V THE BEGINNINGS IN AMERICA 22

The American Revival of Religion in 1857–58. Mrs. Marshall O. Roberts and the New York ladies (1858). The first factory meeting. The first boarding home (1860).

CONTENTS

PART II—1866 TO 1906

LOCAL AND NATIONAL ORGANIZATIONS IN THE UNITED STATES

LOCAL

CHAPTER PAGE

VI THE FIRST YOUNG WOMEN'S CHRISTIAN ASSOCIATION IN AMERICA 29

Two attempts in Boston. Organization (1866). Rooms. The Beach Street and Warrenton Street buildings. Pioneer departments —Cooking, Physical Education, Traveler's Aid.

VII OTHER PIONEER CITY ASSOCIATIONS 50

Women's Christian Associations in Hartford, Providence, Pittsburg, and Allegheny (1867); Cincinnati, Cleveland, St. Louis (1868). Nine others in 1870 and 1871. Varieties of interests.

VIII THE YOUNG WOMEN'S CITY ORGANIZATIONS . . 57

Origin. Nature of membership. Influences of student Associations. St. Joseph, Scranton, Kansas City, Minneapolis, Toledo.

IX CITY DEVELOPMENT AND STANDARDIZATION . . 64

Rise of departments and phases of work: religious meetings, Bible classes, workers' training classes, religious work directors; lunch rooms and cafeterias; social features, clubs; libraries, educational classes, sewing, cooking, nursing, physical education; Traveler's Aid; industrial extension; administration buildings.

X THE ORIGIN OF STUDENT ASSOCIATIONS . . . 108

Middle West co-educational colleges. Spontaneous student Associations (1873–1880). Women members of college Young Men's Christian Associations. Student Christian Association, University of Michigan (1858), Young Men's Christian Association, University of Virginia (1858). Men's Intercollegiate Movement, Princeton (1877). Mr. Wishard and

CONTENTS

CHAPTER PAGE

the student Young Women's Christian Association. Appeal to the Women's Christian Association conference. Segregation. Formation of State Associations (1884).

XI THE INTENSIVE GROWTH OF STUDENT ASSOCIATIONS 138

Membership, social features, religious meetings, Bible study. The Student Volunteer Movement for Foreign Missions. The World's Student Christian Federation. Community service. Equipment. Secretaries.

XII COUNTRY ASSOCIATIONS 153

Pleasant Valley township, Johnson County, Iowa (1884). Small towns in western states. County organizations in Minnesota (1898).

NATIONAL

XIII THE CONFERENCES OF THE WOMEN'S CHRISTIAN ASSOCIATIONS 159

First national meeting at Hartford (1871). International meeting at Pittsburg (1875). Constitution, scope of work, programs, etc.

XIV THE NATIONAL ASSOCIATION—LATER THE AMERICAN COMMITTEE 167

Reasons for organization. Establishment of headquarters (1886). Summer conferences. World's and foreign work. Secretarial training.

XV THE INTERNATIONAL BOARD OF WOMEN'S AND YOUNG WOMEN'S CHRISTIAN ASSOCIATIONS . 196

Outgrowth of the International Conference (1891). Explanation of name. World's Columbian Exposition. Other expositions. Traveler's Aid. Chautauqua and Monteagle headquarters. "The International Messenger" and "The Bulletin."

XVI THE JOINT COMMITTEE PREPARING THE WAY FOR ONE NATIONAL MOVEMENT 206

Miss Grace H. Dodge. The Manhattan Conference of 1905. Decision to attempt union.

CONTENTS

CHAPTER PAGE

International Board Conference and American Committee special convention. Applications for charter membership. Organization Convention and election of National Board (December, 1906).

PART III—1906 TO 1916

THE YOUNG WOMEN'S CHRISTIAN ASSOCIATIONS OF THE UNITED STATES OF AMERICA

XVII THE PRESENT NATIONAL MOVEMENT 233

Adoption of policies. Development of departments: Office; Publication; Field Work; Finance; Conventions and Conferences; Secretarial Training; Home and Foreign. St. Paul Convention (1909). Adoption of constitution. The Portland definition of evangelical churches. The Federal Council of Churches.

XVIII THE YOUNG WOMEN OF THE CHRISTIAN ASSOCIATIONS 260

Zirkus Busch gathering at Berlin World's Conference (1910). Emphasis on membership at Indianapolis (1911) and Richmond Convention (1913). National Headquarters. San Francisco Exposition.

XIX THE STUDENTS 269

State universities and other groups. The Studio Club; Central Club for Nurses. Negro and Indian students. Student activities, religious campaigns, voluntary Bible study, social service, student initiative and cooperation. North American Student Council. Commission on Restatement of Basis. World's Student Christian Federation Conference, Lake Mohonk (1913). Student Volunteer Movement Convention, Kansas City (1913).

XX THE CITY GIRLS 281

Membership, not buildings. Forms of cooperation. Building campaigns. Community

CONTENTS

CHAPTER PAGE

service. Activities inside and outside the building. Summer programs.

XXI The Girls in Industry 289

Statement of field. Industrial clubs and Associations. Federations of industrial clubs. Club Councils at conferences and camps.

XXII The Country Girls 292

County Associations in Illinois and elsewhere. Eight Week Clubs. The county summer conference.

XXIII The Young Girls 297

First branches; their laggard development. Study of adolescence. Camp Fire Girls' Council.

XXIV The Strangers Within Our Gates . . . 300

English classes for foreigners. International Institutes.

XXV Girls in Other Countries 303

Recapitulation of openings in India. American work in China and Japan, South America and Turkey. Foreign students in the United States. American secretaries abroad. Contrasts in World's Conferences (1898–1914).

XXVI The Secretaries 316

Origin of name. Scope and remuneration of office. Association of Employed Officers. System of training.

XXVII A Prophet Among Women 326

Miss Dodge as president. Her colleagues and successors.

XXVIII Mottoes and Spirit 330

Zech. iv, 6—Prayer Union, American Committee, World's Committee. Gal. v, 13—British Associates, International Board. John iv, 10 —Young Women's Christian Associations of the United States of America.

Appendix 335

LIST OF ILLUSTRATIONS

OPPOSITE PAGE

Emma Robarts, Founder of the Prayer Union Branch in Great Britain 10

Lady Kinnaird, Founder of the Home and Institute Branch in Great Britain 16

Mrs. Marshall O. Roberts, first directress of the Ladies' Christian Association, New York City 22

Congregational House, where the Boston Association first had rooms 32

Sewing Class in New York City Association, 1889 . . . 106

Founders of the first Student Association 116

Ruth Rouse, when representing the Student Volunteer Movement 148

Women's Christian Association, Hartford, Conn. First building constructed for Association purposes . . 160

Facsimile of autographs of delegates who formed the "National Association," August, 1886 172

Mrs. John V. Farwell, first president of the National Association (later The American Committee) 174

Annie M. Reynolds, while visiting Russia as World's Secretary 182

Morse Hall, Headquarters and Hostel of the Association of Lahore, India 188

Secretaries and Students, Secretaries' Training Institute, Winter Term, 1904 194

South Church, New York City, where present national movement was formed 226

LIST OF ILLUSTRATIONS

OPPOSITE PAGE

The Auditorium, Asilomar Conference Grounds, California 248

Michi Kawai, Secretary of the National Committee of Japan 262

Delegates to the Fourth Biennial Convention, Richmond, Virginia, 1913 264

Headquarters Building of the National Board of the Young Women's Christian Associations 266

Young Women's Christian Association, St. Louis, Mo. Modern type of administration building 282

Mary A. Clark Memorial Home, Los Angeles, California . 284

Eastern City Conference, Silver Bay, New York, 1915 . . 288

First County Conference, Conference Point, Lake Geneva, Wisconsin 294

Ying Mei Chun, directing gymnastic drill in Shanghai, China 308

Clarissa H. Spencer, General Secretary of the World's Committee 314

Mabel Cratty, General Secretary of the National Board . 322

Class of 1915, National Training School 324

Letter sent by Miss Dodge to all the National Board staff 326

PART I. BEFORE 1866

PRELIMINARY ORGANIZATIONS IN GREAT BRITAIN AND AMERICA

FIFTY YEARS OF ASSOCIATION WORK AMONG YOUNG WOMEN

CHAPTER I

INTRODUCTION

FIFTY years ago woman's work was in the home. And such faculty for organization had the mistress of the home that she could order the tasks of each season and of each day of the week, could assign suitable duties to the elder and younger daughters, and teach them the varied processes until they became in turn as proficient as she.

Up to the middle of the nineteenth century the three chief occupations for women, "gainful occupations" they were termed, in spite of the meager remuneration for each, were: domestic service, where an American born girl helped in another person's home; teaching school, where the teacher boarded around from house to house in many country districts; and sewing, where the seamstress usually came to the house of her employer for a longer or shorter time, or in the case of well to do families was a regular member of the household staff.

Even outside employments such as working in cotton mills were under a semi-domestic régime. The corporations owned boarding houses for the women operatives, and established in each a matron, usually a widow with daughters in the mill. There was little financial risk in conducting this sort of an establishment, for the mill corporation deducted the weekly board rate from the wages of each employee and paid the amount directly to the landlady. Such was the position held by Lucy Larcom's mother in Lowell, which fact accounted for the eleven year old child going into the mill.

The hours of labor ran, or dragged, from five in the morning to seven in the evening, which tallied with domestic rather than business working time. The very church attendance was likewise regulated in paternal fashion, for the mill directors charged up "pew rent" to each employee, under their system of paying wages partly in commodities.

Millwork dovetailed also into the public school system, because in those early years, teaching was for many mill hands a "by employment" for the few months in the year when "school kept."

When the weaving and spinning went out of the house, and the weavers and spinners followed on into the mills, there was still a link between factory and home in the hand processes of manufacture carried on in the family living rooms. There is an economic basis of fact as well as poetic fancy in the verses containing, "Hannah's at the window binding shoes."

If the situation in the first half of the nineteenth century, with few girls away from home, and a limited range of occupations open to women, did not seem such as to require what we are pleased to call Association work in cities, neither were women college students feeling the need of voluntary religious organizations. Most of the seminaries and colleges to which women were admitted were built on Christian foundations by the prayers and labors and sacrifices of godly men and women, and consecrated to the "Christian nurture of youth." Such was Mt. Holyoke Seminary, where Mary Lyon saw visions come true from 1837 to 1849. Such was Oberlin Collegiate Institute, later College, where the influence of Charles G. Finney was felt from 1835 to 1875. Here in 1841 three young ladies graduated from the regular four years' college course, "the first young women in the country to receive a degree in the arts."

The personal piety of such students and their missionary service here or abroad after graduation, were accepted as a matter of course, by those who arranged the curriculum, prescribed the use of week days and Sundays and rejoiced that the students received inspiration as well as training to carry out the college ideals.

Women had not yet learned to work together in a large way. They were achieving, but by acting as individual forces, not as social elements. Like Lucy Larcom, Harriet Beecher Stowe and Louisa May Alcott, they were writing; like Maria White Lowell they were stirring others to write; or like Ann Greene Phillips they were heartening others to efforts on behalf of oppressed humanity. Women came together within parish circles, for ladies' prayer meetings and "Dorcas

Societies'' which made coats and garments and did other good works and alms deeds, but these were almost entirely local activities. Even the ''Female Cent'' societies did not burgeon into any general foreign missionary society until 1861, when the Women's Union Missionary Society of America for Heathen Lands came into being.

What changed these conditions? Many things; among them stand out three totally unlike factors: the invention of the sewing machine in 1846; the great revival of 1857–1858; and the Civil War, from 1861 to 1865.

CHAPTER II

UNITED PRAYER IN THE UNITED KINGDOM

IN England the early Victorian situation was not unlike that in America at this same time. Some noted achievements there were, due to the fact of the long established civilization, but on the other hand some social delays were occasioned by the conservatism of that very same settled order of things. There is, thereby, all the more credit to those who had faith enough to regard these mountains as removable, wisdom enough to know where to begin, and grace enough to associate themselves with many others in accomplishing their original purpose or that larger purpose that is sure to develop when like-minded people cooperate.

One such pioneer was George Williams, who came up to London from the provinces in the fall of 1841. That was a noteworthy year in religious history, for the Oxford Movement was at its height; but the young draper's assistant found his religious reading not in the polemic pamphlets of the Tractarian leaders, but in two of Charles G. Finney's books, "Letters to Professing Christians," and "Lectures on Revivals." His place of employment, Hitchcock and Rogers, in St. Paul's Churchyard, was of the usual type of "living in'' drapery establishments, with dormitories on the top floor for assistants and apprentices. These young fellows worked off what spirits were left after their day of fourteen to seventeen hours behind the counter, in a way that left much to be desired. None of George Williams' five roommates professed himself a Christian, but we are told that there was a Christian fellow in the adjoining inner bedroom who had only four roommates, whom he got to leave so that the two like-minded souls might have a place of prayer. Soon others joined them; they read together the Finney books, many were converted, larger rooms were used. Then they interested the head of the firm, who provided a chaplain to conduct daily prayers. Life at Hitchcock and Rogers was changed. Young men in other shops also put these ideas into operation. Finally, or to speak more correctly, as a beginning of the story, on June 6, 1844, twelve young men from four different church connections formed a Young Men's Christian Association with religious and social features, rented rooms, and engaged a salaried organizing secretary and missionary to administer and extend the work.

This was the origin of the Association idea, that is, young men and young women uniting from different Christian churches for higher all-round development and service and using both religious and secular means therefor. The new movement was so timely and its emphasis so distinct that leading clergy and laymen gave their assistance.

His biographer found among George Williams'

papers a circular formulating a scheme for a Young Ladies' Christian Association which seems to have been sent out by him in the '40s. But the time for such an appeal to be listened to was not yet come. In the next decade the Crimean War set in motion waves which permanently affected the thought and the work of British womenkind—girls, young women, ladies, and ladies of title, in country and in city, down in the provinces and up in London.

Barnet stands in English history as a battle field in the Wars of the Roses; in Association history it appears as the residence of the Robarts and the Pennefather families. Rev. William Pennefather, vicar of Christ Church, known as the founder of the Interdenominational Christian Conference and the Mildmay deaconess house and many similar institutions, had been given spiritual charge of hundreds of the orphans of the Crimean War, who had been gathered together by the Patriotic Fund workers; and Mrs. Pennefather was deeply interested in them also. The Robarts family included five unmarried sisters, devoted to works of charity and education. Besides the infant school which their father had built and placed under trustees the daughters supported a school for girls held on their own estate. Many years before Tennyson had said, through King Arthur, "more things are wrought by prayer than the world dreams of," Emma Robarts, the youngest sister, was roused by such a realization of the vast possibilities of prayer, that she asked some of her friends in 1855 to pray on Saturday evenings for young women, either for those in their own circle or for young women as a class. "What can we do for them," she wrote, "how reach and act on them, scattered as they are in every sphere of life? Look at the young women of our day and remember their number, their present and future influence. Look at the several divisions of the class:

1. Our Princesses and all who are in the glitter of fashionable life
2. Daughters at home of the middle classes
3. Young wives and mothers
4. Governesses in families and teachers in Day and Sunday Schools
5. Shop women, Dressmakers, Milliners and Seamstresses
6. Domestic Servants
7. Factory Girls
8. Young Women in our Unions, Hospitals, and Reformatories, the Criminal and the Fallen
9. Those who are enchained by Judaism, Popery and heathenism

"What can be done for them? What means can be used to win their souls to Christ?" As her friends, assenting to this request, sent in their names, she copied these in a list.

Heading the first list of twenty-three names in this Prayer Union is that of Mrs. Horatius Bonar of Kelso, Scotland. Each member notes her religious activities and Mrs. Bonar's record is, "District and workhouse visiting; class of girls on Monday at 5 P. M. for Scripture Instruction; Maternal meeting every fortnight; meeting in another district for Mothers every alternate Tuesday at 3." Seven other Scotch names follow, then Mrs. Pennefather's and Miss Robarts' own

Miss Emma Robarts,
Founder of the Prayer Union Branch in Great Britain

names. Their reports credit Mrs. Pennefather with "Parish and workhouse visiting, Superintendence of Patriotic Orphan Homes, and of Homes in connection with Society for the Rescue of Young Women, Scripture Class every Thursday for young ladies," and show Miss Robarts' work to be, "Sunday morning class of servants and dressmakers, Intercourse and correspondence with former scholars." Several of the early members lived in Ireland. A Bradford, England, member reports a class of "adult factory girls." Classes for "apprentices," "grown girls," "shop girls," "milk girls," appear. George Müller's daughter belonged, and Frances Ridley Havergal, who wrote the Young Women's Christian Association hymn, "True Hearted, Whole Hearted."

"In the course of 1859 the first Branch was formed," wrote Miss Robarts; "a band of Christian girls uniting in the name of Jesus for their mutual benefit, and for that of any young women in their respective spheres whom they might be enabled to influence for good." These members were largely girls of leisure and education who wanted to become more efficient workers for God. Miss Robarts also explained in the same circular that "the title of Young Women's Christian Association was assumed simply as the feminine of Young Men's," which had already become known to many of the same friends. The local units, however, were called Branches, not Young Women's Christian Associations. That term was usually reserved for the membership as a whole and the usage is steadily adhered to by many British ladies, among them Miss Lucy M. Moor, the friend of Miss Robarts and Mrs. Pennefather and the historian of the British movement.

CHAPTER III

AN OPEN DOOR IN LONDON

MISS ROBARTS' classification of young women was no doubt made more from observation than from statistics. However, the British census of 1851 reported 3,000,000 young women in Great Britain (excluding Ireland) engaged in industrial occupations; of this number 500,000 were wives helping their husbands either behind the counter, at the desk, or in manufacturing processes.

The 39,139 nurses in domestic service largely outnumbered nurses in hospitals and on cases, but the age of those nurses—half of them were from five to twenty years old—helps us to understand that Tilly Slowboy was as true to life as Sairey Gamp or Betsey Prig, who have come to the front as the representative English nurses of that period. As to the living-in system which prevailed for young women shop assistants as well as for youths, it was probably a survival from the time when one extra pair of hands was called in to help the shop keeper, of whose family the owner of the pair of hands then became a part. But the family idea had long since been abandoned. The girl shop assistants spent most of every week-day waking hour in the shop itself. Recesses for meals were of the shortest and even on Sunday the girls were not allowed to stay in their own rooms.

That knight of womanhood, who has been called the most spiritual Christian of his age, Antony Ashley Cooper, later the seventh Earl of Shaftesbury, had spoken with alarm a few years before of the displacement of male by the substitution of female labor in industrial occupations at large. Although he had led Parliament to put a stop to the degrading colliery practices where women and girls crawled through dangerous passages, harnessed like beasts of burden, dragging after them heavily loaded carts, yet women were still laboring in fields and factories.

Young girls in dressmaking and millinery trades were working from fifteen to eighteen hours per day. There is no hint at this time of those occupations in business houses which were certainly lighter, but which were monopolized by men. In 1854 telegraph clerkships were first opened to women, in 1870 the post office used a mixed staff in its clearing house branch.

Only one occupation was genteel enough to engage the well born young woman whose need to earn her bread was sometimes as severe as that of a girl in the lower classes. She might be a governess in a home. For this as for the other gainful occupations no professional preparation was required, and what she made of the position depended entirely upon her own personality and the character of the family where she lived.

Ladies as well as hired nurses went out to the Crimean hospitals under the leadership of Florence

Nightingale, that gentlewoman trained in the best institutions of Europe.

The Honorable Mrs. Arthur Kinnaird, so says her biographer, "cooperated with Viscountess Strangford and Miss Nightingale in sending out nurses." Various institutions were recruiting places, among them a home in Fitzroy Square, London, where nurses might board and prepare for sailing.

But the Crimean War had still another effect upon the woman's movement. The Fitzroy Square home suggested to Mrs. Kinnaird a more permanent effort for the benefit of all girls coming up to London from the provinces.

To no avail does one search for minutes of a meeting where a resolution was passed to establish a Young Women's Christian Association. "Ladies did not do much with making and seconding motions. They had a cup of tea together, talked about things, prayed over them and then did what seemed best," explained Lady Kinnaird's daughter, the Hon. Emily Kinnaird, upon whose shoulders her mother's mantle rests. "You could hardly say when it was organized." But sometime during the year 1855 the decision was reached to enlarge the scope of the Home, and in January of 1856, the Hon. Arthur Kinnaird sent out a circular saying that he had taken over the responsibility of the late "Nurses Home," although "as nurses will benefit by it equally with other classes, we are still in a condition to carry out the design of the Nurses Association." By implication one learns that Mrs. Kinnaird was the head of this enterprise, but according to the English custom that where gentlemen are contributing funds to women's societies they also administer those funds, the name of the Hon. Arthur Kinnaird is signed as treasurer, with his address and that of his bankers.

So the work was begun. During the first year there entered the home for longer or shorter periods thirty-nine persons classified as follows:

21 Governesses, Matrons, etc.
2 School mistresses
3 Matrons of Emigrant ships
9 Nurses from the East
2 Foreigners
1 Young Person in Training for a school mistress
1 Lady in Distress

There was a lady superintendent in residence, but as her services were gratuitous she could hardly be called the first employed officer.

Neither had the name Young Women's Christian Association been officially assumed, for the circular called the place "North London Home, Late Nurses Home, or General Female Home and Training Institution."

However, the main departments of an Association were already outlined. Besides the boarding home there was an employment bureau for "Matrons, Protestant Bonnes, etc." Intellectual needs were recognized and partly supplied through the lending library. Social features were combined with the religious activities; tea was always served in the friendly hour which followed the Sunday afternoon Bible class; there was an afternoon missionary meeting each month; and the lady superintendent was at home every Tuesday and

Lady Kinnaird,
Founder of the Home and Institute Branch in Great Britain

Friday evening to young women from any part of London.

These departments were emphasized by organizing in the Home a Young Women's Christian Improvement Association in 1858, when the second superintendent, a nurse returned from the East, came into contact with the girls in business houses who needed a "Sunday Home" and opportunities for recreation, instruction, and Christian companionship. By 1861 there were four homes: one offered full board and lodging for five shillings a week; two were serving the double purpose of residence and general headquarters. Next came (1861) the Institute at 118 Pall Mall, the first experiment of opening rooms for offices and class rooms independent of any residence. Mr. Kinnaird in a public address made the following distinctions:

> In what we simply call an Institute no young persons are boarded and lodged. It would be utterly impossible to provide more than a few homes, however valuable these are, and when established they of course are involving household cares, so that a resident superintendent in a Home must, like a lady in a private household, have less time for aggressive missionary work than the superintendent of an Institute, who has comparatively speaking no home cares and very few household duties involving her energy. The moral machinery, which is the sole machinery of an Institute, is applicable to every part of the metropolis as well as to country towns and to districts where facilities for lodging may not be needed. And we also think that some friends who might shrink from the responsibility of starting new homes might more readily be induced to start Institutes, when the work would solely consist in the loving and patient endeavor to gain access to the hearts of those whom the Association is designed to win. (Cheers.)

People who complain of the length of the name Young Women's Christian Association may care to know that the general circular sent out in 1861 showed the title "United Association for the Christian and Domestic Improvement of Young Women." The religious and philanthropic leaders of the day appeared on this directorate, headed by the Earl of Shaftesbury, President.

It was now a metropolitan movement. "While there are a few leading ideas emanating from the centre, giving harmony to the work, there is a great deal of practical diversity in the way of carrying it on!" But a larger federation was ahead.

CHAPTER IV

FEDERATION LOOKING TOWARD THE FUTURE

IN several parts of England the leaders of the Prayer Union branches had been thinking of "a sort of outer circle, or an organization for reaching and keeping an influence over girls not eligible for the Prayer Union." Some of these leaders were interested in the developments which led to the founding of the Girls' Friendly Society in 1875, and thought about an organic connection of the two societies, abandoning the plan, however, because of the Interdenominational basis of the one, and the Church of England basis of the other. The leader of the London Prayer Union branch was also identified with Mrs. Kinnaird's rapidly expanding work, and since Mrs. Kinnaird was projecting a prayer union in connection with that it seemed reasonable to amalgamate the two.

The secretary thus relates the action:—"One day, quite unexpectedly, Mrs. Kinnaird called at 19A (Young Women's Christian Association Prayer Union Office at 19A Great Portland Street, London, West) and Miss Robarts and she met for the first time. They settled the name and the card then, and the union of the two Associations in London was effected." This was in January, 1877. In May Miss Robarts died, having willed to Mrs. Pennefather the presidency of the Prayer Unions, which numbered beside the forty-eight branches in London, about fifty elsewhere in England, sixteen in Scotland, twenty in Ireland, with some form of contact also with the continent of Europe and British possessions in America, Asia and Australia. Perhaps 12,000 members in all were enrolled.

Not only had the Prayer Unions increased, but many Homes and Institutes all over England had spontaneously sprung up, as Birmingham (1860), Bristol (1861), Liverpool (1864), Manchester (1866), etc., etc., so that when reorganization was at hand its outlines naturally became, a London division with Mrs. Kinnaird as vice-president, and a country and foreign division with Mrs. Pennefather as vice-president. The Earl of Shaftesbury, who had been president of the Pall Mall Institute, was of course elected president. His autograph letter of acceptance is on file.

St. Gile's House, Cranborne,
Salisbury.

Dear Mrs. Kinnaird:

My services to the Single Association are so small that they will be nothing to the Double one. Nevertheless, if you desire me as President I will accept the honourable office, and give what time I can when you summon me to its services.

I urged a similar Institute the other day on the good ladies of Glasgow. They have a Society for young women, but it is a very "wee" insignificant thing.

Yours truly,
(Signed) SHAFTESBURY.

November 1, 1877.

This combination provided definitely for country and foreign branches. The nearness of Great Britain to the continent, the familiar acquaintance of English women with foreign people and languages, and the Christian responsibility felt for British colonists by the wives of civil and military officials, led on to the Foreign and Continental Division and the Extra European and Colonial Division when the United Central Council was formed in 1884, and this was the germ from which the present World's Young Women's Christian Association developed. Invitations to the April, 1892, meeting of this United Central Council were sent to America, asking representatives skilled in national administration to attend and remain to form, if the time were ripe, a World's Young Women's Christian Association. Further, when in 1894 preliminaries had been arranged and Great Britain, the United States of America, Norway and Sweden had united as the active members of a World's Association, the chairman of the British Foreign and Continental Division, Mrs. J. Herbert Tritton, was made president.

CHAPTER V

THE BEGINNINGS IN AMERICA

EVERY great revival of religion has certain features which distinguish it from similar manifestations upon other occasions. The historic American revival of 1857–1858 showed three outstanding characteristics: the number and value of prayer circles; the unity of Christians of different denominations; and the large place filled by women as leaders of organized Christian forces.

Doctor Nathan Bangs, writing a series of articles in the phraseology of the day, declared that the help of the "pious female" should not be spurned. One of the famous union prayer circles of that winter in New York City was led in the Church of the Puritans on the corner of Union Square and 15th Street by a member of the Broadway Tabernacle, a young woman of splendid intellect, personal charm and fervent religious life, Mrs. Marshall O. Roberts.

The Young Men's Christian Association, organized half a dozen years before, had maintained remarkable meetings in the Reformed Church on Fulton and William Streets, and the Methodist Episcopal Church on John Street, and hence it was not strange for the women connected with this ladies' prayer meeting to

Mrs. Marshall O. Roberts,
First Directress of the Ladies' Christian Association,
New York City

contemplate an organization with aims and methods somewhat akin to those of the men.

Accordingly, a meeting was called in the chapel of the New York University on November 24, 1858, and a Ladies' Christian Association was formed with thirty-five charter members, who elected Mrs. Roberts as "first directress." The first constitution, printed in a tiny booklet four by five inches in dimensions, is of historic interest.

> We, the undersigned, believing that increase of social virtues, elevation of character, intellectual excellence and the spread of Evangelical Religion can be best accomplished by associated effort, do hereby adopt for our mutual government the following:
>
> CONSTITUTION
>
> Any lady who is in a good standing of an Evangelical church, may become an active member by paying one dollar annually in advance.
>
> Any lady not a communicant may become an associate member—except voting and holding office.
>
> DUTIES OF MEMBERS
>
> They shall seek out especially young women of the operative class, aid them in procuring employment and in obtaining suitable boarding places, furnish them with proper reading matter, establish Bible classes and meetings for religious exercises at such times and places as shall be most convenient for them during the week, secure their attendance at places of public worship on the Sabbath, surround them with Christian influences and use all practicable means for the increase of true piety in themselves and others.

One can but notice that the next year after the members had been conducting meetings in churches, homes, mission chapels, and elsewhere as well as assembling in their general Association prayer service, they amended part of this preamble to read, "fully impressed with the belief that their own personal piety may be greatly promoted by associated effort, and that greater influence can thereby be brought to bear upon many of their own sex in this city (who are without those means of social and religious education enjoyed by them)." They had recognized that their first duty was "to be" before they assumed the responsibility "to do," and the Spirit of God opened their eyes to some unusual opportunities for the service they were prepared to render. New York City led in the printing trades and clothing manufactures and there were sufficiently large forces of young women employed by some of these establishments to attract the attention of the Ladies' Christian Association as a field for their efforts. Their 1860 report speaks of religious services for the one hundred women employed in the Tract House, and the five hundred women employees in a skirt factory. A later report sustains the conjecture that this was a hoop skirt factory. A casual observer of that decade would have been surprised if any one had said that the hoop skirt and its manufacture would soon become laughably out of date, but that the fashion of religious services among young women in mills and factories would become universally prevalent. This innovation of the New York ladies antedated by a dozen years any other recorded effort of systematic extension of the Christian Association into young women's work places at the noon hour.

All this may have been more or less inconspicuous, but their next venture brought them into great prominence. The Rev. Heman Dyer had been asked to find a comfortable, safe boarding place for a young woman from out of town. She was, it is said, a minister's daughter who wanted to study for self support and could not afford the prices charged by respectable families and boarding houses. Dr. Dyer reported this to the new Association and added, "Now ladies, here is your work; open such a Home for such young girls." They had no precedent, but they had faith. So they hired a house at 21 Amity Place for $850 a year rental and opened it on June 1, 1860. Twenty-one found their way into the family the first year; for the most part students of wood-engraving, drawing and painting in the School of Design for Women, and teachers and needlewomen. Other homes in other localities were later rented and properties purchased. This required incorporation, which took place in 1866 under the name Ladies' Christian Union, but the aim of the members and their double devotion to their Wednesday prayer meeting and to the Christian welfare of young women did not vary. Mrs. Roberts' enlistment of young girls of leisure in this enterprise finds place in a later chapter.

PART II. 1866 TO 1906

LOCAL AND NATIONAL ORGANIZATIONS IN THE UNITED STATES

CHAPTER VI

THE FIRST YOUNG WOMEN'S CHRISTIAN ASSOCIATION IN AMERICA

"CANNOT something be done by benevolent ladies that shall remain a permanent institution?" This was the question asked by Mrs. Lucretia Boyd, a city missionary of Boston, depressed by the deplorable state of things existing among the self supporting girls whom she met. Her regular duties took her from house to house, from street to street, month after month, and she knew that many young women were rooming and boarding themselves in the attics of lodging houses where the better rooms of the lower stories were occupied by young men. Few made a part of any pleasant social circle, but were either lonely and discouraged or ready for chance acquaintance at railroad stations, on the street or in places of worldliness and folly. Some of these girls had been religiously educated and had sufficient inherent strength to resist the downward tendencies of city life, but others were unconscious of their own danger. Young women were continually coming from all parts of New England and the Maritime provinces to earn their living in Boston, but there was no agency offering protection or advice to them as strangers.

When ill they were neglected, when out of work they were helpless. Mrs. Boyd set in order the facts made up from her diary entries of several years, and roused the interest of some of the leading Christian women. She received a hearing at the Boston City Missionary Society as she outlined the plan of a Young Women's Christian Association, and it looked as if the desired permanent institution were to be compassed in 1859.

One of the women, Mrs. Edwin Lamson of the Park Street Church, discussed the plans with her pastor. He thought the women could not do all this alone, and that the men would not help in the undertaking, yet he presented the matter to the ministers' meeting. His brethren evidently saw eye to eye with him, for they decided that it would be hazardous for the ladies to undertake such a scheme, and seemed to believe that in advising them against it they were kindly preventing them from making a failure. Nonplussed, the women saw no way to go ahead in establishing a Christian organization in opposition to the leaders of Christian affairs, and action was indefinitely postponed.

This unfavorable response from the clergy was all the more unexpected because they had been most active a few years before in forming the local Young Men's Christian Association, although a sea captain, Thomas V. Sullivan, was the real moving spirit. He had read in his denominational paper, *The Watchman and Reflector,* an account of the London Young Men's Christian Association written by an American theological student visiting London and reporting upon this novel organization, "where there is no turning a crank, no doing good by proxy, a society which asks for sympathy, prayers and active cooperation, which asks for men, young men, nothing more.'' Captain Sullivan is said to have visited the London Association, to have become as enthusiastic as the previous American visitor and to have lost no time in imparting his knowledge and enthusiasm to the young men in his own home city. They advised with their pastors and Boston organized on December 29, 1851, the first Young Men's Christian Association in the United States. They afterwards heard that Montreal, Canada had taken the same step some weeks before. Within a year, 1,200 men had joined and the first quarters had been outgrown.

Only one conclusion can be drawn from this unhappy attempt at interdenominational work for girls, namely, that the pastors knew the needs of the young men of the community much better than the needs of the young women. They probably had not realized that young women were entering the business world to such an extent that the reasons for ''the combination of effective religious appeal with a humanitarian social-service emphasis upon a better environment for the tempted young man'' were becoming valid also in the case of young women. This realization came a little later when some one said, ''The considerations that have led to the formation of a Young Men's Christian Association apply, if possible, with increasing force in the case of young women, who from their position and sex are more unprotected and more helpless.'' And the next time the call for the young women of Boston was sounded, it was heard and heeded.

Another city missionary had become aroused to the interest of orphaned, homeless and otherwise unprotected girls. There was thought of establishing a home for young women who came to the city in search of instruction or employment, but that particular feature was postponed and decision made "to organize on the plan of the Young Men's Christian Association." On March 3, 1866, thirty ladies met at the home of Mrs. Henry F. Durant in Mt. Vernon Street and adopted a constitution under the name of the Boston Young Women's Christian Association.

Its object was "the temporal, moral and religious welfare of young women who are dependent on their own exertions for support."

Its basis of membership was that "Any Christian woman who is a member in regular standing of an Evangelical Church may become an active member of this Association by the payment of one dollar annually."

Its duty, as carried into effect by the board of managers, was "to seek out young women taking up their residences in Boston, endeavor to bring them under moral and religious influences, by aiding them in the selection of suitable boarding places and employment, by introducing them to the members and privileges of this Association, securing their attendance at some place of worship on the Sabbath, and by every means in their power surrounding them with Christian associates. It shall be their duty also to exert them-

Congregational House,
Where the Boston Association First had Rooms
(By permission)

selves to interest the churches to which they respectively belong in the objects and welfare of the Association, and to use all practicable means for increasing its membership, activity and usefulness.'' The hostess of that day, Mrs. Durant, was unanimously elected president.

The new society had a name. It was soon to find a local habitation. Two rooms were secured in the Congregational building at 23 Chauncey Street; these were comfortably furnished by the generosity of friends and were opened in May. The reading room was particularly large and airy, and with papers and magazines, a few books and a loaned piano, it was a cheerful place to which to ask young women. The general secretary, Mary Foster, with her attractive personality and lovable disposition, was a wise counsellor to the many girls who came in complaining of low wages or no work or loneliness in the city, and at each weekly meeting of the board of managers she was able to bring to the members opportunities for the personal service they had enlisted to do. Miss Foster advised about getting positions and homes. In six months she had found boarding places for fifty girls. Light drinks and luncheons were served in the rooms, which were open day and evening except Sunday. Although ''such healthful recreation as might be offered'' was provided, yet the chief social resource seemed to have been that of finding a ready listener accessible at all times, ''A heart at leisure from itself, to soothe and sympathize.''

During the first year a singing class was started as

well as the Bible class and the Thursday prayer meeting. Another of the dreams of the projectors came true in that the Good Samaritan Hospital offered free care to members who might be ill.

So seriously did the managers accept their self imposed obligation that they sent a circular letter to the pastors of country churches that first season, relating how the duty of extending sympathy and protection to young working women in Boston had been recognized, and how they stood ready to fulfill all the terms of their constitution. An embarrassment of riches followed. More applications for rooms and board resulted than they could satisfy with the places they were able to recommend.

By this time the sentiment for a Home was unanimous, and a second circular was issued calling for financial help, which was the means of securing the two houses at 25 and 27 Beach Street. When alterations and furnishings were completed at a cost of about $40,000 the property was dedicated on February 19, 1868. On the list of subscribers to this fund is the name of Professor Henry W. Longfellow.

Here were found lodgings for eighty, and immediately questions of eligibility arose which were decided as follows:

> In admitting young women to the privilege of the Home, the managers feel that they are called upon to discriminate in favor of the younger class of applicants and of those who do not receive large compensations. It is obvious that these classes need the aid, protection and sympathy of such an Institution. Those who are older, and whose principles are more firmly established, can better take care of themselves

elsewhere. A few such as are intelligent and truly religious belonging to this class will be especially welcome on account of their influence upon their associates at the Home. As the Institution is not designed to be a reformatory, no one will be admitted whose references in regard to character are not perfectly satisfactory.

A list of the occupations followed by members of the Beach Street family a few years later suggests rather accurately, no doubt, the openings for self supporting women of that day, though the fact that the record was made shortly after the great Boston fire may affect somewhat the classification as given:

Seamstresses	114
Clerks in Stores	27
Compositors	7
Machine workers	7
Milliners	10
Bookfolders	6
Vest makers	5
Book keepers	4
Tailoresses	2
Copyists	2
Cap makers	2
Teachers	2
Artists	2
Telegraph operators	1
Students of Music	2
Students of Book-keeping, Drawing and Elocution	10
Blind Girls	2
	205

If the family had diversified occupations by day they were at night a homogeneous group as far as age was concerned, for few more than twenty-five years old were received, and suitable homelike customs could be maintained. The ten o'clock closing hour pleased one New Hampshire mother. "I have been so glad," she wrote, "that such a restraint was about my child living in your city; I could wish you closed even earlier."

The evenings at home offered much that was pleasant to do. Besides what had been begun in Chauncey Street there were classes in Astronomy, Botany, Physiology, Penmanship, and Bookkeeping. The library was constantly enjoyed in spite of its regretted deficiency in books of poetry, and there were two home evenings each week aside from the special times of "social amusement during the hours of leisure."

A provision for associate membership among any young women of good moral character, and the fact that the dining room of the house was conducted on the restaurant plan, meant that many young women in addition to the lodgers in the home had a part in the Association. Many more wished to take advantage of the employment bureau who were practically unassistable. It may be that no such word is found as yet in the dictionaries, but the condition it describes is familiar to even amateurs in social organizations. At a time when Boston was credited with 20,828 needlewomen the annual report records the "need of competent dressmakers, seamstresses, machine workers, and capable nurses," the feasibility of "a department of instruction in these branches of employment for young women that require time and experience in preparation for them," and a desire to "open and maintain a Training School."

Not only because Boston was the first city in America to use the name Young Women's Christian Association does this history go into details that cannot be repeated in other instances, but also because from the first it has had a rather symmetrical development, not emphasizing one department inordinately above another. It also originated many lines of work which have been adopted into the whole movement, its basis has been one which guarantees its purpose in spite of changing personnel of working force, it has adhered to formative instead of reformative measures and it has been of large service to other Young Women's Christian Associations and other betterment agencies by training women for their administrative and teaching staffs. It has still another distinction—it was the field in which Charlotte V. Drinkwater poured out unstintingly thirty-two years of service. Hers was a leadership so unselfish one wonders how it could be efficient, but so efficient one realizes it must have been unselfish.

When the city wished to widen Beach Street and offered the Association a reasonable sum for its property, the managers decided to plan and erect a new building. Although the Hartford Women's Christian Association, whose organization had been inspired by Boston, had in October, 1872, entered its new home, the first in the country to be constructed for such a purpose, yet the Boston Association undertook as its own original problem to devise a structure so appropriate to the needs of girls that they should find in it a typical Christian home after the New England pattern. One means of raising the $120,000 needed for the new property was a mammoth ten days' fair at which $38,000 was cleared; this included the sale of a piano for $850, of a valuable India shawl and other expensive articles, since the memory of the great Sanitary Commission Fairs of Civil War days still lingered with the public. Further funds were raised by subscription, and on October 14, 1874, the new Warrenton Street Home opened its doors for two hundred residents, who could secure board at the family table, and room, light, heat and personal laundry for $3.00 up to $5.50 a week. An adjoining house on Carver Street was purchased at the time for the employment bureau. Nothing could be further desired as to physical equipment, but the person to make it serve the young women was yet to seek.

Mrs. Edwin Lamson of the Boston Association Board of Managers was also a trustee of the Lancaster Girls' Industrial School, where Miss Drinkwater had been as teacher and matron for six years and had been developing among the girls heretofore untried plans. With the invitation which the Boston board extended to her to become superintendent of the building came these carte blanche instructions: "Build it up by your own originality; no one can tell you how to do it, and the men's prophecy of women's failure must not be fulfilled." Accordingly when Miss Drinkwater arrived on the first of April, 1875, she began to take account of stock and discovered amid the bills payable a coal bill for $500. When she went down to lead the sixty-six boarders in their evening devotions, she began to learn the next secret, that the thirty or more girls who had come in from Beach Street were truly loyal to the Association, but the others seemed to consider their presence there as a favor. She soon put the pieces of the puzzle together; an unpaid bill for coal resulted in sparing use of it, a cold house, and an all-round chilly atmosphere. While the loyal members endured this discomfort as manfully as possible the others frowned, murmured and complained incessantly. The janitor when ordered to put on more steam said that the boiler would burst if the pressure ran above seventy pounds, and he would not go beyond that. On his next day out the new superintendent called in the steam fitter who had installed the heating system, learned every detail of it and kept her own counsel. Soon there came a wretchedly cold, stormy day when she knew the girls would be coming home drenched and dismal. She called the janitor to her office, told him to make a grate fire in the company back parlor, and put on seventy-eight pounds of steam. "But seventy is all the boiler will stand." "You may put on seventy-eight and I will be responsible for the consequences." The house began to warm up. As Miss Drinkwater saw the girls returning, she opened the basement street door, saying, "Come in here and lay off your wet wraps, and then after supper come down to the back parlor." Adverse sentiment began to melt. Soon the girls told others in their places of business that the Warrenton Street Home was a good place to live in, and by the May board meeting the number had risen from sixty-six to ninety-one.

But summer was ahead, with probably a more difficult situation as to vacant rooms. The residents and staff wrote letters to friends all about, extolling the merits of this new building and asking that they and their friends come and see them in town at one dollar a day. "The few newcomers who ventured to test our accommodations were reckoned as so many trophies for the cause, and we spared neither time nor strength in entertaining them." This summer campaign was as effective as the original letter to the New England ministers in 1866, for when fall came on the house was filled with the girls for whom it had been put up. In fact, some fastidious young persons who had announced that they "didn't like the street" and "didn't want to be considered objects of charity" now competed with each other for rooms for the coming year. Convention delegates and other transient guests poured in and were glad to obtain cots for the nights, or even to get bedrooms outside and come in to join the family in parlors and dining room.

Yet there was something more than good management which was making that home a success: "sanctified common sense," the owner of this quality called it, common sense evidenced by care in assigning the one or two roommates so that the necessary companionship would be enjoyable and beneficial; delicacy in gaining and retaining the confidence of members of the family; alertness in anticipating and gratifying wishes; resourcefulness in providing home amusements; cordiality in inviting young men friends to the house; tact in promoting voluntary literary, social and religious organizations in the home; and dependence upon the Spirit of God for daily wisdom in reaching and elevating the soul, which was the primary object of her work.

Out of the employment bureau and its perplexing problems rose much of the strongest future work. Again and again had the demand for good household helpers overwhelmed the secretary, who saw only a meager number of women for whom the Association could conscientiously vouch among the crowd awaiting positions. Some who might have been efficient, were not, because of personal discrepancies; some could not take places, some would not take them, others took them but did not keep them. Again and again the question of a training school for domestic service, or a kindred institution, was before the managers. Finally, a little later, a house next door was rented for a bureau of instruction, with a boarding department and arrangements for girls of sixteen years or more to secure a three to six months' course in all domestic branches, including sewing and laundry work. As the plan progressed it seemed wise to grant compensation to students after a certain duration of residence, and as the course included some study of English subjects as well as religious instruction the graduates went out with a good economic and moral preparation for a calling in which the demand was unabating.

In 1879 were held, three times weekly, cooking classes taught by Madame Favier and attended by women of leisure, or any who wished domestic instruction but could not come into the three months' residence required in the domestic training school, of which some six or eight were taking advantage. But the most interesting development of this cooking régime was that a donor—a man, as might be reasonably expected—offered a course of twelve lessons in cookery to a class from the public schools, and Mr. Swan, head master of the Winthrop School, sent twelve girls from the senior class, who finished their studies with a May Day Exhibit, in 1880, and with enough general satisfaction so that this course was followed the next season by another taught by Mrs. Webb, a graduate of Miss Parloa's normal class. This was experimental work in a double sense, as the subject had not before been taught in the Boston schools. The combination of boarding house and bureau of instruction was favorable to the training school class, but the other students hoped for a place distinct from that where meals were being prepared. All of this was due in good season.

Then too, the employment bureau, while dealing exclusively with domestic occupations, could not be of much help to the steady stream of young women whose strength or aptitude fitted them better for other duties, and for these some systematic effort must be made. One day three Canadian sisters, all wearing mourning, came in asking advice as to how to begin making their way in the world. The eldest had applied for a position at the post office, thinking that would be congenial and remunerative. She learned that there were no vacancies and already several thousand applications on file. Upon the superintendent's advice the elder began the study of bookkeeping, the second entered nurse's training and the youngest worked for her board in the home and went to public school. This incident of girls unfitted for anything, searching everywhere for a chance to earn their bread, determined the opening of a Business Register, which ever afterwards sought places for girls, as the domestic employment bureau continued to seek girls for places. With this registry the Mercantile School, as the business classes were termed, and other educational departments closely cooperated. Dr. Edward O. Otis inaugurated a course of Emergency Lectures in 1883 which were so popular as to be immediately repeated.

On December 8, 1884, the new building at 40 Berkeley Street was dedicated. It contained the training school and other educational departments, and the employment bureau, assembly hall, offices of administration, parlors, and reading room, large dining room and sleeping rooms for one hundred and fifty-six residents. On the fifth floor was the Durant gymnasium, the first to be incorporated into a Young Women's Christian Association building. Physical education as now conducted was the outgrowth of a class in calisthenics taught by one of the boarders in 1877, of athletics in the park in 1882, and of a few simple exercises originally prepared for the residents in the Warrenton Street Home, with a few chest weights on closet doors and in the corners of hallways as apparatus, in 1882. That same year free instruction was offered a class from the Association in Miss Allen's famous gymnasium. The board of managers had heartily accepted and made the uniform suits required, and the superintendent accompanied the class during the first season. The first teacher in the Durant gymnasium was Anna Wood of the Wellesley College gymnasium faculty.

The calls for domestic help kept growing louder. Sometimes Miss Drinkwater would count twenty housekeepers looking for maids where she could see one girl whom she could recommend, with almost any price put upon her services. She knew there were girls coming into the city who needed the very kind of work in homes here offered and who needed still more the protection and advantages of other departments in the Association. So one April morning in 1887, Miss Drinkwater rose at five o'clock and walked to one of the docks. An old wharf hand stopped his sweeping to hold speech with her. "Every steamer brings girls who don't know where to look for work. Well, well, am I not glad to know that the women of Boston have awakened to the needs of these girls!" The way opened later to have one secretary give her time to meeting steamers and following up the various and unfolding needs of the young women who came. In July, 1887, Miss M. E. Blodgett of Mt. Holyoke College, a girlhood friend of Miss Drinkwater, assumed this new position. Girls who were helpless because they could not speak English, learned how to talk and act and think like Americans. Circulars and newspapers carried the address of this unusual "Intelligence Office" into German and Scandinavian communities of both continents, and strangers began to look it up on arrival. As the Young Traveler's Aid

Association of Boston had already begun to be of use in the same way, so far as receiving travelers was concerned, a meeting was held to divide the territory. This society remained in charge of the railroad stations and the Boston Young Women's Christian Association of the docks, where boats from Atlantic coast states and provinces and transatlantic ocean steamers landed hundreds of women passengers on a day. In the first three months Miss Blodgett was able to serve five hundred and eight girls through channels within and without the Association.

Every year there was a keener desire for a school of domestic economy and industrial arts, or, as some one termed it, "a college for mental, spiritual and physical culture." This should train girls in housewifery as a ladylike accomplishment, as a means of self support in families or institutions, or as a profession in training others in schools or missions. Mrs. Ellen H. Richards of the Massachusetts Institute of Technology and a personal friend of the superintendent advised on the prospectus which Miss Drinkwater drew up before it was presented to the managers for adoption. "It's all right," she said, "but what you have put into this curriculum requires five years." The impossibility of a one year course attaining the end was sure; to keep students five years was equally impossible, so a compromise was made on a two years' course.

Though the board of managers was somewhat appalled, Mrs. Durant, the president, whose name is known in academic circles in connection with the founding of Wellesley College, believed in it, and in the fall of 1888 the school opened with a month of public demonstration lectures by Mrs. Emma P. Ewing of Purdue University. Instruction in domestic economy covered cooking and general household management, purchase and care of family supplies, home sanitation, home dressmaking, home millinery and economical selection of wearing material. Instruction in industrial arts embraced industrial drawing, clay modeling, carpentry for household needs, wood carving and light upholstery.

The experimental kitchen was a model of its kind, for it was a large airy room fitted up as a laboratory with individual equipment for each student and with charts, a food museum, and other teaching appliances. The regular classes met here day and evening for cooking lessons, the normal class secured their advance instruction here and twice a week, the twenty girls in the Training School for Domestics were taught here.

Among the teachers and lecturers in Domestic Science in various years have been Miss Emily Huntington, Mrs. Mary A. Lincoln and Miss Anna Barrows. The Normal pupils were resident and paid inclusive charges from October to June as in any girls' school for general culture.

Of course religious education was not overlooked and presently from the original Bible classes there developed an evening Bible school with prescribed courses leading to examinations. On Saturday evenings, the Rev. James M. Gray of the Gordon Training School, which at that time had no evening classes, offered a

Synthetic Study of the Bible. On Tuesdays there was Bible Geography and History by Miss Lucinda J. Gregg, and on Thursdays Bible Interpretation by the Rev. J. M. Orrock. Naturally this led to a department for Christian workers as a part of the Normal Training School and the whole was formally termed "School of Domestic Science and Christian Workers." Nor was it strange that Miss Drinkwater, who was in constant demand for preparing papers and other program duties for Association conventions, should be considered the natural head for a department of Association Organization. This she gave in two months' courses for five years (1897 to 1901 inclusive), and from the forty or more students there went out some devoted and capable secretaries to Women's and Young Women's Christian Associations throughout the country.

Thus for thirty-three years of nearly continuous labors Miss Drinkwater's mind, might, soul and body strove for young women, her neighbors in the gospel sense. After the presentation of the secular departments upon one occasion, the question was asked her, "What is the Boston Young Women's Christian Association doing in the line of religious work?" This answer was given: "Soul winning and Christian character building through a score of means." These were cited in a paper read at the International Board Conference in 1893.

1. Personal efforts of directors and resident officials to bring strangers under moral and religious influence.
2. By aiding them in the selection of suitable boarding places, and by friendly visits and relief in trouble.

3. By securing their attendance at some place of worship on the Sabbath.
4. By introducing them to Sabbath School and Church Socials and surrounding them as far as possible with Christian associates.
5. By a free distribution of printed cards of invitation to religious services held in the Berkeley Street building, also by tracts and leaflets.
6. By meeting girls at the wharves who arrive as strangers on our shores and ministering to their bodily and spiritual needs.
7. By daily family worship in each of the Homes.
8. By weekly home prayer-meetings and Sabbath morning devotions conducted by Christian young women of the Home. Bible classes for all.
9. By object teaching in Bible study through models, charts, maps and blackboard work.
10. By practical application of the truth to individuals.
11. By personal appeals to the unconverted.
12. By letters of transfer from one Association to another.
13. By loans and gifts of money to poor but worthy girls, temporarily ill or out of work, or otherwise in special need.
14. By aiding ambitious girls to an education with the hope that their talents will be consecrated to God's service.
15. By the aid and influence of Christian teachers in Schools and Class Department.
16. By equipping young women with a systematic course of Bible Study and Scientific Homemaking, and sending them out as Missionaries, Teachers, Young Women's Christian Association Secretaries, Pastors' Assistants and organizers of different kinds of religious works throughout the country.
17. By practical training in all forms of Mission Work under the leadership of a Christian worker, in Girls' Clubs, Free Kitchen Gardens and Industrial Classes conducted and sustained by the Association.
18. By teaching young women the proper relation of body to mind and spirit and their personal responsibility to God in its care and development.

19. By placing the unskilled under religious influences while being trained in some branch of industry.
20. By teaching the ignorant to read, and furnishing them with Bibles.
21. By warning the willful of danger and pointing them to Christ.
22. By letters of sympathy and counsel to the absent.
23. By private seasons of prayer with inquirers.
24. By the truth of God unfolded to doubters and skeptics.

By the above means the entire work of the Boston Young Women's Christian Association is permeated with general religious instruction.

CHAPTER VII

OTHER PIONEER CITY ASSOCIATIONS

WHEN these two groups of Christian women in New York and Boston who had organized on behalf of self supporting girls were augmented in June, 1867, by a similar society in Hartford, Connecticut, a third title had been introduced, Women's Christian Association, but the aim, "improving the welfare of self supporting young women," the active membership within Evangelical churches, and the duties of managers, were almost identical with those of the two Associations previously established.

This was not strange. The first president, Mrs. Charles B. Smith, in a reminiscent anniversary address forty years later, told how her husband's niece, Mrs. Marshall O. Roberts of New York City, had spoken at the Ladies' Union prayer meeting in the Pearl Street Church of Hartford upon the text, "The Master is come and calleth for thee," in the winter of 1867. The recently organized Young Men's Christian Association of Hartford, the knowledge of what Mrs. Roberts was doing in New York City, and correspondence with Mrs. Durant, president of the one-year-old Boston Association, helped the ladies of the Hartford prayer band in deciding whether to undertake preventive or reformatory work. "Each was a great work, but they must be separate, and in our infancy we could undertake but one." When the preventive policy had won the day and a home for self supporting girls was in prospect Mrs. Isabella Beecher Hooker, one of the leaders, remarked, "I'm going to lobby to be matron of that home."

But they did not wait for that home. A few hundred dollars was raised to lease rooms in a business block on Asylum Street from which the landlord who lived near by really received more than his rent, for he said he delighted to sit and listen to the singing of the girls at the rooms. That very autumn a lady subscribed $1,000 for the nucleus of a building fund. To this, the first organization of ladies in the city, much help came from the clergy and well known occasional speakers, such as H. Clay Trumbull and D. L. Moody and the famous "Singing Evangelist," Philip Phillips.

Reckoning exactly, the Women's Christian Association of Providence, Rhode Island, antedated Hartford by about six weeks, but the deliberations of the managers as to reformatory *versus* preventive measures ended in a compromise, and the home which was opened in Providence on July 23, 1867, combined the two features. But the experiment proved the undesirability of the arrangement, a separation was made and a new constitution adopted so that the Association might really in its present form be said to date from March, 1868. Other cities organizing Women's

Christian Associations in the years immediately following covered both these branches and other forms of institutional work. In this connection it has been said,

> While many of the Associations at their origin took the work of the Young Men's Christian Associations as a type for their own, it was soon found out that the requirements for successful work among women were much more varied than for men. In the newer communities where few charitable societies existed the Associations must embrace and sometimes confine themselves to fields of labor already filled by societies in older cities. Thus the charge often made, that "the Young Women's Christian Associations and Women's Christian Associations embrace all sorts of things," appears on the surface to have truth, but underneath all the variety lies the one common purpose, never lost sight of by any Association, to do all things possible for the elevation of women physically, mentally, morally and spiritually.

To the establishment of a third Young Women's Christian Association in Pittsburgh, which dates from 1867, the productive religious sentiment of that decade also contributes, as is seen by the following extract from one of its reports:

> During the session of a Christian Convention under the direction of Rev. Mr. D. L. Moody and the Young Men's Christian Association, when the spirit of God, invoked by the presence and prayer of these lovers of God and their fellow men seemed present in power, a request was made to Rev. Mr. Moody that he would tell of the wonderful work of the women of London for their own sex, and so instruct the women of Pittsburgh and Allegheny that they too might lend a helping hand to the destitute and suffering and save the tempted.

He addressed a large meeting of interested men and

women, who were anxious for this new departure for the cause of God and humanity, and thus on the spot a Women's Christian Association was organized and $1,640 subscribed as an initial offering.

So powerful was this impulse that in 1875, when Pittsburgh entertained the Third International Conference of Women's Christian Associations, reports were submitted from ten distinct branches in order of their date of organization,—the Temporary Home for Destitute Women, Home for Aged Protestant Women, Boarding Home for Working Women, Sheltering Arms, Women's Foreign Union Missionary Society, Gilmore Mission, Bible Reader's Mission, Ladies' Depository and Employment Office, Hospital Committee and the Young Women's Christian Association of East Liberty.

Westward the star of empire continued and in 1868 two Women's Christian Associations were formed in Ohio, Cincinnati, and Cleveland. Of the former Mrs. John Davis, its first president, said, "The instrument under God in the formation of this Association was a member of the Young Men's Christian Association of Cincinnati who saw the need and suggested the work. This young man, now a missionary in China, has the satisfaction of knowing we are reaping a rich harvest from the small seed he planted." The first result for girls was the opening of a home in March, 1869. "They have a well ordered, contented household with a good table, neat rooms, and a general compliance with rules. But the work of the Association is not limited to the care of young women at the Home.

They have organized a city missionary work, visiting in the hospitals, county jail, city prison for women, house of refuge, work house, etc., seeking to cheer and encourage a class so much neglected, to lead better lives." Public sentiment was so strong in Cleveland that the old hall at the corner of Superior and Seneca Streets, then the home of the Cleveland Young Men's Christian Association, was crowded to its utmost capacity at the initial meeting. "Almost immediately a Missionary Committee was formed, the city was redistricted and a certain definite tract assigned for visitation to each patronizing church." The next year they secured property and opened a boarding home in November, 1869.

And still further to the west St. Louis women had been saying, "There should be a place of safety in this great western city for young women thrown upon their own resources for maintenance." A vacant building had appealed to them as particularly available for such a home, and they had even fixed upon a clergyman and his wife to be its proper guardians. Presently the way opened, as is recorded in the first report. In November, 1868, Mr. H. Thane Miller of Cincinnati, who was in attendance at a Christian convention in St. Louis, invited the ladies of that city together that he might urge upon them the necessity of Christian labor among and for their own sex. This call was responded to by seventy-five or more ladies, among them many earnest Christian workers with the inquiry in their hearts, "Lord, what wilt thou have me to do?"

His earnest appeals for sympathy, for counsel, for aid, for a Christian Home for Women, made more forcible, if possible, by a recital of incidents that had fallen under his own observation, entranced the audience and led them to feel that his lips were touched with pentecostal fire and his soul clothed with poetry as with a garment attuned to the very essence of holy song. Could this be lost, his zeal, his song, which might be said "to animate the dead and move the lips of poets cast in lead"! Let the sequel tell.

The sequel was the organization of the Women's Christian Association of St. Louis, which within four months had leased, furnished and opened a boarding home.

Under a still further variety of circumstances did the other pioneer city Associations come into being. Mrs. Marshall O. Roberts, first directress of the Ladies' Christian Union of New York City, invited a company of young women of leisure to meet at her home at 107 Fifth Avenue on February 10, 1870, where they formed a Young Ladies' Branch of this Union which next year became the Young Ladies' Christian Association of the City of New York, and in 1876 changed the title to Young Women's Christian Association. Utica also dates from 1870, and Philadelphia, which "received its first call and inspiration from Mr. Miller, who addressed Christian women on 'Women's Work for Her Own Sex,' " also Washington, D. C., Dayton, and Buffalo. In 1871 Newark, New Jersey, Germantown, Pennsylvania, and Springfield, Massachusetts, wheeled into line. Some eight or ten other cities were listed up to this time as carrying on work which either lapsed shortly afterwards, or became absorbed in other general movements where the features they had been emphasizing rightly belonged.

Because of the variety of purpose and method indicated above, it was natural that the constitutions of the later pioneers varied more than did the three first formulated. In a number "any woman upon the payment of the membership fee" might become an active member.

Almost every one of the pioneer Associations started some work which later became a prominent independent philanthropy or charity in the city. Examples of this are the Woman's Exchanges for sale of women's handwork which the Women's Christian Association of Cincinnati, St. Louis and many other cities evolved and put upon a paying basis before they were independently maintained. The Board of Associated Charities in Cincinnati and many other relief organizations elsewhere had their rise in a Women's Christian Association. For eleven years the Young Ladies' Branch of the Women's Christian Association of Cleveland developed work for children, until in 1893, the Day Nursery and Kindergarten Society of Cleveland became a chartered institution in care of the five day nurseries and six kindergartens thus originated. This roll might be indefinitely extended.

"The elevation of women physically, mentally, morally and spiritually" was not only forcing women into unsuspected fields of opportunity; it was also revealing unsuspected capacities that were henceforth abundantly made use of.

CHAPTER VIII

THE YOUNG WOMEN'S CITY ORGANIZATIONS

IN certain cities, the Young Women's Christian Association expressed the maternal concern which Christian women felt for young women getting a foothold or making their way in unfamiliar surroundings; in other cities the Association resulted from the sense of sisterhood through which a few earnest Christian young women were led to work for the things which they and the others wanted.

Some of these beginnings were rather humble. The St. Joseph, Missouri, Association, organized in 1888, said in an anniversary meeting that there was "a list of about twenty names as charter members, with no money and little time," but the secretary of the prosperous Association, Martha Fisher, remembered to add, "but many promptings of the Holy Spirit born from the consciousness of an effort put forth 'in His name.'" Some of the methods may have been amateurish, as this survey shows. "In our own city there are 1,500 *self supporting* young women—375 are not under home influences, 515 are in factories, 238 in offices, 184 are teachers, 173 seamstresses and 390 domestics." But if the premises were perhaps inaccurate the conclusion was correct enough. "With these statistics before us, can *any one* doubt the need of a Young Women's Christian Association!"

This was indigenous growth: Kalamazoo, Michigan (1885), Lawrence, Kansas (1886), Ypsilanti, Michigan (1887), and Topeka, Kansas (1887), started before the days of State secretaries. The influence of graduates of Mississippi Valley coeducational colleges was felt by many of the early city Associations, even Scranton, Pennsylvania, organized in 1888; for the first president, Mrs. L. M. Gates, who made Scranton the model for a period of years, was Helen Dunn of Hillsdale College, Michigan.

Mingled with the spirit of consecration which was really the motive power of these capable young women, there was frequently a feminine outburst of envy. "I don't see why we girls can't have a place like the Young Men's Christian Association to go to." And through their own struggles they did come to possess such a place in one city after another, a place where they could work together and where the workers themselves shared in the objects of the Association as stated in the constitution almost universally adopted—"The object of this Association shall be the improvement of the spiritual, mental, social and physical condition of young women."

In some cities there were already women's organizations including in their various activities the housing of young women or specializing in that. This was the case in Minneapolis in 1890 where the Women's Christian Association, an outgrowth of the Ladies' Christian Aid Society, had for twenty years represented the evangelical churches of the city in relief work for families, an industrial school for children, and other good work. At that time it was devoting its energies to homes for self supporting young women, for transients, for aged women and aged ministers. In the churches there was a very active Christian Endeavor Union and the young women of its Central Committee sought in vain for some quiet spot down town where they might meet at noon for consultation and prayer. Plenty of places they found for obtaining food and even talking at the table, but no place where they could have a committee meeting with prayer. Again it was said, "The young men can go to the Young Men's Christian Association, I wish we had a place of our own."

These Christian Endeavor leaders called an evening meeting in February when the new state secretary of Minnesota was to be in town, and begged the State Committee for guidance in opening a "real city Young Women's Christian Association." The State Committee promised help on condition that they could show they were in earnest by holding a Young Women's Sunday afternoon meeting regularly until spring, and the girls responded by electing a provisional committee to have charge of this. This committee was made up of a recent graduate from coeducational Carleton College, at home for a year or two, another girl of leisure, a practising oculist, a business girl, and the young wife of the general secretary of the Young Men's Christian Association. They kept up the meeting and their determination grew week by week. When spring came their state secretary returned from the convention of the International Young Women's Christian Associations (see Chapter XIV) held in Scranton, with abounding revelations of that work, which served as both pattern and inspiration, and Miss Nettie Dunn, general secretary of the International Committee, was able to make a promised visit at the same time. After consultations with the ladies of the Women's Christian Association who had been hoping for such an institution in Minneapolis, but had felt unable to add another department of their own, after evening committee meetings of girls and day committee meetings of women, the Young Women's Christian Association was formed and began to look about for a location. This was secured in October "in an attractive suite of rooms," so the first annual report said, and although some callous people called it an ordinary apartment or even a flat, to the enthusiastic charter members it contained "a secretary's office, reading room, parlor, class room, committee room, kitchen and bath."

It was furnished by donations of things new and old, including a library of 380 books, and was opened at once for the religious and social occasions which formed most of their early program. It certainly was a place in which to work together, for out of the 127 active members, there were twelve standing committees, counting in all 102 names, but it was not a place of general resort, and any skilled financier will see that these two initial departments were not revenue-provoking. Even the references to employment were gratuitous. One of the dearest illusions was early dispelled, that is, that by opening a room, putting a name on a door and asking a hostess to be present to receive, troops of shy strange girls would thereby appear to make the acquaintance of the hostess and be entertained by her. Definite invitations were accepted, indefinite invitations were not.

"Are you reaching the factory girls?" inquired one patient business man, writing out a check because he had confidence in the lady who presented the little red leather subscription book to him. "My sister went up to your rooms to entertain them one evening last week, and she said nobody came except some of the regular members for something else." The embarrassed secretary accompanying the board member explained that two girls from the shoe factory and one from the woolen mills had attended a sociable a few evenings later and said they had a splendid time. However, the kindly criticism set them to thinking and later on quarters were secured with regard to the gymnasium classes which Abby Shaw Mayhew taught, and to the lunch room and those other features which girls always know they want, and the location was on a street to which one did not have to be personally conducted.

Out in the middle west the term "working girls" was conspicuous for its absence. In a newer civilization and especially in college towns, so many girls worked or were making themselves capable of doing so that the participle was generally omitted. In many cities which were rapidly increasing in population during the period of 1880–1890 and thereabouts, such responsible positions were being held by young women in railroad and newspaper offices, in wholesale and retail business houses and elsewhere, that when the Kansas City, Missouri, Young Women's Christian Association in 1890 launched the expressions "business women" and "business girls," other communities gladly followed that example in nomenclature.

Two or three young business women in Toledo had formed an independent Young Women's Christian Association with a score or so of members, and had rented a small upper room where they met for religious meetings and an occasional social festivity, inviting others to join them as opportunity offered. They were not affiliated with any state or national body, fearing that they might be taxed in proportion to their membership. Still they were so desirous of uniting with the International Committee that they sent to Chicago for a traveling secretary to come and explain matters. There was a full meeting, to which was presented the plan of financing state and national work by voluntary gifts, and when the speaker closed with the patriotic principle that these budgets were "Millions for defense, but not one cent for tribute," there was a unanimous vote in favor of affiliation. That was December, 1891; in a few months the Toledo Association had a new suite of rooms, nearer the center of town and nearer the ground, and called Agnes Gale Hill as general secretary. They increased their membership in a year more than five times over, entertained the International Convention in 1893, and in 1894 of their own will and upon their own initiative sent out their beloved secretary as the first American representative to a foreign field and never since relinquished that support.

CHAPTER IX

CITY DEVELOPMENT AND STANDARDIZATION

THROUGHOUT all the early years the satisfaction of local divergencies was giving way to the effectiveness of reasonable similarity. Christian Associations for young women, whether conducted by women or by young women, were growing more like each other as experience taught the value of cooperation between elder and younger. The Women's Christian Associations were forming Young Ladies' Branches or Junior Committees or adding daughters' names where mothers' names had been enrolled. The young women's organizations were depending more and more upon the older women on boards of management, and the "heavy committees, like those on Finance, Rooms, and Noon Rest." Young women were studying a city, learning what a Young Women's Christian Association was doing in other comparable places, and might do in their own communities, and then challenging with these facts and prospects the older women to work with them in bringing these things to pass. And when a petition signed by hundreds of girls had been the means of bringing a Young Women's Christian Association into being, the signers were naturally the charter members, and still more naturally, no question was raised as to whether self supporting girls might be members either active or associate. These charter members from home, schools, factories, offices, shops and stores were the Association itself, active for the most part, looking for all the help which the older Christian women, clergy, heads of local movements, and secretaries of State and National Committees, could give, but not waiting for the action of any of these, nor dependent upon the strength or weakness of any of these, in attempting to plant the institution which they felt they and the other girls needed.

What did they expect to realize? There are certain Association features which are the deposits of decade after decade. Others come in or go out with the civic or economic or educational manifestations, local or nation-wide, but the permanent features change only in aspect, or emphasis, and even the temporary are seen to respond to some fundamental need of a girl, her respect for her body or the expansion of her mind or the realization of her soul.

As has already been seen, the North London Home of 1855 and the Boston Association of 1866 contained the germ of almost all the departments which forty or fifty years have only served to develop. Each of these departments has a miniature history of its own which properly finds its place in any account of the rise of city Associations, for while "a Young Women's Christian Association is greater than the sum of its parts," these parts have yet to be taken into account.

Prayer meetings were the atmosphere in which the Young Women's Christian Associations were born and grew into usefulness.

Because the need for housing young women under a hospitable Christian roof seemed paramount, all the seventeen Associations listed as pioneers soon made a Boarding Home the center of their interests, with the exception of the New York City Young Women's Christian Association, which, beginning as a branch of the Ladies' Christian Union, did not duplicate the work the latter had been carrying on for a decade. This is one reason why it is difficult to classify the religious elements of the early programs, since the meetings for the young women at large cannot always be distinguished from the family prayers of any Christian household.

But from the very first, before any homes were opened, there were weekly devotional meetings. The board members met for spiritual communion and found in their hours of intercession light for the path ahead and a deepening confidence in the divine leader in whose name they had assumed unusual responsibilities. Many a woman has acknowledged that in these Ladies' Prayer Meetings where week after week the same familiar company gathered, pleading requests common to all, she learned how to speak to God aloud in prayer and found courage to lead such meetings or to conduct larger assemblies as the way opened up later on.

The Thursday evening prayer meeting in the very first rooms of the Boston Association was another type of devotional meeting which has been followed by weekly prayer services in probably every Association throughout the country.

How the religious element permeated the boarding homes of a city has already been seen from Miss Drinkwater's summary of means used in the Boston Association.

But the first large attempt to build up a religious service for young women of the whole city was that of the New York City Association. In 1872 there met for a Sunday afternoon Bible class seven women; six of these were young women without Sunday school relations, the seventh, the teacher, was Ella Doheny. As became the custom those present on that first day left their names and addresses and from this record of attendance grew up the membership roll. Miss Doheny gave herself unsparingly to preparation for the lesson, usually a continued exposition of one book of the Bible with special application to the members of the class; workers in other departments cooperated heartily in extending to young women who came into the library, the employment bureau and other parts of the building, personal and cordial invitations to this meeting. In time this class grew to an enrollment of 2,000 with an average attendance of 600. The chaplain, as Miss Doheny soon became, went regularly with a group of members before the service, but later these United Workers, as they called themselves, held their devotional meeting on an evening during the week. Thousands of women visiting New York found their way into this Sunday Bible class and carried into many states the memory of the dignified service from which radiated uncounted lines of helpfulness to its members and visitors. The Easter observances were so largely attended that two overflow meetings were sometimes provided in other rooms after the spacious chapel was filled. It is not strange that on the south wall of this assembly room close to the platform where as teacher and leader she had dominated the life of that influential Association, there should have been erected by the class a bronze tablet bearing these words:

IN LOVING MEMORY OF
ELLA DOHENY.

ENTERED INTO LIFE ETERNAL FEBRUARY 3, 1910. WON IN YOUTH BY THE SCRIPTURE, CALLED BY THIS ASSOCIATION AND IDENTIFIED WITH ALL PHASES OF ITS WORK FOR FORTY YEARS. SHE SERVED THE LORD CHRIST AS A MINISTER TO WOMEN IN THE TEACHING OF THE WORD AND IN THE CURE OF SOULS.

I HAVE CHOSEN YOU, AND ORDAINED YOU, THAT YE SHOULD GO AND BRING FORTH FRUIT AND THAT YOUR FRUIT SHOULD REMAIN.

Somewhat after the English terminology this service was called a Bible class, although its teachers presented the lesson in the form of an address and others took part only in the verse reading and opening and closing exercises.

In most of the Associations which began work with only a suite of rooms for headquarters, the Sunday afternoon "gospel meeting" was the heart of the whole organization. It was a taken-for-granted appointment; one did not say "a" gospel meeting but "the" gospel meeting. In 1888, when the state of Kansas reported twenty-one Associations, twelve in cities and nine in colleges, the Gospel meeting was the main element of each local report, with an attendance of twenty, thirty-four, sixty-five, etc., as the case might be. These little gatherings were very simple. The music was chiefly singing from a Gospel Hymns collection accompanied upon a cabinet organ. A different leader took charge each week, opening the topic announced for the day in such a way as to elicit the cooperation of the other young women in testimony and prayer. Sometimes a "Bible Reading" was given, either prepared by the leader or carefully selected from some of the religious periodicals to which it had been contributed by a well known Biblical student. Sometimes a decision meeting was held where girls determined to follow Christ and "come out on the Lord's side." The power of the meeting was often inverse to the self confidence of the leader, just as it was often out of proportion to the size of the town.

Indispensable to the gospel meeting was the invitation committee, thus charted in the first model constitution adopted by most of the Associations of that era. "The Committee on Invitation shall seek to promote the attendance of young women at the rooms and meetings of the Association by personal solicitation and distribution of invitations and in every other available way." These available ways measured the ingenuity and the consecration of the committee.

When Associations grew larger and multiplied departments, the religious emphasis was more distributed, yet in certain cities, as Aurora, Detroit, Omaha, and Harlem, one felt that she had not really visited the Associations, unless she had met with them on Sunday afternoon. The preliminary circle of prayer for God's blessing on the meeting, the decorations of the assembly room, the ushering, the reception committee, the leader of the singing, the choral class in evidence as choir, the cordial presiding officer, the speaker of the afternoon (usually a prominent Christian worker from within or without the city), the audience of members, friends, and strangers and the after meeting, strengthened the belief that Christ himself is the solution of every girl's every problem, and that it is the business of the Young Women's Christian Association to help girls find this out.

A hospitality offered for many years by the Brooklyn Young Women's Christian Association was the Sunday evening supper after the Bible class, to which thirty-five guests remained each week after the general social hour which followed the assembly room service. The vesper tea of Association House, Chicago, played a great part in the history of the Sunday meetings, and these two examples other Associations have imitated, though frequently the breaking of bread together could mean little more than a social cup of tea and a sandwich or wafer.

As to the early Bible classes, they were of two kinds. One was the open Bible class where a text book or printed outline might or might not be used, but where there was always an opportunity for the members to answer and ask questions based upon a study of a prescribed topic or portion of Scripture assigned for the lesson. The class period was usually some week day evening hour, the teacher some earnest but probably self taught Bible student and the attendance at the class large or small, dependent almost entirely upon the personality of the teacher. Such Bible classes have had the most direct evangelistic results. Out of one class in Connecticut where the average attendance for four years was twenty-five, it was said that twenty-three had become Christians, and many others were brought back into Christian allegiance.

On the other hand the Worker's Training Class was preferably small, composed of women of spiritual experience who wanted to do the work of personal evangelism. Upon most of the early convention programs this subject was placed to be treated by the strongest person available. The names of Mr. C. K. Ober, Mr. L. Wilbur Messer and Mr. John R. Mott appear in this connection. The latter thus defined a Worker's Bible Training class as "a class which enables Christians by special Bible studies and by actual participation in personal work to lead others one by one to Christ." Because of its confidential character, this class was almost invariably led by the general secretary; manuals were used which had been published by these men and others.

Once a month the missionary meeting might be found on the topic cards for the Sunday afternoon. If the meetings were notoriously poor they occurred less often, if they were notably good, ten or twelve a year were not too many. In states where the recognized leaders were Student Volunteers for the foreign field who after reaching their appointed posts kept up a large personal correspondence, missionary spirit was easily cultivated. Kansas and Michigan and Illinois owe much to Jennie Sherman, Annie Laurie Adams, Jean and Nellie Dick, Emma Silver, Bernice Hunting, Belle Richards and Eula Bates in this connection.

Not until 1894 after the formation of the World's Young Women's Christian Association did missionary giving focus upon distinctly Young Women's Christian Association objects. That was after Miss R. F. Morse had begun to collect money for the support of work done by American secretaries on the foreign field and by the first general secretary of the World's Committee, herself an American.

About the year 1900 there seemed a great enlargement of religious activities throughout all the city Associations. Such as had been content with one or two small classes were multiplying these to meet all sorts and conditions of Bible students. Drop-in classes were held at the noon hour; clubs were organized which gave the first part of the evening to Bible study. Women's morning classes were securing the leadership of the best Bible students among the pastors and whole departments were succeeding the single committee which had been expected to carry this essential burden. More Associations began to call employed officers to administer this department under the title of Bible Secretary or Religious Work Director, retaining elsewhere the former title of Chaplain. In such capacities Charlotte H. Adams had come to Pittsburgh in 1894 and Dr. Anna L. Brown to Boston in 1899.

Even if the first Young Women's Christian Association had not undertaken to help young women find places in which to work they would have been asked to do it both by the young women and by the general public. Yet probably in no other department has there been expressed more lively dissatisfaction than here, because in securing a position for an applicant there is a double obligation: the bureau hopes to satisfy both the employer and employee; repeatedly neither is satisfied. Even in the best administered offices this is bound to happen, since many applicants are not qualified by health, training or disposition to earn a respectable weekly wage, but they and their friends are sure "the society ought to do something for them," because the Young Women's Christian Association name includes the word Christian, and they return after each failure not disappointed in themselves, but a little critical of the society which has disappointed them. Otherwise keen-sighted people are often slow to appraise the market value of the working capacities of dependent members of their own families. Since the only permanent employed officer in many of the early Associations was the matron of the boarding home, whose waking hours were filled with discharging her first duties to the residents, volunteer committees on employment kept certain hours at the Employment Bureau, meeting would-be employers, and girls and women looking for work, all the while depending upon the records on the desk for continuity of treatment. This method, which seems so haphazard and lamentably unscientific as to be wholly inadequate, had at least two arguments in its favor. The ladies of the committee and board knew as individuals the exact situation with which they as an organization were trying to cope, and further, there was a personal acquaintance revealing sympathy and desire to help, which often reached a happy outcome even if not the outcome either had at first anticipated. Many a girl who came to learn "how to make a living" has found through the employment bureau "how to make a life." Mrs. E. P. Terhune, president of the Women's Christian Association of Newark, New Jersey, read a paper at the Pittsburgh conference in 1875, pleading for the moral courage in American families to have the daughters taught some useful trade, not profession, to be selected with wise regard to her taste and aptitude. So much more difficult was it also considered to find places for teachers, governesses, saleswomen, seamstresses, etc., than for domestic helpers that Philadelphia, New York and other Associations exerted all their energies within these and similar occupations, leaving the other placings to agencies already established. Certain other Associations held, however, that many of the existing agencies were commercial and that the Association had more to give an applicant than a mere statement of how many there were in the family and the weekly remuneration she might expect.

Contrasts between labor conditions in the home and out of the home were constantly discussed and philosophies were based upon the advantages and disadvantages of both. One analysis of the domestic worker's position was made in 1873 with the greatest frankness. "It must be admitted that the amount of absolute labor required of a housemaid is often entirely disproportioned to her strength. Think of a single girl doing the washing and ironing for a family of ten people, more than half of whom are adults; and at the same time, with only the help of a nurse girl, who must be ready to take baby at any time, doing all the other work of the family, the cooking, sweeping, scrubbing, dusting, washing dishes and tending. To do this she must begin work two hours before male laborers, and continue at it until two hours after they are through, unless she be one of the exceptionally quick handed. For this she is fortunate if she receives the sum of three dollars per week, an amount entirely inadequate to the amount of service rendered. Why, even the washing and ironing of such a family is of itself enough to occupy a girl for full three days in the week, if the labor were as equally parcelled out to her as it is by the contractor to his men who sweep the streets. The sewing machine has added immensely to the work of the laundress in multiplying tucks and puffs and ruffles. The complications of trimming with which even one garment is adorned, require as much time in crimping and pressing and fluting as would have served for half an ironing in an old fashioned family. If we are told that pecuniary circumstances will not justify the employment of a laundress, or indeed of any more expenditure in the direction of help, we inquire, why must restrictions in expense be confined to this particular department of a home? If clean clothing, well cooked food and prompt and orderly service is a necessity why not curtail from the luxuries in order to secure it? We think there will have to be concessions before we can expect cheerful and contented helpers in our families. The drudgeries will have to be provided for, even if it be at the expense of indulgence in other directions." It is humiliating to realize that forty years later this is still an unstandardized occupation, although the Commission on Domestic Service appointed by the National Board to report at the Convention of 1915 showed that it was not disregarded.

All the three earliest Associations carried on work for a couple of years before a boarding house was opened and in this time were mindful of that clause in their constitution about aiding young women "in the selection of suitable boarding places," but there was a basic conviction in the hearts of members of the administrative boards that to provide a Christian home for girls was an obligation they might not long postpone.

The story of how the Women's Christian Association of St. Louis achieved its end might almost be a chapter from the recording secretary's minutes or the annual report of any of the pioneer Associations. A committee was appointed to lease a building suitable both to the wants of a large growing city and to the financial ability of the Association. A new building with a sunny corner exposure presented itself. It contained about thirty rooms; there was a dining room extending the width of the building, also pantry, laundry, cellars, etc. In order for the unincorporated society to be able to secure the house for a year, a gentleman interested offered to take the lease from the landlord and receive the rent from the board as it could be raised. An appeal which was then sent to the Protestant churches asking each to furnish one or more rooms met with so prompt a response that in a month the home was formally opened. Inspection showed parlor and library at the left of the main entrance, on the right an office and a sewing room. For the equipment of the sewing room two loaves of cake had been sold "On 'Change" and four sewing machines (Wheeler & Wilson, Singer, Florence, Grover and Baker) had been donated. The many bedrooms were "furnished in a becomingly neat and homelike manner, the walls hung with pictures, the mantels ornamented with vases, the black walnut sets of furniture cosily set in, the table with its bright covering, the beds faultlessly white, all speak of comfort if not of luxury." Within eight months one hundred and nine boarders were received, of whom twenty-three were seamstresses, ten were students, and the others variously employed. The reference committee gave preference to the younger girls as permanent residents, and the price of board ranged from three and a half to five dollars. Change and lack of work made the income uncertain, especially in the summer, and the Executive Committee asked for a contingent fund to relieve specific needs, since some of the members of the family were left at times without means of support except a share of the orders which came in to the sewing room as piece work.

For purposes of administration in this boarding home in St. Louis there were at first committees on the Home, Admission, Supply, Visiting, Lectures, etc. The first September there was added a Committee on Social and Intellectual Culture which assisted in organizing "a club for intellectual improvement by means of reading, etc.," which met each week in the parlor, and arranged social functions for members and friends. There was also a Religious Committee, although the chief religious service was house prayers conducted each evening after supper by the superintendent, Mrs. Shepard Wells. Frequently a city pastor took charge of the devotional hour.

Winter homes began to be a necessity, but summer homes were a luxury. The first venture of this kind was made in 1874 by Philadelphia. Its long cherished hope for an Association residence offering rest and recreation during the summer months was suddenly realized when Mr. James A. Bradley donated a lot at Asbury Park, New Jersey, one of the favorite beaches of the Atlantic Coast, only a short ride distant from Philadelphia. Prompt measures were taken to erect a building and that very season "Sea Rest" was opened. Later additions enabled the house to accommodate one hundred and twelve guests and as the usual stay was limited to two weeks and the inclusive price for board was little over three dollars a week, many hundreds of women every year were able to enjoy the sea air and ocean bathing, to whom a sea side visit or even a change from city life would otherwise have been virtually impossible. On Conanicut Island in Narragansett Bay the Providence Association leased two farm houses in 1878 and furnished them for a vacation home conducted on much the same plan. In some Associations parties were made up to go to Vacation Lodges for week ends, or for a longer stay.

Rest Cottage, which the heroic invalid Jennie Cassiday founded and bequeathed to the Women's Christian Association of Louisville, was like the others in its aim to be a house for which Christ was the recognized head. She herself used each week to send a letter here to be read after Sunday morning prayers, and in this was always a bit of Bible exposition which she had worked out in hours of pain and thought, or as in this one case, had quoted from another: "In Galatians, the fifth chapter, one reads of the fruit of the spirit. Love is the first thing and all else can be put into it. Joy is love exulting; peace is love in repose; long suffering is love on trial; gentleness is love in society; goodness is love in action; faith is love on the battlefield; meekness is love at school, and temperance is love in training."

The personal element which pervaded this Vacation House has also been felt in the Summer Cottage of the Milwaukee Association at Genesee Lake, Wisconsin, which Mr. Walter Lindsay put up in 1896 in memory of his wife, Mary Knowles, one of the charter members in Milwaukee. With its fifty acres of land it is what might be called a "self contained" estate, for rowing, swimming, tramping and extensive nature study may be enjoyed without leaving the premises.

Amazing discoveries were made from time to time by every group of people who thought at all on what people are pleased to call Association problems. One discovery was that not so large a proportion of non-residents in comparison to real citizens as had been superficially supposed made use of even the privileges of the Association, to say nothing of cooperating in such a way that they would initiate further privileges which might be still further extended. Dependent upon this is the second discovery, namely, that there are not, as reckoned by the census, as many non-resident as citizen young women in the majority of cities. If these discoveries were made by the board or accepted by them, which for practical purposes is all the same, their attention was paid to young women who did not need shelter, as generously as it was afforded those for whom this led the train of necessities. Boston recognized this when the Beach Street houses were opened and the dining room was conducted on the restaurant plan open to outsiders, but since that same dining room must cater to the resident family, it fell so far short in that requirement that when the Warrenton Street home was opened the family table was made the unit. The early Associations were too simply organized and too insufficiently equipped to meet the four separate issues which must be faced between eleven and two o'clock daily by an Association actually satisfying its natural constituency, which calls for a large central lunch room with rapid service and low prices to accommodate girls who are down town every day and want to make their noon hour reach around luncheon and errands; a well appointed lunch room with attractive menu and service for people who are willing to spend time and money to obtain them and like to find them in the Association; a seven days in the week dining room arranged as to hours of meals and other features for transient guests whose rooms may be in the same building or in private homes in the neighborhood; and besides these, the family table of the Association residence, where menu, service, grace at meals, personal acquaintance and conversation are such as might be found in any Christian household and can be observed here even though this be a family of forty. Much of the bitter criticism of the Young Women's Christian Association which, so far as the public press is concerned, is usually limited to the boarding home, comes from trying to unite these four features with one dining room, one matron and one domestic staff.

The first conspicuous attempt to afford a woman's hotel to distinctly transient guests was made by the New York City Young Women's Christian Association in 1891, when the "Margaret Louisa" was opened at 14 East 16th Street. The beautiful building contained rooms for seventy young women, a restaurant seating one hundred and twelve and was given entirely equipped, by the one donor, Mrs. Elliott F. Shepard.

When the Philadelphia boarding home department was well under way a lodging home under another roof was added and a restaurant was opened in 1872, which was visited within a year by one hundred or more girls and women each noon. A substantial dinner of meat and vegetables was served for from ten to twenty cents or soup with bread at a charge of five cents. One day when a record was kept it was found that forty-three persons had secured a meal for five cents and the other seventy-one had dined at an average price of not more than seven or eight cents. After a time one corner of the room was railed in, carpeted and supplied with reading matter and made into a pleasant waiting or lounging place.

At its very organization in 1883 Baltimore decided to offer both mental and physical food, and the committee appointed to secure rooms were charged to find such as were suitable for reading room, lunch room and kitchen. In less than two months these rooms were found in the central part of the city and scores of girls had enjoyed the savory meals, the few minutes' peaceful loitering in the bright cozy parlor where newspapers, magazines, and books were at hand, and the personal acquaintance with members of the employment and lunch committees who were always present. It is worthy of notice that five years later when the Baltimore Association had entered its new building it referred to these first quarters as the shabby upper room, approached through a dark alley up a rickety flight of outside steps, where the Young Women's Christian Association established herself, a veritable Cinderella among her elder sisters, treated with contempt by many of those whom she wished to serve.

Perhaps the credit of naming this combination of luncheon with other features may be awarded to Poughkeepsie, which in 1886 described its "Noon Hour Rest" as a place "where neatly spread lunch tables are in readiness every noon from twelve to one o'clock for the accommodation of girls who bring their lunch to their places of employment. Hot coffee, tea and milk are served at a very small fee. From its lunch room the girls bring their work into our sunny pleasant parlor, where music, reading and conversation make the noon hour the shortest of the day." Soon the Noon Rest had swept the country; the name was popular, the idea back of it was exactly what many had been looking for—an invitation to bring or buy luncheon as one preferred and to expect to remain for the rest of the noon hour. Concerts, Bible classes, popular talks, brief programs by artists entertaining in the city, fancy work instruction, every imaginable Association propaganda could be introduced, in case the guest could finish her luncheon in time to enjoy some of these features and get back to desk or counter within sixty minutes.

Private school alumnæ associations helped annihilate the time difficulty with the self service plan called "Cafeteria." Probably Kansas City, Missouri, was the first Young Women's Christian Association to install this system, modelled after the Ogontz Club in the Pontiac Building in Chicago, and its neighbor, the Wildwood Club, maintained by Miss Kirkland's School. The room first opened in March, 1891, and was soon exchanged for a larger one, where the members passed between the brass rail and the counter, studied the menu poster, selected tray, cold foods, hot foods, waited for the penciled check, spread the table, ate and talked, carried back dishes and paid their way out at the other door in the same time they would ordinarily have spent waiting for a table and the return of the waitress with the food they had ordered. The novelty attracted attention, small cities with limited equipment and few departments of wide appeal could do a service to the women of the town which was readily appreciated, and the small expense of supervision and labor made it pay almost without exception.

"To have a good time, to get to know each other" —these were the goals to which the social department committees set their united front, even when an Association was so small that one person as a committee of the whole planned most of the good times and the members already knew each other.

A cardinal point of the Association compass was the feeling against calling entertainments for revenue only, social affairs. If the scheme for such had arisen in the finance committee or in a ways and means committee hoping for a new building or despairing over an old mortgage, to such committee should belong the labor and glory of putting it through. Both labor and glory were of a surety involved in such mammoth manœuvres as the Exposition of Authors in St. Louis in 1875, and the Great Bazaar which the New York Association held ten years later in the Academy of Music, opened by the chairman, Mrs. D. H. McAlpin, and the Governor of the State, Samuel J. Tilden, for which Mr. R. C. Morse was chairman of the Press Committee, and which printed a daily paper to which Bryant, Holmes, Holland and other eminent authors contributed.

Entertainments in which members took part or to which membership tickets admitted them, or which collected a small sum for delegates' expenses, something for which no appeal was made to the outside public, and yet from which the young women gained real pleasure, were not barred out of this category, as the returns were measured by a good time, not by increased funds. Holidays have always been scrupulously observed and the best publicity on behalf of membership was found to be the souvenirs which girls carried home from Hallowe'en or Valentine festivities and exhibited to their friends the next day.

But the Associations kept growing larger and the social committees which had been arranging one gathering each month and worrying over the budget basis therefor, realized that the occasions most enjoyed were not those when they had tried to cater to the entire membership, although their concept of democracy tried so to convince them. The times most keenly enjoyed were the social hours in connection with some regular work through which girls had begun to know each other, and whose acquaintance could be deepened, where newcomers could be welcomed into a circle which they would meet again and again. The picnic supper of the bicycle club, the birthday party for a teacher or secretary, the celebration for which guests were invited to the boarding home, all these could be planned for by the participants with as much hilarity as was actually enjoyed on the evening in question, and the social committee proper could concentrate on the large affairs. The lunch room equipment was put to use, and banquets brought out the members for the annual business meeting of the Association. Open house on New Year's Day or on Washington's Birthday was a time for cooperating with the Young Men's Christian Association. Summer picnics in parks and winter picnics in gymnasiums—every season was utilized.

A new conception of democracy was acknowledged. That democracy in which girls could plan their good times in connection with their classes led on to the clubs, where working together made a short cut to a new social life, or playing together. Outside of the Girls' Branches, where the children's office-holding had the club flavor, the first real self governing club may have been that resulting from Miss Grace H. Dodge's visit to Baltimore in 1887. In the Harlem Association in 1894 the prevailing spirit seemed to be club spirit, for that year the Birthday Building Club, the Literary Club, and the Annex Choral Club all voted themselves into life, to be followed in 1895 by the Colgate Chrysanthemum Club, which either because of its brilliant name, or of the relation held to it by Miss R. F. Morse, who had been associated in club life with Miss Dodge, seemed to hold the front of the platform for many years.

In the days when there were no free public libraries, and memberships in corporate libraries or rentals for books were costly, in the days when there were no free evening schools, in the days when there was no available trade or technical instruction for girls, in the days when household arts had not been academically formulated, the Christian Association, which recognized mental culture as a necessity in the whole development of young womanhood, undertook to collect libraries, teach English branches and general subjects, provide classes preparing the pupils for self support, and gather the untrained into classes in sewing, cooking and other domestic accomplishments. But even when these educational agencies appeared in community after community the city Associations had still their task before them in making books accessible to busy girls, or cultivating or guiding their choice in reading; in supplying evening classes at the hours when employed young women could attend, and for such blocks of time as they could devote to study, also in stimulating them to begin and heartening them to continue; in studying the labor market and opening classes from which graduates could reasonably hope to go into occupations for which they had showed natural aptitude; and in seizing the first opportunity to secure teachers of the common household subjects which everybody declared all girls should understand, but for teaching which no provision had apparently ever been made.

For many years the word "Library," as applied to Young Women's Christian Associations, customarily presented to the mental vision a room containing shelves and a table for reading matter, not a collection of books for which shelf space had been provided. Lacking a library endowment, the supply of books depended upon occasional "book socials" where friends cheerfully parted with books they thought girls ought to read, because they knew they themselves did not wish to read them, or upon spasmodic efforts of the library committee to secure the price of a certain new book from an individual donor. Lacking a librarian the distribution was restricted too often to fixed hours of attendance by the library committee, hours which were not always frequent enough to accommodate many people whose weekly visits to the building might not coincide with them, though for those who could attend it was very satisfactory. The other method, free access to the shelves at all times by the patrons, who selected their own books and made note of such as they withdrew, resulted in a more general use. More books were taken out and vastly more failed to come back.

Just as a pleasing notion once prevailed that organized Christian work for young women could be postponed until the young men of a city had been adequately and permanently taken care of in these respects, so there seemed to be an unwritten declaration of confidence that any girl who would be attracted to a Young Women's Christian Association by a library was of such serious tastes that she "did not really need the Association" so much as others, and hence efforts that might have built up a library were directed toward equipping a gymnasium or putting an addition on the boarding home. Occasional exceptions to this state of things were York, Pennsylvania, among the smaller, and New York City among the larger Associations.

> Go teach the orphan boy to read,
> The orphan girl to sew,

was the scathing advice meted out to Lady Clara Vere de Vere by the first person in Tennyson's poem. Not the orphan, however, but the Lady Clara was to benefit from the process, and so in the primitive years of Association education where a class was formed because there was an available volunteer teacher, where there was no thought of payment, where the number of lessons in the term depended on how soon a class could be got under way, and how long the teacher would meet the class or could hold it together, the benefit accruing was as often to the teacher as the class. For example, a tall school teacher all through a long cold winter regularly met a class in which a little dressmaker was the most devoted student. By spring the dressmaker had found her chance in a preparatory school where she could partly earn her way, and the teacher was communicating with a home mission board concerning a new sort of teaching. Statistical reports would have been too voluminous to print if all the similar incidents in fifty years of educational classes could have been written out.

Without question common English branches and fancy needle work were taught to small groups in almost every city Young Women's Christian Association, and many of those which bore the name Women's Christian Association, but Boston definitely reports a class in singing the first year (1866), and a little later classes in astronomy, physiology, penmanship, bookkeeping, botany and history. Leaving at one side for a moment the trade or teachnical classes, we find in New Haven and other cities classes in entertaining reading, then German, current events, drawing, English literature, First Aid to the Injured, choir music, elocution, Latin, and French. Most of the Boston topics are repeated here and there except astronomy. No other educational committee seemed ever to have the ambition to hitch its wagon to a star. As work went on and courses were more definitely outlined, fixed school terms, class fees, paid teachers, both day and evening sessions, and certificates for completed courses were gradually introduced.

But it is in the realm of classes in which students prepared for remunerative positions that the service of the Young Women's Christian Association has been most hugely appreciated by young women, and by the community at large. The need for encouraging young women to fit themselves for self support was one of the first lessons borne in upon employment committees and boards of directors, and they determined in offering such classes to make the hours, scope of work, rates, and all circumstances convenient and beneficial to intending students. As early as 1868 bookkeeping was taught in connection with penmanship. The Civil War had called women into offices and clerical training was in demand. In 1874 Philadelphia introduced telegraphy. In 1880 New York City made a success of a class in phonography, the practice of which in connection with typewriting was said to be the "most remunerative for their sex"; later on typewriting alone was advertised with the explanation that "some firms prefer typewriting to penmanship." In 1880 retouching photograph negatives was taught and a class of eight competent women graduated, then photo coloring, crayons, and India ink drawing, and in 1884 technical design and free hand enlarging.

In Boston and New York and elsewhere the business branches soon grew into a commercial department or mercantile school. After eight years the superintendent in the former city was able to say they had as yet had no pupil returned to them as incompetent. Care was always taken to inculcate a sense of the responsibility of a stenographer's position and the confidential nature of the information of her employer's affairs which she possessed. Most pronounced has been the success of the art department or school of the New York City Association, which in course of time offered a three years' course fitting graduates for positions in numerous fields of art and applied design. Silver and gold medals have repeatedly been given this Association for exhibits at International Fairs and Expositions here and abroad.

No doubt the parallel of Lady Clara Vere de Vere's efforts—if she did make the attempt—to teach the orphan girl to sew, would have been found in the many industrial schools undertaken by churches and missions and by many Women's Christian Associations. But the instruction in sewing, dressmaking, and millinery given to young women who wished this skill as a personal accomplishment, or a means of earning a living, is the more natural theme in this study of Industrial Education in the Christian Association movement.

If the Crystal Palace Exhibition of 1851 was to have a permanent effect upon industrial and mechanical arts, there was also an American event of that same year which affected women's industrial relations in a degree previously unbelievable. This was the perfection of the sewing machine, by which in that one year Wheeler & Wilson brought out the circular bobbin type, Singer the vertical needle and shuttle type, and Grover and Baker the double needle and two spools type of machine, all based upon certain of the original features which Elias Howe, commonly called "the father of the sewing machine," had patented in 1846. These were followed in 1857 by Wilcox and Gibbs' single thread machines, and after 1867, when royalties were removed, many others appeared in the market. Pessimistic communications of the period indicate that "woman's weapon, the needle," had somehow been turned against her. Machines were so expensive that two dollars was paid for daily rent of one, if a seamstress wished, or was obliged to cater to customers who looked for modish machine stitching instead of hand sewing.

In every boarding home where the occupations of the residents were enumerated in any available record, seamstresses always headed the list, and needlewomen might also be listed under other classifications as well, when they were machine operators upon one specified product, such as vest makers and cap makers. This proportion would have been higher if the seamstresses, who were given room and board during their engagements in private homes, could have had rooms over Sunday regularly reserved for them by the Association and thus have been enrolled, but there were usually so many applicants for the full seven days of the week that any two day plan seemed impossible, although the hardship it worked to the seamstresses was recognized by the Association and openly regretted. The sewing room in the St. Louis boarding home has already been noted as one means in helping the seamstresses to keep their economic footing in these perilous transition times.

One remembers that the Ladies' Christian Union of New York City had been organized twelve years before it established the Young Ladies' Branch. As was both desirable and inevitable, maintenance of their Association boarding home had led to the establishment of an employment bureau and this was transferred to the Branch, which endeavored to find places for teachers, housekeepers, first class seamstresses, etc. More than this, they set aside quarters for a fine needlework department for which were donated "One best Wheeler and Wilson sewing machine from Honorable Peter Cooper, one best Singer sewing machine donated from the French Fair by the subscription of several ladies, one Elliptic best sewing machine from St. Luke's department of the Methodist Fair voted to the Association by numerous friends." A dozen more Elliptic machines were furnished by a gentleman who also gave the services of a competent teacher. In February, 1872, a class in machine sewing began, which later on graduated thirty-two members, most of whom at once secured good positions. That fall Wheeler and Wilson extended a similar courtesy in furnishing machines and teachers, but later on the department paid its instructors and bought machines of various makes. The class beginning that fall worked four hours daily for four weeks, and supplemented the mechanical instruction with a hand finishing course in order to learn the nicer details of sewing and become fully prepared to enter families as seamstresses. Springfield, Massachusetts, taught machine operating as women came in with their own sewing to the rooms for a social evening. Germantown, Pennsylvania, conducted a sewing school regularly four evenings of the week for girls employed in mills during the day.

A three months' period of instruction from 8 A. M. to 5 P. M. was required in the industrial school which the Young Ladies' Branch of the Cincinnati Association conducted at this time. It had both a primary and a dressmaking department. Sewing was included in the curriculum of both the Boston and St. Louis training schools and out of sewing classes came the students for the dressmaking classes, and the cutting and fitting classes with costume design as an ultimate goal.

While "almost every one" could teach sewing in popular estimation, if she were herself a skilled seamstress and dressmaker, the science of cooking waited for its general presentation until there were competent professional teachers of the subject.

It is said that the modern form of instruction in the Household Arts sprang from the renewed interest in all these lines at the time of the Centennial Exposition in Philadelphia in 1876, but cooking had been already reduced to academic terms in the State Agricultural College of Iowa at Ames (1869), in the Kansas Agricultural College at Manhattan, and in the Illinois Industrial University (later the University of Illinois) at Urbana in 1874. Here Lou Allen (later Mrs. Gregory) taught household science in the "first college course of high grade in the United States, if not in the world." Eastern progress centered around distinguished teachers of cooking who began as lecturers and demonstrators. One of these authorities was Juliet Corson, who started in 1874 a free Training School for Women in New York City. A ladies' cooking class was formed the next year and in 1876 in her own home she opened the New York Cooking School. From January to April, 1879, there was an attendance of 6,560 in public and private classes under her direction. In 1877 she copyrighted a Cooking School Text Book. New England was led in this movement by Maria Parloa who lectured in New London in 1876 and in Boston in 1877, opening that fall a school on Tremont Street. The next year she organized a Domestic Science department in Lasell Seminary, Auburndale, Mass., and the following year she lectured at the assembly of the Chautauqua Literary and Scientific Circle, at Chautauqua, New York, and at the Boston Cooking School which had been founded that same year. Its principal was Mrs. D. A. Lincoln.

Attention has already been given to the instruction in cooking which the Boston Association in 1879 gave to members of the Training School for Domestics, also the day and evening classes for general students, and the class from the Winthrop School in the spring of

1880. Educational authorities say that instruction in household subjects in Boston was at its start supported by private funds in classes outside the school, and the claim that this Boston Association class was the beginning of cooking lessons in the Boston public schools has never been disproved.

In the city of St. Louis there was public sentiment favoring the establishment of a cooking school, and the Association had been hoping and working for a training school in which cooking instruction should find a place. Consequently at their invitation Miss Corson came out in April, 1881, and gave a series of ten morning and afternoon lessons which were so well attended as to net $1,200 for the Association treasury, and the interest in cooking as a domestic accomplishment as well as a trade was extended. By the fall of 1882 a house had been leased and various ladies had gathered up classes from among their own acquaintance to start the movement.

Young ladies' cooking clubs in the early eighties were popular social functions throughout the country and many of the Association classes were more social than technical in character. One finds records that "six brides-to-be" or "six young men going camping" were enrolled here and there. In 1887 there were already Association classes in Cincinnati, Worcester, Poughkeepsie and New Haven, usually under teachers trained in Boston. The Connecticut city held a course during July and August for a class composed of sixty-eight pupils, largely girls employed by the day in stores and factories.

While the laboratory method was partially employed, in that every pupil had a hand in the preparation of the food, yet individual equipment was rarely introduced before the late nineties, after which time it was considered essential. Milwaukee made an innovation by including a model apartment of parlor, bedroom, dining room and kitchen in its building, dedicated in 1901, and here housekeeping as well as cooking could be properly demonstrated.

As the local Associations became better equipped they were in a position to receive classes in dietetics from nurses' training schools and other public institutions. Up to the present time (1916) no Association has undertaken to give complete training for nurses, but the need in every home of at least one member able to give something better than the over-devoted, under-intelligent care of the sick common in most families has led many Associations to offer a trained attendant's course. The Brooklyn Association gave much attention to discovering new types of women's work and in 1890 opened a course of training to fit women for convalescent and chronic cases as a salaried occupation. Dr. Eliza Mosher and other physicians helped lay out the course and gave part of the lectures. Qualified women who completed the course of forty lessons were able even at first to secure salaries of from eight to twelve dollars per week. Others discovered their own talents and began regular hospital training.

While it would be a gratification to study the merits of the different systems of physical education, and to believe that the various Associations discussed these before introducing this department, yet the truth is that the Young Women's Christian Associations were largely following in the wake of all sorts of influences and practices already active in the communities. To some people physical education meant gymnastics as strenuously exemplified by the Turn Vereins of the resident German-Americans. This meant to them a hall with heavy apparatus, acrobatic feats and Sunday parades. To others it meant a Young Men's Christian Association building with a gymnasium, baths, a salaried director and a large budget. To many others it meant that misconception or dilution or caricature of Dr. Dio Lewis' adaptation of the Swedish free movements which under the name of "calisthenics" appeared on the daily program of the public schools. This succeeded through the first commands of "stand up straight, shoulders back," in curving the spines of the executors of the orders, until the violent thumping of clenched fists upon flat little chests, accompanied by vocal counting 4-4 time, had somewhat counter-balanced the affliction. To some a little later it meant "Delsarte," which being commonly interpreted by a young woman who had "taken a course of lessons" meant throwing the weight on the ball of the foot, and with the wrist leading, and the eye following the hand, going rhythmically and to soft, slow, sad music, through classic postures of the torso where must be strength, and angelic wavings of the extremities where must be freedom.

When gymnasium classes were formed the system adopted depended upon the physical director secured, and the extent of her teaching depended upon the place which was called gymnasium and the amount of equipment it could or did contain. Hope Narey in Boston, Mary S. Dunn in Kansas City, and Abby S. Mayhew in Minneapolis were three creative physical directors to whom the entire Young Women's Christian Association movement in America and abroad owes deference and gratitude. As Boston had shown ingenuity in fastening up chest weights—the first practical developing appliance in this field—to the doorways of a boarding home, so other Associations used their rented rooms in such a way that every square foot of floor space served a multiple purpose, for the one large area must be lunch room at noon, assembly hall on Sunday, social center at the demand of the entertainment committee and gymnasium whenever classes were scheduled.

By 1887 Philadelphia, Poughkeepsie, and New York City reported classes in light calisthenics accompanied by the piano. The next year Coldwater, Michigan, and Newburgh, New York, had the same, but Scranton, Pennsylvania, had fitted up a room for a gymnasium with rings, Indian clubs, dumb bells, wands and a chestweight. Worcester was holding four classes weekly in "physical culture including voice training." More than in any other department democracy was felt here. A gymnasium suit and team play obliterated social and educational partitions. With the recognition of the body as the temple of the Holy Spirit old members got a new vision of a complete life and new members began to "believe in the Young Women's Christian Association." After this time a gymnasium must be reckoned with in organizing an Association and in renting rooms or planning a new building. Board members realized its value and glibly answered questions and argued that the work itself combined strength and elasticity of muscle with beauty and grace of movement.

Worcester, Brooklyn and Newburgh were among the early owners of gymnasiums constructed in their buildings, but not till Buffalo and Montgomery in 1905 succeeded to Young Men's Christian Association buildings did any Young Women's Christian Association give swimming instruction in their swimming pool. Later on a pool, or merely a plunge, began to be thought a requisite for any organization of this character.

Lord Shaftesbury showed his interest in the protection of young girls by paying for placards which the several railroad companies allowed to be put up in the terminal stations of London in 1885. These gave addresses of Young Women's Christian Association Homes and Institutes both in London and provincial towns, from which representatives would come to meet upon application any girls arriving in the city who had no friends there to look after them. This was in connection with a Traveler's Aid department and secretary working at 17 Old Cavendish Street, when that address was headquarters of the London Association. So strongly was the pressing need for protection brought out by the press at that time, that the necessity of a movement to unite forces willing to help and to avoid overlapping was felt. A meeting was called at Exeter Hall of some twenty-two different societies engaged among women and girls and a permanent union effected under the name of the Traveler's Aid Society, with a standing committee of men and women. Lady Frances Balfour was president and her associates represented the Girls' Friendly Society, Young Women's Help Society, Metropolitan Association for Befriending Young Servants, the Reformatory and Refuge Union, Protective and Rescue Society for Jewish Girls, National Vigilance Association and Girls' Helpful Society. One might say that it was "in bound" travelers whom this society was to assist, but for "out bound" passengers the British ladies had already been concerned for nearly thirty years through their connection with the British Ladies' Female Emigration Society. But the outbound travelers of the old world became the inbound travelers of the new, and both British agencies had been long in communication with Association homes and friends in America before the Boston Young Women's Christian Association actually formed a department in charge of a secretary (1887). The Chicago Association in 1888 had a Traveler's Aid department and a transient home in connection with it. Matrons at stations and ferries were provided in Kansas City and St. Louis, Missouri and San Francisco as a beginning. It frequently occurred that long after the necessity of this work had so appealed to the station officials that they had added the matron to the pay rolls of the company, the Association was asked to nominate suitable persons to the vacancies, and to advise with them about matters much as if she represented only the Association.

In the ceaseless debate between the advocates of domestic and factory labor, the anti-factory speakers have cited not only the long hours but the unpleasant surroundings of factory and mill operatives. In this regard the same error exists that always makes trouble when people generalize about any human beings, young *versus* old, native *versus* foreign, rich *versus* poor, and attach to hundreds of thousands, the characteristics or the circumstances that may have pertained to a few individuals. The ease with which statistics are gathered about manufacturing establishments aids this. People easily fancy so many girls, coming from such-looking mills, where they have been doing such and such things, going along such streets to such homes, and flatter themselves that they "know factory girls."

It was not with such a spirit that the devoted women of the New York Ladies' Christian Association had visited at noon in the American Tract House and a hoop skirt factory. They were fresh from an uplifting, regenerating, rejuvenating religious experience, which made the whole city of New York a place for which Christ had died, and although timid and hesitant over the ordeal, they found their way to the places where girls were and at a time when they were at liberty. Probably they had personal acquaintances in these places through whom the visits were arranged. It was not such a spirit which caused the Germantown Association as soon as it was organized to open a night school where sewing and other womanly arts were taught, where social life was enjoyed and where a Bible class held the main place in the weekly program. Many Associations had regular campaigns of invitation into workrooms and places of business. If it was convenient for the girls they boarded at the Association homes and had a hand in everything that was going on. There was no distinction in membership, but the fact finally had to be faced that in many cities the home and business localities of thousands of girls were too far away from the Association for the rank and file of industrial workers to know or care whether there were any Young Women's Christian Associations.

It was then that the people at the center who really did know, and really did care, began to think of "extending" the Association to where the girls really were. Some Associations, Baltimore (1889), Scranton (1891) and Milwaukee (1893) found rooms for a miniature Association in a part of town nearer the homes or the factories.

Dayton went even further in 1892, and their workers had a regular Monday appointment at the National Cash Register factory, for what was called the "Busy Girls' Half Hour" in the workroom after luncheons were eaten. Health, dress and morals were themes for practical talks—Bible verses were memorized. The meetings, which always opened with prayer, were mutual exchanges of ideas about Christian helpfulness, for many of the group were leaders in their own church organizations. One November day the "Busy Girls" showed one hundred and seventy-five jars and glasses of fruit which they had collected for the Deaconess Hospital; at Easter a similar offering was ready. More cities worked out the same plan. Charlotte Adams made regular visits to bakeries and cigar factories in Pittsburgh, from 1894 on. Maude Wolff's visits in the Milwaukee factories in 1895 are another paragraph, as is Isabel Smith's picturesque bicycle trip to a Kalamazoo paper mill one May day in 1897, carrying a large baker's roll as her text book for a talk on the Feeding of the Five Thousand. Her comrade was a board member bearing her guitar to accompany the gospel hymns sung heartily by men, boys, women and girls all seated on bales of rags and piles of paper. The clubs that grew out of these, the revelations of leadership, the addition of a member to the secretarial staff whose sole duty was in industrial plants, such as Neva Chappell in Minneapolis in 1900—all this is but the preface of a story of which we are even now living only the beginning.

As has been seen, the first building erected contained dormitories, but in New York City in 1887 a new type of structure made its appearance. Under the title, "Certain Forms of Women's Work for Women," Helen Campbell contributed an article to "The Century Magazine" for June, 1889, which was splendidly illustrated and aroused attention all over the country. The bare description of the building follows.

January 18, 1887, saw the dedicatory ceremonies and the simple but beautiful building, five stories in height, was thrown open for public inspection. Brick with red freestone arches and trimmings was the material employed, terra cotta ornamentation being freely used, the result being one of the most attractive façades among the many examples of good work which New York now offers in this direction. A vestibule with tiled floor gives access to a broad hall, finished like the entire interior in ash, stained to produce the effect of antique oak. Wide double doors open on the west side to the social parlor, thirty feet square, with carved mantel and cheerful open fire, on the east to the employment room and their various offices, while back of both is the chapel, running completely across the building and some 70 x 40 feet. On the second story is the library running across the entire front, two small rooms at each side being partitioned off—that on the east as reading and reference room, on the west for magazines and periodicals.

The third, fourth and fifth stories are devoted to the class rooms, including typewriting, stenography, machine and hand sewing, dress cutting and fitting, bookkeeping and arithmetic, and technical design; in short, all the branches in which women engaged in over thirty trades may desire to fit themselves for more efficient work. In all these, save dress cutting and fitting, instruction is free to members whose small yearly fee gives opportunities in every direction.

On the fifth floor are two art rooms with artists' skylights, one of them occupying the entire back of the building which is slightly narrower than the front.

An Industrial Room gives seamstresses an opportunity of exhibiting their work, fancy and otherwise, and orders are taken for every variety. Monthly entertainments, concerts, recitations, et cetera, give needed diversion, and a small gymnasium with a skilled teacher is the satisfactory climax of the work undertaken.

Sewing Class in New York City Association, 1889

(By permission)

This type of administration building was found practicable for small as well as large cities, which Newburgh and other places soon proved.

Almost all these departments were matters of evolution, as were indeed the whole city Associations; in a way the Associations were led on, one by one, to meet the fundamental necessities of girls: religious fellowship and instruction, individual needs of employment, protection, housing and food, acquaintance with the right kind of friends and books, study for culture and self support, physical preparedness for life, and a chance to work together in being useful to the whole community.

CHAPTER X

THE ORIGIN OF STUDENT ASSOCIATIONS

THE Woman's Student Movement within the Young Women's Christian Association had its beginning in the coeducational colleges of the Middle West.

Among these may be included the colleges closely related to one religious denomination even if not controlled by it; the state universities of which only the undergraduate department was taken into account (for the graduate departments were chiefly the schools of law, medicine and dentistry, often situated at the metropolis of the State, away from the main seat of the university, at the state capital or other smaller city); and the normal schools, which offered an academic course of two years beyond college entrance requirements. Both colleges and normal schools had large preparatory departments enrolling more or less mature students who were accepted into college life in accordance with their age and ability, not their class rating. The exact functions of university, college and normal school were not always consciously distinguished. Young women chose the state university because of the variety of courses offered, the better equipment and the larger faculty. They attended their denominational college in their own State as a matter of course, or because they lived near by such in case they were of another church connection. Aside from the young women who wanted to teach school and attended the normal school as the logical preparation for their chosen profession, there were also the daughters of educationally thrifty parents who went to a normal school because they could fit themselves for self support there in half the time it would take if they went to college, a quantitative rather than a qualitative analysis of the matter, one might almost say.

For the person seeking the bachelor's degree in arts or science in the '70's or '80's there was slight variation in the courses of most colleges except that Greek, in the classical course, added a third year in the "prep" department as the scientific course meant only two years' preparatory work in which there was no Greek. The weekly schedule ran along in solid blocks of five,—each of the five days of the week an hour long recitation in Latin, one in some other language, one in mathematics, until history and mental philosophy and moral philosophy and the other higher studies were reached. Alterations in the curriculum were gradual and were accomplished mainly by the advent of a new professor "from the East" or the return of some distinguished alumnus who "had been East" fitting himself for an alumni chair. That electives were slow in finding a place was not due alone to fondness of the Board of Trustees for those subjects which must be dropped from a student's course in order to allow him a choice—one does not easily forget the consternation over the rumor that a college proposed to graduate a student without Latin—but the delay was also due to the meager resources of library and laboratory and the short list of faculty members as well.

Perhaps the faculty was small, but in instance after instance it was a faculty of great teachers and great men.

The president was usually an ordained man, from some New England storehouse of learning; his classes in logic and evidences of Christianity were the meeting places of souls and minds for students possessed of both. When the president did not play the part of guide, philosopher and friend, an intellectual giant with the heart of a friendly child, there was always sure to be some "grand old man" on the faculty, from whose steadfast personality the character of individuals and the very character of the college caught their tone. In two or three instances this ranking personality was a woman. Usually the preceptress, or lady principal, was content to teach four classes in modern languages each day, preside over the ladies' dormitory and administer the rules of the college both for town and out of town girls, interpreting and enforcing the regulations "concerning the Association of ladies and gentlemen." The faculty sat in a row on the rostrum at chapel, and the men took turns in giving out the hymns, reading the scripture lesson and offering prayer; but it was the president, or in his absence on preaching or financing tours, the vice-president, who gave the notices and made talks beginning, "It has been brought to my attention—"

The college building occupied little space on the ample campus which had been laid out in the early days of the town. Perhaps the college had been the motive for building the town. If the chapel were larger than the church of the corresponding denomination it was the main community audience room. If the church were larger it was upon that platform that students rehearsed in the unaccustomed rainbow colored light of a mid-week afternoon, those orations and prize declamations, which admiring relatives from all over the state would come to hear.

The men's dormitories rarely had commons, but the students made up boarding clubs at private houses, or took their meals at the women's hall, or boarded themselves. Sometimes young women were granted permission by the faculty to set up their own housekeeping in furnished rooms, and a few girls lived with even less expense by working for their board in a family which understood and accepted the college hours, namely, morning recitations at eight, nine, ten and eleven, afternoon classes at two and three o'clock and chapel at four. Sometimes chapel began the day instead of closing it.

In the denominational college many of the faculty felt very deeply their responsibility for the "cure of souls" and expressed this not so much in the required chapel services as in the mid-week college prayer meeting, in the Day of Prayer services on the holiday granted the last Thursday of January, and in those revivals of religion which sometimes followed upon that day of prayer or upon the Evangelical Alliance Week of Prayer in which the churches united the first week of January. To these general services must be added the young ladies' prayer meeting, which the preceptress led each week and in which many a girl, who had made a decision for Christ in a larger meeting began that religious expression which she found not only a result of growth, but a means to growth. Back of this the constant intercession of parents and pastors at home could be reckoned on for certain young folks whose careers had been guided toward college in the hope that they would not be disobedient to the heavenly vision to which they had not before responded or had followed only haltingly.

The last call of the whole college course was some service during Commencement Sunday, led, perhaps, by an alumnus, when some one who had been apparently uninfluenced by any manifestation of religious life or teaching during the past four or six or seven years would rise and say, "I could not leave this college without testifying that I go out as a disciple of Jesus Christ." Then the professors forgot their heavy schedules and their scant salaries irregularly paid, and their remoteness from intellectual resources and the faintness of any hope of bettering these conditions, they forgot the tedious faculty meetings, and the indifference of undergraduates and the criticisms from within and without; they thanked God for one more student ready to live, and took courage for the next incoming generation.

Commencement Day was the brightest jewel of Commencement Week, which crowned the year. Each member of the graduating class delivered an oration, and the valedictory and salutatory honor speakers could indulge in a few words of Latin to match the sonorous sentences of the president, as with dignity he placed his silk beaver hat upon his head, rose and bestowed the diplomas upon men in frock coats and girls in puffed and trained white muslin dresses, and wearing pink roses in their hair. Bunches of garden roses and bouquets of vari-colored flowers had greeted the close of each address, they came in showers from galleries and seats in the old chapel, but if in the new church were carried up by ushers and banked up the whole corner where the class received the congratulations of their friends. Then came Commencement dinner with toasts. Some one must represent the graduating class, but rarely a girl, although she might be intellectually gifted enough to have just produced the valedictory oration. But in the evening when the alumni (where now the class truly belonged) and faculty and townspeople met at the president's "Levee," as this annual reception was called, the white muslins and pink roses were the center of attraction. Education was Coeducation.

Each college was divided into halves, not by academic standing, nor by sex, but by two rival camps known as literary societies. Subdivisions were by sex, for as the men were lined up into Philalatheans and Adelphians, so were the young women into Athenas and Hesperians. The Philalatheans and their sister

Athenas collaborated not only in the college year, but during vacation skirmished to bring in the members equally coveted by the Hesperians and their brothers the Adelphians. The decorations of their halls, the solidity of their Friday night debates, even their participation in religious and general college issues, were conducted on the strictest partisan lines if society spirit was running high.

The social life of the undergraduates centered around the receptions, sleighing parties and boat-rides of these societies more than around class matters. Other voluntary organizations such as the college newspaper board, the foreign missionary society, the oratorical society, the college chorus, lacked flavor in comparison.

This same competitive spirit marked the intercollegiate relations, which were in early days limited almost entirely to the state oratorical contest, from which champions were sent to the inter-state contests, and the winning speakers and winning orations were never forgotten by a grateful constituency. But knowing each other, appreciating each other, co-operating in anything at home or abroad—that was not dreamed of. Had it been dreamed of, would it have been desired?

On the main line of the Chicago and Alton railroad, two miles north of Bloomington, the state of Illinois had established in 1857 the Illinois State Normal University, and the village had taken the name of Normal. Here in 1872 the cultural features of education were fully recognized and the faculty were interested in graduating not simply teachers, but men and women with a working idealism that would stir them to take a hand wherever they might find themselves. It was a congenial soil in which a voluntary religious organization of young women might spring up and flourish. Some of the student girls realized a need for a meeting for Bible study, Christian conversation and prayer where no restraint would be felt and which would not interfere with attendance at church services or Sunday school. Three other students and two friends from one of the churches met with Lida Brown in her room, Sunday afternoon, November 12, and after all had prayed they talked over the possibility of a regular meeting in a larger place where more would feel free to attend than might come to a private house. The committee appointed that afternoon reported during the week that the vestibule of the Congregational Church had been offered, and here they met regularly, with increase in both attendance and interest owing largely to revival meetings held in town under the preaching of Mr. Hammond the revivalist. To make these meetings permanent an organization seemed desirable and a committee brought in a constitution on January 19, 1873, in which they had hoped to be original, but at the last moment could produce nothing better than the borrowed constitution of the Young Men's Christian Association of the school. They styled themselves the Young Ladies' Christian Association of Normal, Illinois, but in September, 1881, after a new constitution had been adopted in the spring, were satisfied to become merely Young Women.

Their officers were president, Ida E. Brown (Mrs. James Cary); vice president, Ida Witbeck (Mrs. Charles De Garmo); secretary, Emma V. Stewart (Mrs. I. E. Brown); treasurer, Lida A. Brown (Mrs. William P. McMurry). The secretary was very emphatic as to their relation to the Men's Christian Association and repeatedly explained, "This Young Women's Christian Association is not an offshoot of the Young Men's Christian Association. The only part they took in the formation of our Association was that of a goad. They wearied us by saying continually: 'Why don't you form an Association similar to ours?' This was after our prayer meeting had grown too large to be handled without some system and we were debating about what it was best to do. They also kindly lent us their constitution and bylaws, upon our application. With the organization of the prayer meeting they had nothing to do, not even the part of the importunate widow."

Soon the attendance outgrew the vestibule and the body of the church was used for meetings, until it burned in the spring of 1873, when the basement of the Methodist church was placed at their disposal. These meetings were usually led by one of the members, each appointed by her predecessor, and upon such topics as The Love of God, Faith, Prayer, Praise, Christian Work, Christ, the Rock. All present were invited to speak. Both men and women led the evening meetings, which they held with the Young Men's Christian Association. Soon these were held each Tuesday evening and a twenty minute noon prayer

Ida A. Brown — Emma V. Stewart

Lida A. Brown

Jennie Leonard — Hattie A. Lawson

Founders of the First Student Association

meeting for girls met twice a week in the White Room of the University Building. In this same building the business meetings found a place in the recitation room of the preceptress or of one of the professors.

The leadership of these services and the rotation in office occasioned by electing new officers and executive committee each of the three terms of the school, with an extra committee for the vacation term, certainly gave to all of the members a chance for development of their gifts. There were also several standing committees, and special committees from time to time, as for example, "a committee consisting of two members from each of the churches was appointed to confer with those who had recently become Christians, about joining some church." "Each of the churches" meant Presbyterian, Baptist, Congregational, Methodist and Christian. Other special committees planned neighborhood work.

The minutes were faithfully kept as may be seen from some of the entries.

A Committee of three was elected to appoint one person in each row of seats (evidently in the Normal Assembly Hall) to speak with those sitting in that row and ask them to join our Association and to attend the meetings.

The Association passed the following resolution, whereas Mr. D. C. Elliott had procured for the Y. L. C. A. free of expense a Record Book which is even better than they had expected to get for themselves, therefore

Resolved, that this Association tender him sincere thanks for his kindness and that a copy of this Resolution be presented to him.

A Committee was appointed to join with a similar committee from the Young Men's Association in providing a literary entertainment for the Association. These committees decided it would be better to hold a sociable, which was accordingly provided for by the two Associations with the assistance of some of the Normal residents in preparing supper for the evening. The music, toasts, speeches and supper passed off very pleasantly. (This was at the opening of the school year, 1875.) As the young ladies had been aiding the poor by soliciting such things as were thought necessary for them a motion was made and carried that such work should be made a part of the permanent work of the Y. L. C. A.

Term after term the minutes show the evangelistic temper of the meetings.

"At the close of the meeting a chance was given for those who wished to become Christians to manifest it by rising. Several availed themselves of the opportunity. An inquiry meeting was held at the close of the meeting." "An after meeting for young Christians was held in the parlor." "Two of our students asked for prayer for themselves." "Voted that a committee be appointed to see the pastors and working members of the different churches to see if they will not enter heartily into union with us and have meetings for the promotion of Christ's kingdom." "Our last Association of this term—The topic was, 'The Christian on his vacation.' An earnest appeal was made to the young people not to stop work after leaving Normal, but to form other Associations wherever they might go. An invitation was given for any to identify themselves with God's people. One young lady rose for prayers. In the after meeting several very earnest prayers were offered." "Five expressed their desire to become God's children."

Further cooperation with the Young Men's Christian Association was the work of supplying current periodicals for the students' reading table, furnishing reading material for the racks at the railroad station, posting bulletins of church and Association services and holding joint prayer meetings at the homes of members. They also attended state conventions as regular delegates from 1873 to 1881 and as corresponding members or visitors from 1882 to 1884, and made financial contributions.

Young Men's Christian Association conferences held in Normal and Bloomington early in 1881 and again in 1884 had also brought the whole membership into touch with the broader Association field, its aims and policies. Mr. L. D. Wishard, student secretary of the International Committee of the Young Men's Christian Associations, addressed the girls, speaking of the Intercollegiate Movement and stating reasons for the Young Women's Christian Association's existence, independent of the Young Men's Christian Association, congratulating the young women of Normal that their student Young Women's Christian Association was the first of its kind in the country. It was not until after these addresses that the position of corresponding secretary was created and the new officer was asked to correspond with as many other Associations as possible. One of the first communications she read before the Association was a letter from Mrs. H. Thane Miller of Cincinnati, "encouraging us in our efforts to do Christian work." The Normal Association, now in its second decade, was ready to meet that fall with its sister Associations in Illinois and the word Intercollegiate was to be translated into terms of young women's work.

Four other student Young Women's Christian Associations are known to have come up spontaneously in the '70s and others in the early '80s before there was any outside suggestion toward organization. At Northwestern College, conducted by the Evangelical Association at Naperville, Illinois, an hour's ride west of Chicago, the preceptress, Miss Cunningham, met the young women students in her own room every week for an hour of religious worship and fellowship. Timid girls felt free to participate in this informal meeting and finally, with her cooperation on November 4, 1875, "they formed an organization for their own growth and the salvation of unsaved girls and the promotion of Christian work." This they called The Young Ladies' Christian Association until 1884, when they changed their name and became a part of the Illinois State Association. One who entered college as a freshman in 1880 found the letters Y. L. C. A. painted on the doors of the long narrow room which the faculty had given the Association, and which they used for prayer service and business meetings. It would have seemed a sacrilege to use it as a study room and it was too small for social purposes.

The Association at Olivet College, Olivet, Michigan, dates from October 21, 1876. The constitution adopted that day stated their object; "to promote the spiritual and social welfare of the young women of Olivet." One of the prime movers in this effort was Miss Mary Burnham, at that time principal of the Female Department of the college. The first president was Minnie Cameron (Mrs. J. V. Hartness), later president of the Lansing City Association. Rosamond Hunt (Gordon), Flora Lewis (Gallup) and Ella Starkweather were the other officers. They held meettings of their own within and outside the college, also combined with the college Young Men's Christian Association and the Women's Missionary Society of Olivet in other services.

The State Normal School Association at Carbondale, Illinois, dates from the same year, as will be seen by the first entry in their minute book.

> Young Women's Christian Association
> Model Room S. I. N. U.
> Tuesday, Oct. 17, 1876.
>
> At the close of the Young Ladies' Prayer Meeting a proposition was made to change the prayer meeting into a Young Women's Christian Association, which met with general favor. The following officers were elected for the first term: Miss M. Beech, President, Miss Debbie Decker, Secretary, Miss Lizzie Sheppard, Treasurer. A committee consisting of Misses Middleton, McAnally and Mason was appointed to form a constitution and by-laws to be presented at the next meeting.

Then followed the names of twenty-four charter members.

On October 30, 1877, the Lenox College Young Women's Christian Association at Hopkinton, Iowa, was formed after consultation with the officers of one of the Illinois Associations. The Young Men's Christian Association of Lenox College, which had been organized the year before, was the first of its kind in Iowa and its constitution was the basis of that which the young women formed.

Another interesting beginning was made at Doane College, Crete, Nebraska, in 1880 under the name of Young Ladies' Society of Co-workers. The band of girls held at first a daily noon prayer meeting of their own and had a Sunday afternoon prayer meeting with the Young Men's Christian Association. This in time became the regular college prayer meeting, and the girls maintained their own service at the Sunday hour. They led in the Nebraska State Association, changing their name in 1883 to Young Women's Christian Association.

There were other college young women even more closely in touch with the Intercollegiate Student Movement, however, than these; they were the women students in colleges where the words Young Men's Christian Association were construed to mean Students' Christian Association, and they were members in good and regular standing; they became officers, committee members, leaders of meetings and regular delegates to state conventions. It would be more easy to detect this phenomenon were it not that in Young Men's Christian Association reports, *initials* of these persons' names were printed instead of the sex-betraying Christian names. The table of student Associations in the International Young Men's Christian Association Year Book under the date of 1882–83, lists its officers in this manner: "Lawrence University, Appleton, Wisconsin, president, A. Wilson; corresponding secretary, C. Althouse." It does not indicate that *Miss* Annis Wilson was a prize mathematician then in her sophomore year, and that *Miss* Carrie Althouse was the best soprano singer on the campus.

Those two titles, Young Men's Christian Association and Students' Christian Association, had been in vogue since 1858. Mention has already been made of the great revival of 1857–58 and one noteworthy result in New York City, the formation of the Ladies' Christian Association. A most enlightening study might be made of the institutions and organizations originating in revivals of religion which brought to people who walked in darkness a great light, and gave them incentive and power to follow that light. During the revival in Ann Arbor, Michigan, that winter, there arose in the University of Michigan a demand for a Christian organization of a more positive and stimulating type than the Union Missionary Society of Inquiry formed ten years before. A Students' Christian Association was begun in January, 1858. Women had not as yet been admitted to the University, but on their arrival in 1870 were identified fully with this Association.

That same year, 1858, students at the University of Virginia had been attending a series of revival services held in the Baptist church of Charlottesville by the pastor, Dr. John A. Broadus. Some of these students had been conducting mission Sunday schools and they had been thinking of unifying all the voluntary religious work of the university if possible. On October 12, 1858, a Young Men's Christian Association was organized, adopting a constitution based upon copies of those of the Young Men's Christian Associations in London, England, and in Boston. So hearty a determination did this new Association possess to become a part of the world movement that a clause was inserted granting membership privileges to members of other Young Men's Christian Associations while at the university, and almost immediately it entered the confederation of Young Men's Christian Associations in North America. Other student Young Men's Christian Associations arose, some spontaneously, some encouraged by Robert Weidensall, the first employed officer of the International Committee.

In 1877 the leaders at Princeton University, which had just changed its Philadelphian Society into a Young Men's Christian Association, invited students from other colleges to send representatives to the International Convention of the Young Men's Christian Associations at Louisville, Kentucky; twenty-five responded from twenty-one colleges in eleven states. L. D. Wishard, who with William Earl Dodge, Jr., had been active in Princeton, was asked to become a visiting college secretary because of his familiarity with such work when previously an undergraduate in Hanover College, Indiana. Hanover was in a section where coeducational colleges prevailed and Mr. Wishard was perhaps prepared for the interpretation of the words "Young Men" in the title of the Christian Association as he encountered it on the tours he made in the succeeding years.

When he visited Normal, Illinois, he saw the women's Association at work. That was really a young woman's movement for young women, capable of logical expansion, which could not be said of the other situation, for while the active presence of women students might be helpful in certain localities it could hardly carry weight throughout the whole United States, where in some sections coeducation was not even a debatable question, as it had been decided in the negative without debate.

There was at this time no national organization of Young Women's Christian Associations. Delegates from Women's Christian Associations and Young Women's Christian Associations had met at Hartford, Connecticut, in 1871 in a conference which had occurred biennially for the ten years since. At two of these conferences a member of the International Committee of the Young Men's Christian Associations, Mr. H. Thane Miller of Cincinnati, had taken part in the program. Mr. Miller's bride, formerly principal of Mt. Auburn Young Ladies' Seminary, was also corresponding secretary of the Women's Christian Association of Cincinnati. With these friends, it is said, Mr. Wishard discussed the problem of the withdrawal of the young women from the student Young Men's Christian Association without disturbing the local Christian work. Mrs. Miller consented to bring before the Conference of the Women's Christian Association (which had now become International), on October 12–15, 1881, at St. Louis, the question of establishing relations with Young Women's Christian Associations in colleges and seminaries. After Mrs. Miller had reported from the Young Ladies' Christian Association of Mt. Auburn Institute and stated that the object of the organization was the development of Christian life in the members and those over whom they have influence, Mrs. John McDougal, president of the Association in Montreal, Canada, stated that she had received a communication from the Christian Women's Education Union of Scotland requesting that the young women of America be asked to affiliate with them in Christian work in schools. The conference felt that the importance of the work represented by Mrs. Miller could not be over-rated and asked her and Mrs. Lamson of Boston to act as a committee to see what could be done and report at their earliest convenience. The next day Mrs. Miller reported from the Committee upon Work Among School Girls as follows:

> Believing that great good can be accomplished by the organization of Christian Associations in connection with the young ladies' colleges and seminaries of our country, and that thereby the members of such schools will become familiar with and trained in the methods of the Women's Christian Association of our land, therefore
>
> *Resolved:* that a committee of three or five be appointed by this Conference whose duty it shall be, by correspondence and other methods, to encourage the formation of such organizations in young ladies' schools and colleges, and secure from them, as far as possible, a representation in our future conferences.

The resolution was adopted and Mrs. Miller as chairman of the committee collaborated with Mr. Wishard. His duties took him among the coeducational colleges and into the student conferences where women were present. A circular signed by Mrs. Miller and entitled "Young Women's Christian Associations in American Colleges and Seminaries" was sent out widely. This narrated the action of the St. Louis Conference, omitting the phrases limiting its scope to women's institutions, since Mr. Wishard's problem was in coeducational colleges, and stated the objects to be gained by separate organization, and special advantages as well.

> There are special advantages to be desired from the formation of these Associations in co-educational institutions.
>
> *First.* Young women will naturally feel an increased sense of responsibility in the work of an organization bearing their own name.
>
> *Second.* The existence of two Christian Associations in a co-educational institution will secure that healthful, stimulating competition which greatly promotes activity.
>
> *Third.* Many young women will feel more free to *speak and act* in meetings of their own than in those in which young men are present.
>
> *Fourth.* The organization in co-educational institutions of a special Association for young women by doubling the number of officers and committees, will double the number upon whom rests special responsibility.
>
> In schools and colleges exclusively for young women the proposed organization will not in any way interfere with existing societies or methods, but by bringing these societies into relations with those of other institutions will lend increased efficiency to their present methods of work and each society will become a means of help and inspiration to every one.

The circular announced that a constitution especially adapted to the purposes of the Association could be obtained upon application.

This model constitution in its '83 and '84 editions stood for constitution, by-laws and departmental policies all in one, as citations will show.

> "The object of this Association shall be the development of Christian character in its members and the prosecution of active Christian work, particularly among the young women of the institution." "The active membership of the

Association shall consist of lady students and teachers of this institution who are connected with an evangelical church and have been elected by a majority vote of the members present at any meeting. Only active members shall have the right to vote and hold office."

"Any lady student or teacher in the institution may be elected an associate member by a majority vote of the members present at any meeting." "The corresponding secretary shall be chosen from the incoming Junior class. She shall conduct the correspondence of the Association." "Unless otherwise ordered, all standing committees shall consist of one from each class. They shall report to the Association at each regular business meeting." "The Association shall hold a Social Reception for new students at some time during the first two weeks of the college year, for the purpose of impressing them with the advantages to be derived from their union with it."

At both the International Convention of the Young Men's Christian Associations held in Milwaukee in May, 1883, and the International Conference of the Women's Christian Association held in Boston in October of the same year, Mrs. Miller was present and reported sending out the circulars. Mr. Wishard kept up extensive visitations and in many places, as at Otterbein University, Westerville, Ohio, he helped form, from a Young Ladies' Prayer Meeting which had been kept up many years, a parallel Association to that of the young men's organization he was officially assisting.

The Young Women's Christian Association of Merom Christian College (1883) seems to have been the first started in Indiana. Others that year were Illinois Wesleyan at Bloomington, Illinois; Parsons College, Iowa Wesleyan, and Cornell Colleges in Iowa; Albion, Hillsdale and Kalamazoo Colleges in Michigan, and Wooster University, Ohio. The year 1884 saw a great reinforcement: the state universities of Wisconsin, Illinois and Nebraska and many denominational colleges, among them Knox College at Galesburg, Illinois; DePauw University at Greencastle, Indiana, Coe College at Cedar Rapids, Iowa College at Grinnell and Penn College at Oskaloosa, Iowa; Washburn College at Topeka, Kansas; Carleton College, Northfield, Minnesota; Lawrence University in Wisconsin. The first student Association of the south, at Greenville and Tusculum College, Tennessee, also dates from 1884.

As these were coeducational institutions one is not surprised to find that the young men as well as the young women and many of the faculty of both sexes discussed the proposed "special advantages" *pro* and *con*. Little was to be gained locally from segregation, some thought, and they were not sure what might be gained in wider relations. Mr. Wishard's visits were the most tangible evidence of any general body interested in Young Women's Christian Associations, and he represented then and previously the Young Men's Christian Associations, which he was magnanimously advising the women to leave for their own good. He did not publish the fact that his committee, not Mrs. Miller's, had printed the constitutions and circulars which he told them to secure from her in Cincinnati.

But back of all questions of administration it must be remembered that for a strong appeal to the unconverted the young women had looked to the state secretaries of the Young Men's Christian Association, who in their rounds through their territory were accustomed to hold evangelistic services in the college chapel for all students, or in the churches for college and town communities together. For their Bible study courses they looked to the office of "The Watchman," the Young Men's Christian Association organ of that day, in which "Leaves from a Worker's Note Book" and other popular texts were issued. For their intercollegiate fellowship they depended upon the Young Men's Christian Association conferences, state and district, which might be within reach, and in the arrangements for which they had been officially remembered. After state Associations were formed these conferences were sometimes really joint meetings called by the state committees. The men delegates were college faculty and undergraduates, not the general membership from city and railroad Associations. Speakers of international reputation made addresses, students made reports, and Young Men's Christian Association secretaries led discussion upon topics like the following:

"The Opportunities in College Life for Making Religious Impressions upon Young Men; How Is the Y. M. C. A. Improving Them?" "The Adaptability of the Y. W. C. A. to College Girls; What It Is Doing and Can Do." "The Promotion of the Missionary Spirit in College." "The Bible Training Class." "Intercollegiate Relations." "Claims of the General Secretaryship upon College Graduates." "Individual Work, Its Importance and Blessedness." "The Twofold Purpose of Association Work—Saving Men and Qualifying them to Save Others."

On Sunday there were separate consecration meetings in the morning, and gospel meetings in the afternoon, with a great rally at night for state and national presentation. Certain hours on Friday and Saturday were taken by the young women for their own business meetings, when the alumnae, who had been Association leaders in their undergraduate days, unified this year's meeting with its predecessors and the state executive committee was elected for the next year.

This sort of training made the conduct of a state convention of young women alone no matter for alarm or distrust. Even in the sections where the young women assembled for their first state gathering at a separate time and place apart from the men, some of their prominent women workers had attended these coeducational conferences and knew how to build the program, and some of the Young Men's Christian Association leaders would come to speak, to lead the finance meeting and to advise on the general policies in case they should be asked to do so. Perhaps there was an undercurrent of conviction on their part that such effort was well expended and that whatever strengthened the women's Christian organization in any college would also further the interests of the men. Some of these Young Men's Christian Association secretaries had daughters of their own among the undergraduates and counted the girls' convention a good day's work in their year.

Over the signature of Bell Bevier of Wooster University, as chairman, the Ohio State Executive Committee sent greetings to the young women in colleges and seminaries in Ohio telling of the organization of a State Association during the winter of 1884 (February 14–17) and calling a convention of their own at Westerville, the next February. The circular said, "Perhaps never again in our lives will our field of labor be either so *large* or so *personal* as during the days of our college life. The desirability of some organized method of work that can be adopted by the educated Christian young women of our country is evident, and what more pleasant bond of union could be found." Michigan had formed the first State Association at Albion, also in February, 1884 (convention held 7–11), and Iowa, at a convention in Cedar Rapids attended by fifty delegates from college and one country Young Women's Christian Association, formed the third State Association on November 15 of that year. Their far-reaching Iowa spirit was shown by their response to an appeal of one of their number with a subscription of one hundred and five dollars for "an International College Secretary, a young woman," who, they confidently expected, would be secured during the coming year. Their constitution did not confine the organization to student Associations; a group anywhere was eligible. Remember that the Young People's Society of Christian Endeavor had been known less than four years and had not found its way in any appreciable degree into the Mississippi Valley. At joint conventions in January of 1885, at Whitewater, Wisconsin, and at Bloomington, Illinois, the third and fourth State Associations were effected. In April at Greencastle, Indiana, and in December at

St. Paul, Minnesota, the sixth and seventh State Associations were formed; Kansas and Nebraska followed in 1886.

In all these states, an Executive Committee was elected, representing in its membership each local unit. The main officer was the president, some capable undergraduate, who was then at liberty to select one of her friends as secretary, upon whom the duties of the treasurer also fell, for both state and local financing were simple almost to the point of being negligible. By the fall of 1887 prominent alumnae were being called as state secretaries. Ida Schell entered upon her duties at the close of the Iowa Convention in October, and though she was teaching at the same time, managed to report by the fall of 1888 that she had made twenty-three Association visits, occupying thirty-four days and traveling 2,581 miles. For this and other work throughout the year, chiefly correspondence, she received an honorarium of one hundred dollars and about as much for traveling expenses. Nellie Knox, who assumed a similar position in Ohio in December, 1887, had by April visited twenty-seven points and traveled over a thousand miles. Kansas claims the record for full time employment of a secretary; Mrs. L. P. Bradford of the committee served for April and May, 1888, and Jennie Sherman from June on. Illinois was only a few days behind, for Eula Bates commenced work that same April.

Never were four young women more unlike: Miss Knox, quiet, forceful, with a clear vision of the possibilities in the Association; Miss Schell, substantial, unselfish, a natural bearer of other people's burdens; Miss Sherman, keen, alert, giving God the credit for the seeming miracles that constantly resulted; Miss Bates, gentle, gracious, instinctively making the right approach. All were guided by the Spirit of God to whom they looked for guidance in this untried path. None stayed on to watch her work past the pioneer stage, for one married, one studied medicine, one took a missionary appointment in India and another in Turkey under her church board. None broke down from nervous prostration, although the travel was as exacting, the correspondence as taxing, the strain in interviews and meetings as great as in any subsequent era. Three years later (1891) all but two of the thirteen organized states had the full or part time of a secretary. This advance meant, of course, a larger State Committee at a permanent headquarters, a regular treasury, and sub-committees to care for groups of Associations and the various headquarters duties such as planning the secretary's schedule, arranging for conventions and issuing publications.

Now that the intercollegiate idea was expressed through joining like Associations of college women in the State Association, the dependence upon the Young Men's Christian Association was discontinued, as other means became accessible. The young women helped each other and themselves; the results were proving their claim most often made, that the Young Women's Christian Association had as its distinct object "the development of Christian character and the prosecution of active Christian work among young women."

For spiritual appeal to the uninterested girls they had now the visits of their own state secretary, of their own national secretary and of rare Bible teachers like Naomi Knight, who made tours among the Associations. For their Bible study courses and meeting topics of the Young Women's Christian Associations, the national committee (see chapter XIV) was making some provision through *The Quarterly* and *The Evangel,* although the International Committee of the Young Men's Christian Associations kept ahead for many years. For ideas on conducting Association work and for spiritual vigor which the workers craved, they had their own state and national conventions, besides their secretaries' visits, and after 1891 their own summer conferences.

Two styles of railroad connections were afforded to the towns where a large percentage of the first college Associations were to be found. One was the branch railroad, upon which two trains ran daily each way to and from a larger railroad center several hours distant. The other was the main line where local traffic was accommodated—inaccurate use of the word! —upon the through trains which were scheduled for convenience of passengers arriving at Chicago or Pittsburgh or Buffalo, or St. Paul or Omaha or Kansas City, not that of pilgrims to the academic groves which the student secretary was seeking. Street railways were found in few college towns; unseaworthy hackney carriages and very commercial omnibuses were used for depot service at charges that would have seemed too cheap had they not matched the vehicles so exactly. In order to avoid short night journeys and yet not to be *en route* at the afternoon and evening hours when the students were most at liberty to meet with her, the secretary was repeatedly taking local trains due to depart at seven o'clock in the morning, or boarding through trains due to pass through towns at four o'clock, but frequently belated. Dormitory breakfast hours at 6:30 or 7:00 o'clock sometimes fitted in to this schedule, sometimes not. There were no lunch counters at the stations, no dining cars on the trains as a rule, but even if there had been, the state treasury could hardly have afforded to pay for the seventy-five cent and dollar *table d'hôte* meals then obtainable. There was for some years no state office, and even when the state officers were willing to help they were often busy teachers and undergraduates, who had really less time for Association correspondence than had the state secretary.

When the difficulties arising from newness of the position and the secretary's natural diffidence at venturing forth unpiloted upon uncharted seas have been mentioned, all the disadvantages have been swept away and there can be fully acknowledged some of the many pleasures and satisfactions of those visits to the early student Associations. First, the welcome; delegates to the preceding conventions had helped raise and give the money to put a secretary into the field, they believed in the office, and wanted the officer to spend as long a time in their college as she could. Sometimes she stayed a week, rarely speaking in chapel or leading the college prayer meeting, but holding daily meetings with the girls, talking with those who called at the dormitory guest chamber about their own Christian lives, teaching them to pray for themselves as they surrendered themselves into Jesus Christ's keeping. She talked with the president about "how to get the girls to work on committees," and with the treasurer on "how to get the girls to pay their dues," and with the chairman of the devotional committee about "what kind of topics to have," but there was no drawing up of policies for each committee. Often she gave a Bible reading and once at least spoke about the state work, but her main business was to bring the leaders of the Association and the professed Christian workers into the fulness of spiritual light and power which she knew from experience could come only from claiming the outpouring of the Holy Spirit, and to encourage the others whom she might meet to rouse their wills to lay hold on Jesus Christ for salvation. The secretary tried to represent in herself what the Young Women's Christian Association fully meant. One of them once alluded to her first contact with the movement in this way: "We were awakened to a new and vigorous type of personal service in an every day working religion that sought to make every day a day of opportunity." The undergraduates believed that their secretaries were able to make good use of opportunities and sometimes when bidding one good-by at the railroad station would introduce her to a fellow passenger who had not come under the influence of the last few days.

CHAPTER XI

THE INTENSIVE GROWTH OF STUDENT ASSOCIATIONS

RAPID expansion was seen from 1886 on, expansion into new territory, the East, the Pacific Coast, the South; into new types of institutions, such as women's colleges; into more state universities and normal schools and independent secondary schools. The centers least affected were those where a desire for aggressive evangelical women's organizations had not crystallized, and those where the lady principal felt herself so responsible for the spiritual culture of the young women under her charge that she dared not divide this responsibility with a student society of any kind. Every new Association called something forth from the others and added something to them. Good ideas were not copyrighted and few knew the origin of those most eagerly seized upon. Each successive edition of the model constitution incorporated as standing policies what had been independent experiments a little while before.

A natural goal for the membership committee had been "every young woman in college." Faculty members and former members in town were eligible, so that occasionally the total membership exceeded the number of young women registered. More often, however, the membership consisted of as many of the girls in the residence halls, and from those families which had come to town for the sake of the college, as could be secured as members the first term of their college life. Daughters of families with strong local affiliations and of those residing far distant from the university center, members of the schools of music, expression, etc., when not resident in the dormitories might or might not identify themselves with the Association.

Then a new conception was evolved; a Reception Committee was constituted to have charge of the special efforts to reach the new students at the beginning of the year, and also throughout the year plan a social life for the Association which should unite all young women in the institution in a Christian sisterhood. The social program at first had been brief but striking in its innovations upon that most conservative element, college tradition.

For decades the first general social occasion in many colleges had been the formal receptions tendered by the rival literary societies in alternating years or as close together as the faculty would allow. The new students were expected to attend without fail, were judiciously escorted, lavishly entertained, and fulsomely impressed with the master idea of the evening, namely, that a college career would be unendurable unless the student were at once proposed for the entertaining society. When the first delegates reported from some convention that in some colleges the Christian Associations had been given right of way in social matters at the beginning of the year some of the Association leaders faced a painful dilemma. If they fell into line, the literary society of the opposition might get more members than their own, whose turn it was to entertain. If they did not fall into line, they would be justly despised by the colleges which had already made the sacrifice. They usually solved the difficulty by holding the Association reception the first week and offering even more sumptuous entertainments by the literary societies afterwards. Then the informal receptions for the girls alone found place here.

Another innovation was the Student Handbook, sent out to intending students with a letter of welcome through the long vacation or given out at the registrar's office. These pocket manuals were usually issued with the Young Men's Christian Association and gave the current and historical information about the college, the Associations, and the community, which new students were sure to need.

Leadership of the religious meetings grew to be more formal than the occasional custom of assigning each member in alphabetical order had made possible. Topics were more carefully selected, and topic cards were presented in advance, following out a general scheme by which gospel meetings, missionary meetings, opportunities for presentation of religious movements, each had a place. Instead of one noon prayer meeting in an administrative or recitation building, small prayer circles met in the residence halls at an evening hour. The early period of private prayer, The Morning Watch, was becoming known as "the secret of a strong Christian life for a busy student,'' and officers and committee chairmen often met weekly in prayer together even when there was no regular cabinet meeting. For any series of evangelistic meetings projected by college authorities or by the Association as such, there was careful organization of invitation giving and of personal interviews, so that each woman student not known to be a Christian might find help through these meetings. When attendance at chapel and church was voluntary the Association members supported these loyally, as they did the class prayer meetings, separate missionary meetings, or other general religious gatherings not under the Association auspices.

The growth in Bible study was tremendously quickened through summer conference delegates, who often declared they did not know before that the Bible was written for thinking people and were charmed to find that a book that had met the old, old needs of centuries of human lives had anything to say to nineteenth century undergraduates. The distinction made between a general Bible class and a workers' training class has already been noted. There has been no time when a student Young Women's Christian Association could fulfill its obligation unless there were several young women concerned with relating the lives of individual students to their Lord and Master Jesus Christ. But even the best methods became trite and meaningless when followed in the letter and not in the spirit. For this reason the valuable early texts fell into disuse, but the work of personal evangelism which these were designed to further, has again in these later years come to the front, as the real meanings of membership are better construed and the obligations of leadership are being assumed, not with a note of interrogation, but with affirmation of the supremacy of the spirit.

Missionary interests have been almost from the first closely connected with the Student Volunteer Movement for Foreign Missions, which dated from the summer of 1886, the same season in which the State Committees formed the National Young Women's Christian Association (see chapter XIV).

So dear a prerogative is the sending and receiving of greetings at all conventions, that one does not always pay too strict attention to what the content of such messages may be. That could not have been the case, however, with the following communication.

Mt. Hermon, Mass., July 31, 1886.

To the Representatives of the Young Women's Christian Association at Geneva, Wisconsin:

The two hundred and eighty college students representing ninety-eight College Young Men's Christian Associations, now in session in their school for Bible Study at Mt. Hermon, Mass., send Christian greeting to the Young Women's Christian Associations of the United States about to convene at Geneva, Wisconsin, with a view to forming a National organization.

We rejoice to hear of your Convention and its purposes because we believe that God is waiting to show that as He has blest the exclusive Evangelical work of young men for young men so will He also set His seal of approval upon the work of young women for young women. We congratulate you, first, because your meeting will be a notable event in the history of the special Christian work of the age.

Secondly, we congratulate you upon the tact, energy, and

devotion shown in your arrangements for the proposed convention and in the plans which you purpose in it to carry out.

Thirdly, we congratulate you also upon the opportunity you are about to have for receiving the outpouring of God's blessing in a like way to that we have enjoyed.

And we invoke upon you and your deliberations at Geneva, and upon the great work you there may plan and organize, the blessing of our Heavenly Father.

By the Committee:

HOWARD H. RUSSELL, Oberlin College, Chairman
A. M. CUNNINGHAM, Illinois State Normal
S. C. BARTLETT, JR., Dartmouth College
P. B. GUERNSEY, Madison University
O. A. LEWIS, Carleton College
E. H. RAWLINGS, Randolph Macon College
E. C. WHITNEY, Amherst College
JOHN MCDOUGALL, McGill University
J. R. MOTT, Cornell University

This was the historic month of July when at the invitation of Mr. D. L. Moody, men had assembled from universities and colleges in all parts of the United States and Canada to study the Bible in this place apart. This first student summer conference was also the birthplace of the Student Volunteer Movement. It is said that ten days cf the conference had gone by before the subject of missions was even mentioned in the Conference, but some had come with the conviction that out from that large gathering God would call some to consecrate themselves as foreign missionaries. One of this number was Robert P. Wilder of Princeton. He, his sister Grace Wilder, and others of that missionary family had prayed unceasingly for workers not only for India, their home land, but for all other sections of the unevangelized world. When the invitation was given at Mt. Hermon to those thinking seriously of foreign service, twenty-one came together. They began to pray that the Lord of the harvest would separate many of these delegates to the great work. Then the answer began to come. After two weeks of thinking and praying there occurred the "Meeting of the Ten Nations," where sons of missionaries in China, India and Persia, and young men of America, Japan, Siam, Germany, Denmark and Norway, and an American Indian, each told in a three minute address that his country needed more workers from that very group of students and ended by repeating "God is love" in the language of the country he represented. The number of intending missionaries increased from twenty-one to nearly fifty. It is said that missions became the topic of all conversation, everywhere. Each volunteer approached others and one by one men came in to announce that they had won the victory over self which set them free to follow Christ's command. When the farewell meeting of the Conference assembled there were ninety-nine enrolled; when it closed one more had announced his decision and an even one hundred college men stood as volunteers for the foreign mission field.

The Cambridge Band and its tours of the British Universities was then in people's minds. They recalled the dynamic impression made by these seven conspicuous leaders in Cambridge University life as they presented the claim of the unevangelized world to other undergraduates and led the way out to China. Many had been stirred that very winter by J. E. K.

Studd's account of it while he was visiting American universities. The volunteers at Mt. Hermon approved such a scheme of deputations and selected four men to visit throughout the country, laying before other students the reasons which had led them to offer their lives. That year Mr. Wilder and Mr. John N. Forman visited one hundred and seventy-six colleges and divinity schools in the United States and Canada, going two by two for the most part, rallying students around the idea of the evangelizing of the world in this generation; an idea which seemed as visionary in 1886 as it seemed justified in 1913. Like a revelation of the apostles of the primitive church seemed the visit of these two men of prayer to many of the institutions when they came. Like a miracle seemed the response. Twenty-one hundred students volunteered that year; five hundred of these were from the student Young Women's Christian Associations. The percentage was even higher in some later seasons. Robert E. Speer, Lucy Guinness, Clarissa H. Spencer and Horace Tracy Pitkin were among the later traveling secretaries.

How to make the movement permanent seemed to be answered in 1888 by appointing an Executive Committee of one each from the International Committees of the Young Women's Christian Association and Young Men's Christian Association and a third person to represent the Inter-Seminary Missionary Alliance. Mr. John R. Mott, the first chairman, has continued in office ever since. The great Student Volunteer Movement conventions, occurring once in a student generation, the mission study texts, dating from the course on Missions in the Apostolic Church published in "*The Student Volunteer*" in 1893, the missionary institutes at the summer conferences, the instigation to missionary reading and giving on the part of the whole student body, are only means to the end of convincing students of their opportunity and obligation in answering the world challenge for the spread of a world Christianity.

Wherever a college had undertaken, before the Association was organized, the support of a missionary or foreign student or school or other special work under the church board with which the college was affiliated, as was many times the case, the missionary department assumed that obligation before contributing missionary gifts through other channels. After 1894, when the state secretary of Iowa was called to become general secretary of the World's Young Women's Christian Association, and an alumna of the University of Illinois sailed as the first American secretary to India, there was lively interest in these two new avenues for missionary giving. Students who were in college January 20, 1895, will remember the dime banks which were sent out by Miss R. F. Morse, the American member of the World's Committee responsible for raising funds in this country, and the request to hold on that day an Oriental tea, or in some other way to present the interest of foreign Young Women's Christian Association work and collect fifty dimes for the world's treasury.

Intercollegiate relations were most evident at the

time when delegations were being made up for the state and national conventions and for the summer conferences, which began as a Summer Bible and Training School in 1891. These developed more for volunteers than for employed officers and by 1902 had begun a still further specialization, one conference for students only. But the widest reach of intercollegiate fellowship was the inclusion of the Student Young Women's Christian Associations in the World's Student Christian Federation, which was formed in 1895 in the following way: In 1887 Professor Henry Drummond of Edinburgh University visited the Northfield Men's Conference; in 1888 a delegation of twelve students came from the Universities of Oxford, Cambridge and Utrecht. James Bronson Reynolds of Yale made several tours among continental and Levantine universities in 1889 to 1892, concentrating his attention on the student situation in Paris. John R. Mott spent the spring months of 1894 in the British colleges and attended the Keswick student conference when the British College Christian Union was formed. Mr. Wishard had lately returned from his world trip in which student Associations had been developed in mission lands.

Prince Bernadotte of Sweden invited student leaders to Vadstena Castle in the summer of 1895 and two hundred accepted. Delegates came from the United States and Canada, representing the Intercollegiate department of the Young Men's Christian Associations of North America, through which the student organizations affiliated with the International Committee of

Young Women's Christian Associations were given membership; from the British College Christian Union, representing both men and women students in Great Britain and Ireland; from the German Christian Students' Alliance; and from universities in Denmark, Sweden, Norway and Finland, about to unite in the Scandinavian Student Movement. The widely scattered student Associations in non-Christian countries were counted as a fifth Movement, represented by Mr. Wishard as the foreign work secretary. Dr. Karl Fries of Sweden was elected chairman and John R. Mott general secretary. For twenty years they have stood by the task the Federation assumed that day:

1. To unite student Christian movements or organizations throughout the world, and to promote mutual relations among them.
2. To collect information about the religious condition of the students of all lands.
3. To lead students to become disciples of Jesus Christ as their only Saviour and God.
4. To deepen the spiritual life of students.
5. To enlist students in the work of extending the Kingdom of Christ throughout this world.

Ten years later at the Zeist, Holland, Conference, a women's department of this Federation was created and two of the most remarkable women of this generation were appointed to leadership which rallied women students of all types and faculties. Professor Lilavati Singh of Lucknow College, India, was made vice-chairman. She had been introduced at the Ecumenical Missionary Conference of 1900 in New York City as a young woman who had read Green's

Miss Ruth Rouse,
When Representing the Student Volunteer Movement

History of the English People through seven times in her eagerness to acquire the English language. It was after hearing Miss Singh's address on the Results of Higher Education, of which she was herself an exponent, that Ex-President Benjamin Harrison said, "If I had given a million dollars to foreign missions, I should count it wisely invested if it led only to the conversion of that one woman." The western world had little time to see the results of Miss Singh's influence upon the woman's movement, for her death in 1909 cut short that career which would have been a revelation to people unappreciative of Oriental intellect and little acquainted with the history of woman's education in India. Miss Ruth Rouse of Girton College, Cambridge, the general secretary, is well known in America, which she first visited in 1897 as a representative of the Student Volunteer Movement before taking up residence in Bombay in the Missionary Settlement of University Women. Then the International Committee of Young Women's Christian Associations prevailed on her to postpone her plans still another year, and she returned to this country for special student work during the next academic year. It was during this stay that she and Miss Grace H. Dodge talked together at the time of the New York metropolitan conference about what Christian life in educational centers in other lands might be if the student Associations of America would rise to their opportunities, look far afield as well as upon their own campuses and take a share worthy of the name among the women students of the world.

From this interview resulted the more adequate place which American women students have since assumed in foreign student affairs.

It will be remembered that the first organization called itself the Young Ladies' Christian Association of Normal, not of the Illinois State Normal University. Every Association since has felt some call to outside activities, both for the natural expression of an unselfish Christian life, and because many communities have offered appealing fields for the service which could be rendered by college women, endowed as missionaries, speakers, Bible teachers, sympathetic visitors, or organizers of groups for entertainment or study. Mission Sunday schools have been a favorite community enterprise and from these have resulted churches or Young Women's Christian Associations or other permanent institutions. From this training many a girl has gone out from University or normal school, into some isolated town or village so untouched by any organized church that this young teacher has called a Sunday school into being, recruited teachers, herself acted as superintendent, and changed the whole face of affairs. When student Associations are near cities this outside work committee has had literally no end to its opportunities, and when it has been near the open country its response has meant even more self sacrifice on the part of the members, who have made their way along the snowy roads on their Sunday and week-day appointments of winter after winter.

Nothing but preoccupation in the subject of the

meeting, or an enthusiasm which was blind to all physical objects, could have made endurable some of the rooms in which the early student Associations held their meetings. These were chiefly college recitation rooms where settees and the professors' desk were the only furniture, and where the blackboards, covered with geometrical demonstrations with and without the subscription Q. E. D., or corrected French prose sentences, were the only mural decorations. In 1890 only twenty-three Associations reported rooms and only a part of these were large enough for the purposes of an assembly room. In 1900 there were one hundred and forty-nine, many of them dignified and attractive. Although the subject of a building for Association headquarters at the University of Iowa had been broached for some time and pledges had been made to secure one, yet Brinton Hall in Philadelphia was given to the Woman's Medical College of Pennsylvania Association in 1888; the Iowa building, Close Hall, was dedicated in November, 1891; and the next year Stiles Hall was erected for the Association at the University of California. These were both administration buildings for both men's and women's Associations. The Otterbein College building was dedicated in 1893. All sorts of experiences have resulted from renting a large house near the University campus and opening it as Young Women's Christian Association headquarters with home accommodations for the secretary and several members. Other Associations have been amply provided for in the women's building designed for headquarters for all the women's organizations. This assures the general secretary a strategic location for her office.

From the very first every Association has craved for its president a student of outstanding rank, in scholarship as well as in administrative ability and Christian influence. But how to exercise the second requisite without detriment to the first qualification was at times a problem. This led the University of Wisconsin in 1895 to elect a graduate, Mary Armstrong, as general secretary at a nominal salary. Estelle Bennett was called to the University of Minnesota in 1896. Other universities adopted the idea, though they often found that the woman they wanted was a graduate from another university, was commanding a higher salary, and needed a more thorough professional training than was at first taken into consideration. Some of these secretaries have been of the greatest help in introducing student government, or bringing recognition to higher standards of student life as well as in Association administration and in working on vital problems of thought and life with individual students. Each decade placed certain new emphases. Even the terms were being reversed: "The Christian Student" of the nineteenth century became "The Student Christian" in the twentieth.

CHAPTER XII

COUNTRY ASSOCIATIONS

IT may be said that the Young Women's Christian Association in rural communities has been expressed in terms of the college, the city and the county. The time is coming when it will express itself in terms of the country.

The first intimation of country work is found in Iowa. In a letter dated February 9, 1885, one reads,

> The weather with us this winter has been very severe, the thermometer reaching 39° below zero. We have been obliged to give up our Bible class, as the weather has been so very cold we were unable to get to our places of meeting. Some of our members had a distance of four or five miles and it made it almost impossible to attend. To-day the fiercest snow storm that I ever saw has been raging. It commenced yesterday afternoon and I am afraid will rage all night. God pity the poor.

Again under date of April 23, 1885, from the same correspondent there is another communication.

> We feel more encouraged not only by our being able to have our regular Bible class again, but the manner in which the girls have taken hold of the work. They all seem more interested in Bible study than last summer, and we all felt that we were profited by last summer's work. We have held several Gospel meetings with the Young Men's Christian Association of Pleasant Valley lately, and expect to hold them as often as we can, for they have been very well

attended, notwithstanding the usual bad spring roads. At one of these, two started on the right way. In the last year, three or four of my most intimate friends have been brought to Christ. Our Bible class has twenty members and our Association about the same.

This was the Association in Pleasant Valley township, Johnson County, Iowa. The school house, which provided a true religious center, was situated seven miles from Iowa City, the seat of the University of Iowa, and four miles from the nearest church. In the summer of 1884 the young men in the neighborhood organized a Young Men's Christian Association after the pattern of the student Associations to which several belonged, and a few months later the young women adopted a similar institution.

Each organization had its own business meetings and Bible class sessions, for which they came together in private houses. The joint gospel meetings were held every other Sunday evening at the school house, with an average attendance of sixty, and were conducted by leaders chosen alternately from the two Associations. They set an example followed by the young people in adjoining neighborhoods. There were also social gatherings and lectures.

After a few years when some of the leaders had left home for professional service in the Association movement and elsewhere, the Pleasant Valley work lapsed, but the results had already been recorded as "elevating social pleasures, interest in higher literary culture and forming of sterling Christian character."

This Association had also been a charter member of the Iowa State Young Women's Christian Association and one of its officers had been on the committee which drew up the articles of organization of this first State Association in which affiliation was not limited to student Young Women's Christian Associations, but open to any Young Women's Christian Association in the State, provided its object was the maintenance of prayer meetings, Bible study, individual effort and the development of missionary interest.

For a time, enthusiastic Association leaders, going home to villages and small towns or becoming teachers in these small communities, frequently organized what they called local or city Associations, but what were really the spirit and activities of their beloved college organization transplanted bodily into another soil. That all did not flourish was not so much due to the sterility of the soil as to the fact that the plants were not adapted to it, or that the field was often abandoned, though rarely neglected by the gardener. Of the first twenty such Associations listed in five States in 1887, only one had as many as eighty-five members; that was in Kalamazoo, Michigan, which had Association rooms and the beginnings of a genuine city work. Eighteen of these town Associations were found in Iowa, Kansas and Michigan, in which states the Christian Endeavor Movement, started in 1881, was just getting a foothold.

In one or two cities in Ohio there were Women's Christian Associations, conducting a class in sewing for little girls or helping in relief work, but as far removed from genuine Young Women's Christian Association work in small towns on the one hand, as these student Association extensions were on the other. Evidently these were not the right ways.

But not for a moment were the girls forgotten. People were thinking, and occasionally some one wrote out her thoughts:

> Many girls in country regions have ambitions which grow faster than their opportunities; they long for something more than their circumstances will allow, or the place affords; their active spirits grow restless and dissatisfied, and, allured on by bright prospects of good positions, educational and social advantages, they speed city-ward. This is not as it should be. Let no one think because a place is too small to demand and support a full fledged Young Women's Christian Association, that therefore nothing can be done for young women.

Another solution was coming, and as in two preceding plans of Young Women's Christian Association work in country and small towns, coming from the devotion of former student Association leaders. A Carleton college graduate of 1896, teaching in the High School of Preston, Minnesota, was asked to form a class for Bible study. As the interest grew, some of these class members became pupil teachers for other circles in Preston, and hearing of what was going forward in Preston, women in other small towns in Fillmore County formed Bible circles.

The Minnesota State Committee kept in close touch and took counsel with Mr. Robert Weidensall, the pathfinder of the International Young Men's Christian Association, who had added to his pioneer efforts in student and railroad Associations, an exploration of the rural and small town field. The result was that he had brought under way county Associations in Illinois, Nebraska, Kentucky and elsewhere. The state secretary of Minnesota, Helen F. Barnes, arranged a convention of the Bible circles of Fillmore County for December 31, 1897, to January 2, 1898, Mr. Weidensall was one of the speakers, and when the delegates had organized the first county Young Women's Christian Association in the world, he met with the County Committee and helped in outlining their work. The convention, like the Bible circles, gave first attention to study of God's word, but there was a social evening in the Preston Association circle rooms—for Preston was the exception to the rule in having local headquarters—and other helpful convention features. In March, 1898, Dodge County also effected an organization. By spring there was the following County roster in Minnesota:

Fillmore County: Preston—three circles (for seniors, young ladies and juniors), Cherry Grove—a senior and a junior circle, Spring Valley, Etna, Fillmore, Washington, Hamilton, Granger.

Dodge County: West Concord, Kasson, Dodge Center, and a country class near Dodge Center.

Olmstead County: Stewartville, Cummingsville, Eyota.

Other Bible circles on the same plan had been started out of the State.

As the Young Men's Christian Association had made a pre-eminent success of county work with a supervising secretary, so the Minnesota workers learned conversely that a secretary was indispensable, because without one, the local circles lost interest and gradually disbanded, and the county Association disintegrated. The full scheme had not been tried, it ceased, not failed. People still had faith in some far off event, or plan, or leader, which would help the country girls come into their own.

CHAPTER XIII

THE CONFERENCES OF THE WOMEN'S CHRISTIAN ASSOCIATIONS

THE Women's Christian Association of Hartford, Connecticut, invited the officers of all similar Associations known at that time to come and celebrate with them their fourth anniversary, on Sunday, October 8, 1871.

The Sabbath was devoted to the anniversary exercises, held in the Pearl Street Church; the following Monday and Tuesday to the conference, in the same church, for which fifteen delegates had come from Boston, Providence, Lowell, Buffalo, Washington, Cincinnati and Philadelphia.

The presiding officer was that elect lady, Mrs. John Davis, president of the Association in Cincinnati. The program was made up of reports from these eight cities and from thirteen others not represented by delegates, in addition to discussion of the following topics:

1. What are the greatest obstacles to the successful working of our Associations?
2. How shall we secure efficient committees?
3. How shall we establish systematic payments?
4. How shall we best gain a permanent influence over the industrial young woman?

5. What is the best method of Bible teaching in the classes of young women connected with the Homes or Associations?
6. Is it expedient to have a department for the more thorough training of sewing girls in the Homes?
7. Is it economy or promotive of family feeling to have the Home table on the restaurant plan?

Mr. H. Thane Miller of Cincinnati, who had a bent for organization and a gift of song, sang frequently, as well as spoke. One selection was "More Love to Thee, O Christ," which had just appeared. Mrs. Lamson of Boston described the Young Women's Christian Association homes in London which she had lately visited. A trip was made to the still uncompleted Hartford building. The news of the Chicago fire was made known, and resolutions were sent to the women in Chicago.

The call to the conference had emphasized the meetings for prayer, social converse and discussion of important questions which would be both pleasant and profitable for those actively engaged in "striving to protect and to benefit in every way their young sisters, who are toiling for their own and others' support, with many trials and temptations." This was all realized and a resolution was adopted providing for similar meetings to be held at intervals of not more than two years. To carry this resolution into effect a committee of arrangements was appointed, which selected Philadelphia as the place of the next meeting.

Here forty-eight delegates from seventeen other Associations listened to a comprehensive, lucid address

WOMEN'S CHRISTIAN ASSOCIATION,
Hartford, Conn.
First Building Constructed for Association Purposes

by Mrs. Davis, the retiring president, in which she reviewed the work for young women and other kinds of ministry offered by the organizations represented, counting among the results already attained, the extent of the movement and the spirit in which it was carried on. As before, the program was occupied chiefly with reports from cities, and discussion of topics previously announced. These were opened by papers on "Boarding Homes for Young Women, How Can We Best Secure the True Aim of Such Homes?" "American Girls for Domestic Service," and an address on "Personal Consecration to Christ Essential to Success in Association Work," by Mrs. Hannah Whitall Smith. When the question arose as to the eligibility of voters, it was decided that any member present of any Christian Association should be considered a voter; and a list was printed in that report of thirty-two cities where Women's Christian Associations were established, two containing Young Women's Christian Associations, two Young Ladies' Branches were also mentioned, thirty-six city Associations in all in the United States.

So far no organization had been effected for this conference. In Pittsburgh in 1875, however, the question of a more definite form of organization was presented and a constitution was adopted providing —under the name of Conference of the Women's Christian Associations of the United States and British Provinces—for an executive committee "charged with the selection of topics for the conference, with the examination of the credentials of delegates, with the selection of persons to open these topics or to present papers upon them. They shall prepare and publish a report of the conferences, conduct correspondence with, and encourage visitation among the Associations, promote the work of existing societies, stimulate organizations in places where they do not already exist, and transact such other business as may be entrusted to them by the conference.'' There was also provision for a financial policy and for the appointment of a general secretary. In order, however, to have more time for thorough discussion, this constitution was reconsidered before adjournment, and a committee authorized to provide possible substitutes for certain of the sections. In consequence the Montreal Conference of 1877 adopted the following constitution:

Article I—Name

This organization shall be called "The International Conference of Women's Christian Associations."

Article II—Object

Its object shall be mutual conference about the work of these Associations.

Article III—Meetings

The meetings of the conference shall be held once in two years.

Article IV—Representation

Each Association of one hundred members or less shall be entitled to two delegates, and for every one hundred members one additional delegate.

The accompanying rules provided that at the closing session of the conference the president should appoint ''a committee of three whose duty it shall be to arrange for the next conference by making selections of topics for discussion and appointing persons to open the same. They shall also prepare a program for all meetings. The secretaries, with the assistance of the president, shall prepare and publish the proceedings of the conference,'' and further, that ''no standing or special committee shall contract any money indebtedness without previous appropriation from the conference.''

During the Philadelphia Conference of 1873 communications from Rome, Italy and Salt Lake City, Utah, had led to the appointment of a Foreign Committee and a Home Committee to look into the possibility of aiding evangelical work in these two centers. This action and the opening of Associations in Canada, had led the Committee on Arrangements for the following meeting to call for an International Conference, and to invite Associations of other countries to send delegates. Such a delegate was Mrs. P. D. Browne of Montreal, who brought with her an invitation for the 1877 Conference to come over the border into Canada. Quebec and Belleville, Ontario, sent accounts of work. Frances Ridley Havergal wrote a poem for the occasion. Mrs. Pennefather of London (who was afterwards successor to Miss Robarts as head of the Prayer Union) sent a paper on Reformatory Work, and another on The Deaconess House of Mildmay Park. Protestant mission work in France and Holland and Canada was reported and a letter read from Mlle. Anna de Perrot of Neuchatel, Switzerland, with whose name the Union International des Amies de la Jeune Fille is connected. Similar reports were rendered for two or three succeeding conferences.

The Foreign Committee appointed in 1873 recommended later that the work under consideration in Rome be referred to the existing Missionary Societies, and the Home Committee presented a list of Associations in good condition and active sympathy the one with the other.

As truly as the personnel of these Conferences represented the Christian devotion and power of the women of the time, so the papers read by these ladies reflected the economic aspects of women's lives. Mrs. Terhune's brilliant paper on "Our Daughters," read in 1875, has already been cited. A quotation from Mrs. McCollins' paper read in 1877 may find a place here.

> Every conceivable machine for labor-saving is invented. Work that would take days to perform by hand is done in so many hours. Even the devices of Dame Fashion, which were entirely beyond the scope of machinery when first introduced, are at once seized upon by the remorseless inventor, and before the article attains to common use, the iron shaft and buzzing wheel have stolen from human fingers the work that would have secured a competency to hundreds. Every department of labor has been invaded by this inexorable genius, agricultural, manufacturing, mercantile and domestic—yea, even science and art are robbed of much that is pleasant to the eye by the inevitable machine. With all this we are now struggling, but wait until Time, the great harmonizer, shall adjust all these innovations to the needs and capacities of the human family.
>
> Many of us remember the hue and cry raised by the farmers and others when the railroads were first opened

through our country. There would be no work for man or use for horses! What would become of all those connected with the stage coaches, etc., etc.? But look now, and behold the hundreds employed by the railroads where the tens were needed by the stage coach.

The inventor has created this necessity for laborers. Take the sewing machine, which has a place in every family. How loudly it was cried down at first, but with it has come an increased demand for sewing. New styles and stitches, endless hemmings, tuckings, frillings and rufflings, that would never have been dreamed of, are the result. Invention has created the necessity.

Other notable contributions to these conferences were the papers by Miss Juliet Corson in 1879 on "Cooking Schools," and by Miss Grace H. Dodge in 1885 on "Practical Suggestions Relating to Moral Elevation and Preventive Work Among Girls."

Among the visitors to the New York Conference in 1887 were the English party consisting of Lord Kinnaird, who had just succeeded Lord Shaftesbury as president of the British Young Women's Christian Associations, and his sisters the Honorables Emily and Gertrude Kinnaird, Mr. G. L. Dashwood, a generous patron of the London Associations, and Professor Henry Drummond of Edinburgh, who had been teaching Bible classes at the Young Men's Student Conferences at Northfield. Their observations on Christian work, as done by women in the States, were most illuminating, as were their accounts of similar activities on their side of the water.

The steady increase in equipment, forces and results of the constituent Associations was after all the most absorbing topic at all of these ten conferences, shown by the local reports and the practical papers written by the women who had brought these things to pass. This advance has already been noted in the preceding chapters on local city Associations, their organization and development.

The future of the conference will be treated later on.

CHAPTER XIV

THE NATIONAL ASSOCIATION—LATER THE AMERICAN COMMITTEE

PUBLICATIONS, Correspondence, Visitation, Conferences: the members of the Student Young Women's Christian Associations thus dissected their special desires to be realized from a general movement. These had been furnished through their neighborly relations to the Intercollegiate Young Men's Christian Association, but, as the Iowa Convention had voted, they wanted "an Intercollegiate secretary of their own, a young woman." Mrs. Miller's committee did not seem able to help in these regards. The conferences of 1881 and 1883, at which it had been appointed, had neglected to make any appropriation, although most deeply interested in the work for which they held their committee responsible. The monthly periodicals, valuable to the Women's Christian Associations, were primarily the organs of local city Associations and did not approach student questions. The same was true of the biennial conferences, and no representatives from the Women's Christian Association were sent to attend the state conventions where the bulk of the membership came together to discuss topics germane to their particular concerns. The young women felt that these elements might be supplied if back of the International Conference there were an international organization, constituted with both city and student interests in view, and electing at conferences a permanent committee or board, to execute between conferences the wishes there expressed by the representative of the local Associations. With a fixed headquarters and a committee sitting regularly to consider student matters, there could be a large, helpful correspondence and the publication of necessary supplies, and a college secretary could be sent out to visit individual student Associations and meet with the large groups of delegates who attended the state conventions.

Consequently in the fall of 1885 the seven organized states at their conventions or through their executive committees united in framing a resolution to be offered to the conference which was to be entertained by the Women's Christian Association of Cincinnati in October, 1885. Anna Downey, the state chairman of Indiana, and Ida L. Schell, chairman of Iowa, accompanied to this conference Naomi Knight of Nebraska, formerly of the Northwestern College Association of Illinois. Other students were present and gave verbal reports.

It had been the expectation of the committee to present at that same session the following proposition.

1. That a permanent international organization of the Young Women's Christian Associations be formed whose

object shall be to promote the physical, social, mental and spiritual welfare of young women, whose membership shall consist of Young Women's Christian Associations whose active, i.e., voting and office holding membership, shall be limited to young women who are members in good standing of an evangelical church.

2. That a permanent executive committee be appointed by the Convention to oversee the execution of its plans in the development of its work.

However, in many private conversations with leading women at the conference, not one was found willing to support the proposition at that time. It was only eight years before at Montreal that their present working constitution had been substituted for that of 1875, which had proposed a permanent organization. Many Associations were carrying on important departments other than the promotion of the physical, social, mental and spiritual life of young women and might not wish to limit their activities. The large range of work did not call for a uniform basis, and while in most of the earliest formed Associations the active members were communicants of evangelical churches, it would not be feasible to recommend that basis for general adoption. Without such a regularly organized body to define its functions any executive committee would naturally be impossible. The college representatives, fearing that a public presentation would only cause trouble and come to nothing, since they had been informed, unofficially of course, that the resolutions if presented would be laid upon the table indefinitely, did not offer the resolutions they had prepared, and some of the ladies understood that action was to be postponed until 1887 when it would be up for free discussion at the New York Conference. But the girls did not seem to realize that and reported to the State Committees that they had failed in their mission.

That they had come with a mission, and that mission a proposition to unite in a new organization, was unknown to the main body of delegates, who supposed from the local accounts and the report of the Committee on Schools and Colleges, that these student Associations belonged to the conferences in the same sense as the delegates from cities belonged. The invitation to participate in the conference had always been general and hearty and no definite application to join was made by any organization. Societies doing the work of Women's Christian Associations were eligible to send representatives and read reports: only the *number* of delegates from each was limited. These meetings were for the purpose of mutual conference; in fact, it was definitely held that delegates were sent to get information rather than to decide measures. At the students' conventions, however, the regular delegates came from the evangelical Associations which had applied for affiliation. Women guests from other Associations, no matter what their form of organization, were received as corresponding members only. Hence the local Associations did not suppose they belonged to the International Conference, to join which they had not made application, and the State Associations did not suppose they belonged as they had not been encouraged to unfold a plan of joining which they came to the conference to propose. There was complete misunderstanding on both sides.

When the state student conventions were informed that nothing had been accomplished at Cincinnati relative to a National Young Women's Christian Association, they decided to unite among themselves, and elected delegates to a Constitutional Convention, to be held at Lake Geneva, Wisconsin, in August, 1886. Several states, keeping closely in mind their hope for a national woman secretary, pledged funds in advance for the purpose; others followed the example of Iowa still further and amended their constitution so that other than student Associations might be incorporated into the proposed body.

Lake Geneva, like Lake Chautauqua, and other small inland bodies of water, has acquired a reputation from the assemblies congregating there, which carries such weight in certain circles that the question of its own natural beauty is rarely raised, but its contour, its wooded banks and its shining waters had been lovely in themselves long before public attention was called to the place. At one of the promontory-like entrances to Williams Bay, west of the town, a clergyman's family had for some years conducted a camp for Christian people of congenial tastes, and here at Camp Collie, secretaries of the Illinois and Wisconsin Young Men's Christian Associations had planted the first summer conference, under the name Western Secretarial Institute, in 1884. At that time the Chicago trains which afforded the best railroad connection, reached only the town of Lake Geneva at the eastern end of the lake, from whence steamboats carried the passengers to the few hotels and private homes located at other points along the shore. The Association men brought their families and made the season vacational as well as vocational in character. Most of the young women student leaders who had graduated were teaching in high schools or colleges, hence the summer was the propitious time for their meeting. The wives of some of the leading secretaries, interested in the student work, were to be at Camp Collie in August of 1886, hence the invitation to hold this convention at Camp Collie came about very naturally and was accepted all the more readily, since Chicago was the geographical and railroad center of the nine states cooperating and Lake Geneva was only two hours distant.

Nineteen delegates met on August 6 at Bay View Cottage, Camp Collie, and continued in session a full week. Misses Knight and Schell explained the outcome of their visit to Cincinnati, the items of the articles of organization as approved by the state conventions were discussed, there was much prayer and quiet consideration of the whole subject—for it was a solemn responsibility, this launching of a national Christian movement—and then on August 11, 1886, the National Association of the Young Women's Christian Associations of the United States was formed. Its object was the organization and development of Young Women's Christian Associations for the promotion of the social, physical, intellectual and spiritual

OFFICE OF
ROBT WEIDENSALL,
WESTERN SECRETARY OF THE EXECUTIVE COMMITTEE,
YOUNG MEN'S CHRISTIAN ASSOCIATIONS
OF THE UNITED STATES AND BRITISH PROVINCES,
No. 148 MADISON STREET,
CHICAGO, ILL.

List of
Young women delegates who formed The National Organization Young Womans Christian Associations of The United States of America – at Camp Collie Aug. 1886 –

Cassie A Reamer Hillsdale College Hillsdale Mich (Oberlin O.)
Anna P Knight, Normal, Ill.
Nellie M Knappen Albion Coll., Albion, Mich
Marian L. Stacy – Iowa College Grinnell Iowa –
Susie E. Cushman Carleton College, Northfield, Minnesota
Nellie S Knox Otterbein University Westerville O
Carrie Haigh University of Chicago, Chicago Ill
Fanny Blair Mankato State Normal. Winnebago City Minn
Altha J Watson Ill Wesleyan, Normal, Ill
Maud Berggren, Knox College, Galesburg Ill
Cornelia Jones Simpson College Indianola (Des Moines Iowa)
Susie S Goures Wayland Uni Beaver Dam Wis.
Anna M Hervey Wis Univ Madison
Rosa E. Lewis Penn College. Oskaloosa Iowa
Ida L Shell Mt. Vernon Cornell College
Anna E Nicholes. Rockford Seminary.
Emma E. Colville Wooster Univ. y Ohio
Naomi Knight [illegible] Ill

Facsimile of Autographs of Delegates Who Formed the "National Association," August, 1886

condition of young women, its membership was State Associations composed exclusively of evangelical local Associations, its supervisory body was a National Committee of the State Chairman, with at least seven other members, its headquarters were fixed in Chicago and the choice of its officers and agents was left to the National Committee.

One of the four other members then elected was Mrs. John V. Farwell, Jr., of Chicago. Ellen Drummond Farwell had inherited from her father a direct way of approaching matters and the judicial quality of reserving decision until all available information was considered. Her sweet womanly dignity, the humility of her Christian life, and her rare sincerity combined to make her an ideal chairman of this new committee. Association principles were not strange to her, for the Farwell family had always been influential in local and International Young Men's Christian Association councils. Her large circle of friends had confidence in any movement which she could heartily espouse, and so thoroughly did she take hold of all the issues involved, that the state workers immediately recognized her as a providential leader and rejoiced in their headquarters committee.

Three years later, seventy-four delegates from twelve states met in Bloomington, Illinois, for the second convention. Each year in the interim the resident and non-resident members of the National Committee had conferred in three day sessions on the matters entrusted to them, so when they renderd an account of their stewardship at Bloomington, they were able to say, what the delegates knew from their own participation throughout the field, that to some degree the four underlying desires had been met. The new committee had carried on extensive correspondence; they had published model student, city and state constitutions, and had begun issuing a quarterly periodical; they had secured a general secretary, Nettie Dunn, daughter of the president of Hillsdale College, Michigan, and she had made Association visits in eleven states, and attended eighteen of the twenty-nine conventions held by the twelve organized states. Up to this time the office had been the residence of the recording secretary of the National Committee, but one of the recommendations adopted with most satisfaction was that authorizing the securing of an office and engaging of an office secretary. When the one room at 153 La Salle Street was rented the next month, and furnished with purchased carpet and chair and a donated desk, the entire office and publication departments, the correspondence files, literature for sale, printed reports, and all documents were conveyed thither in one clothes hamper.

The biennium of 1889–91 was the period of calling secretaries. Corabel Tarr, preceptress of Napa College, California, came to the Committee in June as associate general secretary, with Miss Dunn. Thirsa F. Hall became the office secretary, succeeding Elizabeth Wilson, who had come temporarily to the position. Michigan, Wisconsin, Minnesota and most of the other states put secretaries into the field for whole or part time. Newly organized cities, like Kansas City, Mis-

MRS. JOHN V. FARWELL, JR.,
First President of the National Association (Later the American Committee)

souri, and Minneapolis, needed capable executive officers and the question of how to find secretaries was one of the most insistent, and its answer the most vital.

The beginning of a financial basis had been made in this biennium also. By '89 the total amount received was $1,200; by '91 it was $5,000, to which Mr. T. W. Phillips' subscription of $1,000 was the largest known at that time. In fact, for a new subscriber to send twenty percent of the budget in one gift might seem monumental even in the later days when supervisory support of Young Women's Christian Associations has been found by many to be a sound investment.

Canada was present at the 1891 convention at Scranton, Pa., in the persons of student and city delegates, for though such Associations had been affiliated before, the constitution had been formally amended in 1889 to read International in place of National Association, and Miss Tarr had recently made a tour in that section.

The answer to the question, "How to find secretaries" came in the summer of 1891. This answer was, "Train them." Near the Straits of Mackinac, on the eastern shore of Lake Michigan, lies Petoskey Bay, and here the Bay View Summer Assembly and University had convened for some years. A great auditorium stood on the grounds, many buildings for various secular and religious classes, a gymnasium, the headquarters of organizations and a real village of summer cottages and boarding houses. The newest of these buildings, Epworth Home, had been obtained for the proposed Summer Bible and Training School for class rooms and dormitories, and a three weeks' program for the Association students was set up. Each student bought a regular assembly ticket for two dollars and a half, and paid five dollars for the Association course for the season, one dollar for room rent weekly, and three fifty for table board. The school had been well advertised, the location was favorably known, the idea was novel and attractive, and people came beyond expectation, sixty-one in all. They filled Epworth Home and overflowed in all directions. Of the sixty-one from nine states, fifteen were secretaries in local or traveling positions, who previously had had no further training than office-bearing in college Associations and volunteer work with the same State Committee, perhaps, which later called them as employed officers.

The unique feature of the School was the secretaries' class conducted by Misses Dunn and Tarr, where the Young Women's Christian Association as an exact science was expounded an hour each day. These lessons covered the history, fundamental principles and methods of the local, state, and International organizations, with particular attention to the secretary's relation to it all. One other daily hour was the Bible training class with ten lessons each by Miss Emma Dryer of the Chicago Bible Society and Mr. J. H. Elliott of the Minneapolis Young Men's Christian Association. Another daily hour was occupied by Professor M. S. Terry of Garret Biblical Institute of Northwestern University. Then there were eighteen lessons by Miss Evelyn MacDougal of Hillsdale College in "Delsarte," light apparatus and free gymnastics, and every evening at sunset a devotional meeting conducted by different leaders.

In addition to this each attendant wished to extract the full value from her Chautauqua ticket and filled in her off hours with lectures and entertainments in the auditorium, where one might hear Doctor James M. Buckley in popular Bible lectures, or the Fisk Jubilee Singers, or Ida Benfey in "Adam Bede" and "The Mill on the Floss," or Mrs. Margaret E. Sangster and "Marion Harland" in the Home Makers Circle, or could sing in the Assembly Chorus or see scientific demonstrations. One could sample but could not exhaust the program. A few tried it and were exhausted thereby, so outings instead of improving lectures were arranged for the interstices between Association engagements. Trips to Mackinac and Oden, and the outdoor sports in charge of Mary S. Dunn were allowed their rights. All Association customs have their beginnings, and credit for the first marshmallow toast is claimed by this outing committee.

Everybody was happy and everybody was benefitted. The conference had come to stay, but several lessons were learned. Three weeks was too long a session. Grounds must be reserved for the Young Women's Christian Association and the purposes of that conference alone. The laity from colleges and cities and State Committees wanted the summer school as much as did secretaries, and the program must be constructed with these in mind.

Two weeks was the duration of the 1892 conference.

It was held on the grounds near Camp Collie, Lake Geneva, which the Western Secretarial Institute had bought and equipped with public buildings and tents for living quarters, and the program was divided into four discussional conferences besides the Secretaries Class and the Bible study and platform meetings in which all united. In the gymnasium department basket ball was the innovation. The attendance was one hundred and forty-two and so carefully were the statistics collated that the ages of the guests were registered, and averaged twenty-four years, varying from fifteen minimum to forty-two maximum. Only a sixth of the delegates were secretaries. The summer conference had come to stay indeed, but the question "How to train secretaries" had also again come to the front.

Notwithstanding the recognition of the several groups and the provision in separate councils for the demands of each, the conference was a unit, and that in a truer sense than the previous year when all attended the same class. The peace and retirement of the conference site effected this. All were of one accord in one place. Those spiritual results possible only when people have somewhat of leisure for the formation of religious habits were manifest.

A girl might have heard for some time of the importance of the Morning Watch. Here she found that it was the practice of most of the people who seemed to be accomplishing things for God, and she discovered for herself the glory and the blessing of a time with her Master in those early summer mornings by the shimmering lake. She had always been preparing lessons for Bible classes as a student or a Sunday school teacher: here the Bible truly seemed to be God's own word to her. His plan for her then was what she wanted to find out. Fresh revelations came in her daily private study as well as in the class hour. Most of the conference attendants were Association workers in some capacity. They knew Jesus Christ as their Saviour and as their Leader. Now they were making his acquaintance anew as their Friend.

Some one said that in the three days' convention where she had been, the new impressions had come so fast and hard that she felt a reaction on her return home, but here she stayed long enough in this rare Christian atmosphere to get her vigorous impressions, her reaction, and gain her balance before going back to the everyday life. Others said that their sense of Christ's presence and his place as the Head of the Conference became so indelibly fixed in their minds that thereafter it was possible always to practice the presence of God. The testimony of later conferences corroborated this year's witness that it was not the deliverance of any one speaker or one sermon or one address which stood out, although every year the ablest preachers and teachers were on the program; but it was the working together of the whole that brought individuals to understand the Christian life and enter into it as they had never done before.

Not one group but the whole conference looked steadily at the task of the evangelization of the world, and some who were at first incredulous at the idea of there being a missionary call for them, heard it at

Geneva and stayed not and stopped not until they had reached that foreign post in which they might serve the Lord of the whole earth.

It may be that this new way of looking at the foreign missionary field was partly due to the presence of Mrs. L. D. Wishard, just returned from a four years' tour around the world, in which a new chapter had been begun in the administration of Christian missions. The first Christian Association in Asia had been formed in 1884 in Jaffna College, Ceylon, by Frank K. Sanders, a teacher there. Two years later Rev. Harlan P. Beach organized another in Tung Chow, China. Appeals were received through the mission boards for city and student Young Men's Christian Associations of the North American pattern in India and elsewhere. The World's and International Committees of the Young Men's Christian Associations authorized Mr. L. D. Wishard to set out on a tour of visitation. Mrs. Wishard accompanied him and had unusual opportunities for seeing the part granted to the Association movement in the foreign missionary enterprise of the churches. The men's convention of 1889 "authorized its Committee to undertake Association extension and expansion abroad through foreign missionary secretaries, provided this were done on invitation from the church agencies and missionaries already on the foreign field, and in cooperation with them in their work, and provided also that the money needed were separately solicited as a distinct fund for this department of the Committee's work." The same day of October, 1889, saw John T.

Swift start West for Tokyo, Japan, and David McConaughy sail East for Madras, India. There were even visions of what Young Women's Christian Association secretaries might do in helping the young women of India and Japan and other remote lands to come into their Christian birthright.

But there had come into being that spring another force tending to draw the interest of members out from any self satisfied, self centered, national concerns into the larger conception of what the word "association" means, when prefaced by the word Christian. It will be remembered that foreign branches were included in the first national scheme of organization in England and that their United Central Council invited delegates from foreign lands to meet with them in London at their annual meeting, April, 1892, to discuss Association work in all parts of the globe and if possible form a World's Association.

Miss R. F. Morse of New York City, chairman of the New York State executive committee and a member of the International Committee, and Miss Tarr were appointed to represent America. They found there both men and women leaders from Australia, France, India, Norway, Sweden, Spain and Switzerland. Since in several lands pastors and other gentlemen were office holders, these gave reports of work done in these several countries and spoke of the industrial and social conditions which would make advance desirable or difficult. When it became evident to all that there was no radical difficulty which made an international organization impossible, a small committee was appointed to take up the details involved. The English and American members of this committee were authorized to draw up a constitution which should leave each nation entirely free as to its own national methods, growth and all national action, and should insist only on the one essential, that the basis of membership for all officers and voting members be such as would embody the fundamental principles of the Young Women's Christian Association.

Two years later the constitution was framed and formally accepted by the British and American executive bodies, which agreed to be responsible for the expenses of the new organization until the first International Conference. The national Associations of Norway and Sweden completed the charter membership.

All Americans were greatly interested in this section of the World's Constitution: "The General Secretary shall be of a nationality other than that where the Headquarters of the Committee are located," for by common consent London was selected as headquarters. That meant a secretary from the States. We in America thought at first that we knew of no one suitable for secretary, but God's providence had been preparing by education in this country and abroad, by experience as a city executive, a state traveling secretary and a member of the staff of the International Committee, the person who was elected and who for ten years thereafter helped to mold Association thought and action. This was Miss Annie M. Reynolds of North Haven, Connecticut, the sister

Miss A. M. Reynolds,
While Visiting Russia as World's Secretary

of the James Bronson Reynolds who had made the basic tour for Christian work in continental universities. But it was not alone Miss Reynolds' trustworthy acquaintance with European tongues, laws and institutions, nor her sympathetic knowledge of Church missions acquired from her youth up; it was her eagerness to see situations from all the angles from which others were seeing them, and to carry out their combined judgment, that made the executive committee in London realize they could now begin attaining their object: "the federation, development, and extension of Young Women's Christian Associations in all lands."

As soon as this new amalgamation was effected, new lines of cleavage appeared, and the Canadian Associations, wishing to join the World's Association as a national unit, withdrew from both their affiliations in the United States. The International Committee thus became The American Committee at its Milwaukee Convention in 1899.

India was the first foreign land to realize the dream of an American woman secretary. Fifteen years before the projection of any World's Association, branches had been started by English ladies in Poona and elsewhere and India was included in the Colonial division of the British National organization. When Dr. George F. Pentecost was holding evangelistic services in India in the early '90s the Honorables Emily and Gertrude Kinnaird were interested in the great numbers of girls gathered in the missions. The city of Calcutta was deeply stirred. A few girls of the

Indian community were beginning to ask for liberty and education under Christian and Brahma Somaj auspices; the Eurasian community was commencing to feel the need of some interdenominational link and of a common ground to meet on; girls from Great Britain coming to houses of business or as governesses needed a home, and the British residents needed something to bring them in contact with the other communities and to take the place of parish work and religious privileges previously enjoyed at home. The need of banding girls together was felt and it was believed that a Young Women's Christian Association could best effect this, hence an organization was formed in Calcutta in 1891 and Miss Emily Kinnaird, the moving spirit, fostered its growth by her visits, her correspondence, the editing of a monthly sheet and by her unforgetting and unforgettable interest. The Madras Association arose in almost identical fashion.

English women came out as early as 1893 as foreign secretaries. These were all voluntary workers and were termed either honorary secretary or president, as the case might be; but the fame of American secretaries, truly trained and professional officers, had reached both England and India. Miss Kinnaird was at home in London on the occasion of the Jubilee World's Convention of the Young Men's Christian Association in 1894 and so concerned for a secretary for Madras that she called together a group of Americans acquainted with India to discuss the possibility of cabling for one of their trained secretaries. After a time of prayer Mr. Bierce of Dayton, Ohio, arose and said:

"My niece Agnes is the girl for it." Mrs. David McConaughy of Madras was present, about to leave for America, and was commissioned to consult Miss Morse, American member of the World's Committee, and urge the claims of Madras.

This was the outcome. Agnes Gale Hill, then general secretary of the Toledo Young Women's Christian Association, had entered into communication with her church board in relation to an appointment to China but nothing had been settled. Miss Morse gave her the call from Madras. Toledo volunteered financial support, for the World's Committee was not as yet fully enough organized to finance any undertaking. Miss Hill spent the early fall of 1894 visiting colleges and state conventions under the Student Volunteer Movement, sailed later in the year and by February, 1895, was safely in Madras, the pioneer of the American foreign department. These were the words of her acceptance: "In college I gave myself to God for Association service; in the Association I gave myself to God for foreign service; in the call of the Madras Association I recognize a combination of these two calls and I give myself willingly."

She found Madras counting at this time, the date of its third anniversary, three hundred and twenty-five members, English, Eurasian and Tamil. There was no headquarters, nor any means of communication between the five places where the five small branches met, except the warm and primitive method of walking. In all the branches there were Bible classes and sewing circles and shortly afterwards some physical and social features were introduced which this good tennis player and ingenious social entertainer knew well how to handle. Her vacation weeks were spent at three of the hill station branches, because there was, of course, no traveling secretary; and this newly arrived American had much to give in Bible exposition and spiritual teaching by way of refreshing these struggling little Associations, as well as in advice upon ways and means which would differ almost as much from those in Madras, as her career as general secretary in Toledo had differed from that as Association president at the University of Illinois.

This combination, or rather the impossibility of continuing such a combination, led her to ask in one of her first letters for reinforcements. Her colleagues were all honorary British workers. She felt that there might be such in America. "God only knows. Perhaps He is turning the heart of some qualified young woman to come out and help me." And the first recruit was her own sister Mary.

One of the charter members of the International Committee of Young Men's Christian Associations, Mr. James Stokes, making a world tour in 1896, wrote home: "I expect to spend the month of October in China, reaching India via Burmah about December first to fifteenth, and we shall probably go direct from Burmah to Calcutta." But plans were changed and late one afternoon Mr. Stokes and his sisters entered the port of Madras instead. Mr. McConaughy, the American secretary of the Men's Association, came on board and escorted them to a missionary conference attended by fifty or sixty missionaries, among them Mary B. Hill, who had arrived a few weeks before. Mr. Stokes knew that the World's Executive Committee had conferred with Miss Morse about Agnes Hill becoming national secretary for India. With Mr. Stokes the future and the present were synonymous. The Young Men's Conference in Calcutta to which he and Mr. and Mrs. McConaughy were bound would also be attended by many ladies connected with the English-formed Young Women's Christian Association branches. He conceived the idea of calling a women's conference at the same time, and invited Agnes Hill to go on with the party, since an extra cabin had been providentially put at his disposal that day. A British account of the founding of the India National Association mentions Mr. Stokes as "acting with the promptitude of an American."

Miss Hill also accepted with the promptitude of an American and the morning after the arrival of Mr. Stokes they were all outward bound for Calcutta. The organization was launched and officered. An office was set aside in the Calcutta building. Agnes Hill was called as National Secretary and sent on to London for a little breathing time between the exhausting local experience in Madras and the still more exhausting labors ahead in her parish of India, Burmah and Ceylon, 1,681,506 square miles and a population of 297,562,876 souls, Brahmanists, Buddhists, Sikhs, Jains, Zoroastrians, Jews, Mohammedans, Roman and Protestant Christians and adherents of still other faiths.

In the year 1899, when the International Committee changed its name to The American Committee of the Young Women's Christian Associations in order to restrict its efforts to the United States alone, Miss Morse, Miss Reynolds and Miss Rouse were all present at the Biennial Convention, speaking of the relation of this American membership to young women in other lands, and a foreign department was created, which, owing to Miss Morse's residence in New York City, was to work from the East, rather than from the Chicago headquarters. Up to that time she had been in herself the whole foreign department, but now she was to associate other ladies with her to help in securing and equipping and maintaining American secretaries whom the World's Association would appoint to the various foreign fields. Miss Morse's own best remembered presentation was at the Nashville Convention of 1901 when she closed an address crammed with information, with this inquiry:

"But you say we are already sending out missionaries to the heathen world. Why should we send the Association? If our Association fills a place of need here as a part of church work which cannot be done within church walls, if it is needed to develop a Christian womanhood in this Christian land, to convict nominal Christian women and awaken them to their responsibility for their sisters here, what shall we say of the need for the women in India and China? Is there less need of the Association work for them?

She had in her hand that day the document signed by women of every influential class in the city of Shanghai, begging The American Committee to open

Morse Hall,
Headquarters and Hostel of the Association of Lahore, India

an Association there. Miss Morse was not present at the Wilkes-Barre Convention of 1903—it was not long before she laid down all her duties and rested forever from her labors—but her successor introduced Martha Berninger, who had accepted this call to China, and Alice Newell, who was to reinforce the little group of American secretaries in India. By 1906 there were ten Americans serving in India, China and Japan and a candidate ready for South America. Miss Morse's memorial stands in Lahore, India, where Morse Hall houses a good general work, a fine educational department and an ample dormitory.

While the International Committee was thus taking its part in extending the Young Women's Christian Association work in the outer circle, the home expansion was also going forward. The pioneer period was passing and the era of specialization had set in. This was noticeable in every way, particularly in the accession of staff members, the opening of additional summer conferences, and the training of employed officers.

At the time of Miss Tarr's retirement in November, 1892, Effie K. Price of the faculty of Northwestern Academy succeeded her as general secretary. This was January first of that "World's Fair Year," as 1893 has always been called by all the people in any way affected by the World's Columbian Exposition in Chicago. The office had been provided for, and the editorial work on "*The Evangel*," which had succeeded "*The Quarterly*" in 1889, had been carried by Elizabeth Wilson in addition to her traveling duties, but the local Association wanted more expert help than these general workers could afford. After a little Florence Simms was called from DePauw University as collegê secretary and Harriet Taylor from the state secretaryship of New York as city secretary. Miss Taylor was enthusiastic and constructive in all the city problems, but her training and experience as a teacher gleamed through the new profession she had chosen and the class work of the city Associations broadened into a true educational system. In 1901 the progress of local Associations undertaking extension into industrial centers was so marked that Helen F. Barnes, state secretary for Michigan and Ohio, was called as a specialist in this field. Mary S. Dunn's work among the city Associations had convinced her that the revenue producing departments in cities were capable of a great improvement and her duties were so rearranged as to give her the title of economic secretary. Esther L. Anderson as general secretary of Detroit had so thoroughly interwoven all the sections of the Association with the religious activities that she was called as religious work secretary. Emma Hays was chiefly occupied aiding state secretaries in communities desiring local organization. In the student department lines were not so closely drawn. Besides visitation, conference preparation was insistent in its demand upon the student staff, consisting after 1889, of Bertha Condé, Ruth Paxson, Frances Bridges, Margaret Kyle and others from time to time.

Ever since the summer of 1892, when the main principles of the summer conferences were crystallized, local and state workers had been valuing them for what they could do for young women through the Association channels, but there were many others both in and out of the organized movement who craved attendance for the inspiration to their own Christian lives and the equipment for better Christian service in any sphere. After the men's student conference, which was organized at Mt. Hermon in 1886, had been increasing in power for each of its seven years, its program and spirit appealed so strongly to the young women who spent their summers in the village of East Northfield that a number of them petitioned Mr. Moody to open a similar conference for young women. Entirely in sympathy with the purpose, but unable to give the matter his personal attention because he was to be engaged almost entirely in the great World's Fair Evangelistic Campaigns through the season, he invited the conference to the Northfield Seminary grounds and put all arrangements into the hands of the International Committee of the Young Women's Christian Associations. Mrs. A. J. Gordon was selected as presiding officer until his arrival. The announcement, supplemented by visits to the Eastern colleges by Miss Price, the leader of the conference, resulted in an attendance of one hundred and eighty-one, who found a program of Bible Training Class, inductive Bible class, Christian Life Work hour, simultaneous college and city conferences, with an afternoon of recreation and the never forgotten Round Top twilight meeting, and the platform addresses by Miss Dodge, Mrs. W. S. Bainbridge and other appealing speakers. A summary may be found in the letter of a Wellesley girl: "It may not be said that one feature was helpful and another not—all were helpful, but some by their very nature were destined to exert a greater influence than others. The interchange of views and suggestions in regard to methods and means of Christian life were of untold value."

So true and wholesome was the Christian influence exerted by this conference, that when its growth pointed to reorganization many Association members could hardly conceive of any change as endurable or of a conference at all apart from the place where it was born. But specialization was again in order and by removing to Silver Bay on Lake George students and city delegates could each have a conference devised and executed to meet their specific needs. Then the crowded Lake Geneva Conference was divided on the same principle. The romantic story of the founding of the Pacific Coast Conference, the swift development of Association interests in the Southern Atlantic and eastern gulf states through the medium of the Southern Conferences, these are definitely beyond the limits of the present available space. Infinitely beyond any written record are the spiritual histories of the thousands and thousands of young women who made their way to these summer conferences and in them found, as a frequent conference speaker had said, "the entrance to the Christian life or a new devotion to Christian tastes and Christian service, habits of Bible study, interest in missions, a straightforward sense of duty, new conceptions of prayer, and deeper love for Christ as personal Lord.''

Every new organization and department made a call for more employed officers. Every conference made a call for qualified women to take up what has for more than twenty years been termed ''a new profession for women.'' The Summer Bible and Training School had become a lay women's conference; an ''International Association School'' board of trustees which was secured by the International Committee, but not organized as an integral part of its work, had established a branch as training ground, and finally confined its work to that branch, relinquishing the school features; direction of practical work in the Association settlement had ended in the supervising secretary carrying the local burdens, and the students becoming neighborhood, not Association, experts; summer terms were too short for professional education, but too long for the strength of the students, chiefly young alumnæ already taxed by their senior year in college or their first year of teaching. In each of these experiments some caught such a vision of Young Women's Christian Association possibilities, that they were soon carrying large responsibilities, such as Clarissa H. Spencer, who succeeded Miss Reynolds as secretary of the World's Committee, Mabel Cratty, general secretary of The American Committee and later of the National Board, and A. Estelle Paddock and Frances Cross of the Foreign Department, all from the summer class of 1902.

Finally the Wilkes-Barre convention of 1903 instructed The American Committee to undertake a permanent Institute under its own auspices. In September a conclave deliberated upon the matter. The chief objections brought out were these. The committee had no money for the purpose. There was no building. There was no suitable provision for practice work. There was no available Bible teacher, nor could a full course of study be set up. Last of all, no students would come. The assets were as follows: The American Committee willing to make an attempt and a secretarial committee chairman, Mrs. Irwin Rew, devoted to the undertaking. A parlor conference in Oak Park, just outside of Chicago, gave encouragement as to funds, a suitable partly furnished house was leased, Bible instructors from the four theological seminaries of Chicago became available, the School of Civics and Philanthropy and the Chicago School of Physical Education were making their initial ventures that same season and gladly opened their classes to our students; factories and churches welcomed noon and evening clubs among their girls and young women.

The house was dedicated by an Extension Secretaries' Conference, December 29 to January 1, and the first term of the Institute proper opened January 2, 1904. Seven students arrived sooner or later and were extremely loyal, reserving their criticism of the meager equipment until the day of their departure, when they politely suggested benefits which might accrue to their successors should certain improvements

Florence Simms   Elizabeth Wilson   Mary S. Dunn

Secretaries and Students, Secretaries' Training Institute, Winter Term, 1904

be made. As the course lasted only three months another group registered in the spring and a still larger group for the next fall. This humble beginning did not convince the Association public of the necessity for professional training and the life of the Institute hung in the balance. But in March of the third year, the house burned, the house, not the Institute—that had just begun to live. A special meeting of The American Committee was called and authorized Elizabeth Wilson, who since her return to the committee in 1900 had looked after secretarial matters, to obtain a furnished house to complete that year's classes and lease another property to accommodate the school the next fall. Mrs. Cyrus H. McCormick, Sr., started a refurnishing fund which other like-minded friends augmented, and when the fourth year opened at the new Ashland Boulevard address, with more than enough students to fill the house, the problem of whether anybody would attend such a school was also a little nearer its solution.

The twenty years from 1886 to 1906 had immeasurably increased the vision of a national organization. It was not merely a body through which local members should be served with "publications, correspondence, visitation and conventions," but a medium which should relate them with other nations bearing mutual obligations.

CHAPTER XV

THE INTERNATIONAL BOARD OF WOMEN'S AND YOUNG WOMEN'S CHRISTIAN ASSOCIATIONS

"TO everything there is a season and a time to every purpose under the heavens."

This was the opening sentence of a paper on "Growth and Perpetuity Necessary to Conference Work," which Mrs. C. R. Springer, President of the Women's Christian Association of Saint Louis, read at the Eleventh International Conference, which met in Chicago in 1891. The argument which she advanced was that while many individual Associations had seen wonderful increase, the Conference as a whole might have been benefited by a centralization of power which could bridge the distance between conventions. The Conference would retain its deliberative functions, but be legislative as well, and the central cabinet would be able to act decisively upon questions that might arise requiring prompt action if the progress and development of the whole Conference were to be ensured. The hearty reception of Mrs. Springer's paper showed that other representative women had been thinking in the same direction, and after much prayer and deliberation a new constitution was made operative and became the basis of incorporation. This called for an organization to be known as The International Board of Women's Christian Associations, its object, to unite in one central body present and future Women's Christian Associations, these and kindred Associations to be admitted to membership by election of the Board in session. There should be an executive committee elected by the Conference, which now became the regular biennial meeting of the Board, this committee to consist of the full quota of officers, including one vice-president for each state, and from the British provinces or other countries entering into international relations. The bylaws provided for membership assessment to meet the expenses of the general work. It was not strange that the Conference, appreciating the grasp Mrs. Springer had of the whole scheme of international organization and knowing her success in relating the many ramifications of the complex St. Louis Association, should have elected her president of the Board, at both this and the succeeding Conference. Her alertness, prodigious faith, and her joy in accomplishment had been proved again and again through the conference days of previous years, as she had been a regular attendant since 1877.

Another important resolution adopted at this time was to the effect that all organizations forming after this time should take the name of Young Women's Christian Association, and those already existing might change to Young Women's Christian Association at their option. This was following the example of Chicago, which had been a Young Women's Christian Association since 1887, although the other Associations from New York State west to the California boundary still kept the title, Women's Christian Association. But it was felt that the purpose of the two, "to promote the spiritual, mental and physical interests of women, together with other Christian work," were identical, hence the resolution. Its natural outcome was the amendment of the constitution at the next meeting to include these new titles, reading "The International Board of Women's and Young Women's Christian Associations."

Two distinguished guests of the Chicago Conference of 1891 were Mrs. Potter Palmer, President of the Board of Lady Managers of the World's Columbian Exposition, and Mrs. Charles Henrotin, Vice-president for the Woman's Branch of the Auxiliary for the World's Congresses of 1893, which formed an important part in the Exposition. Mrs. Palmer spoke particularly of the Woman's Building in which exhibits of women's work of all kinds were to be collected and displayed, and urgently asked for an exhibit from the Associations in the International Conference, that the Exposition, which would in any case be an important moment for women, might become an inspired one for the sex. Mrs. Henrotin spoke of this counciling of the nations as a comparatively new factor in the slow progress of fraternity, and requested that the Women's Christian Association be included in the list of Congresses endeavoring to unite all people in the common cause of the perfection and advancement of humanity. Both invitations were accepted.

All visitors to the Columbian Exposition in Chicago

remember the Woman's Building near the Fifty-Seventh Street entrance to Jackson Park. It stood white and glistening like its neighbors, like them a surprise to matter of fact people who had not realized that apparently solid marble buildings could spring up for one brief season of unreckoned beauty, and then disappear like the flowers of one summer. Unlike its neighbors this white plaster building, while classical and old world in its exterior, was within entirely novel and almost revolutionary. Everything was made by woman's hands, wrought by woman's mind, or called into action by woman's will. Across a whole end of the second story extended a great Organization Room, in which there was found a place for women's organizations, religious, philanthropic and educational in character, corresponding in fact to all women's interests where cooperation had set in. At the end of the main aisle, the observed of all observers, was a wall space covered with decorative shields bearing in rich lettering the name and date of organization of the several Associations affiliated with the International Board. This was supplemented in the booth below by charts and photographs and yearbooks, which were shown and explained to visitors by ladies who had volunteered for that purpose. No labor nor personal expense had been spared by the president of the board in making this a success.

Naturally the presence of so many leaders at the congresses and upon the Fair grounds through the season of 1893 brought very close to their hearts the question of protecting young girls attending such fairs as visitors, or employed upon the grounds in connection with the exhibits, and with the amusement and restaurant concessions. While no other of the large expositions since then erected a Woman's Building which called for so elaborate an exhibit as in Chicago, yet at Buffalo, 1901, Paris, France, 1900, St. Louis, 1904, and Portland, Oregon, 1905, there were opportunities for advertising certain Association features of help to young women and for undertaking Travelers' Aid work either in connection with that department in the local city where the exposition was held or in conjunction with other movements concerned for the welfare of young women.

International cooperation had been gained through the appointment of an American correspondent of Travelers' Aid to the World's Travelers' Aid Society. Her report and that of a special committee on a plan of organization provided perhaps the chief topic of consideration for the St. Louis Conference of 1903. The sense of the meeting was expressed by resolutions which were left to the council to execute.

> The work naturally divides itself into two parts—the agent, and those who are to help the traveler at the commencement of her journey.
>
> First, with regard to the first part, helping the agent, we suggest that there be a directory, for the use of the agent, of all Associations in the United States that would be willing to look after a girl if communicated with.
>
> Second, that every Association should pledge itself never to turn away a girl on any condition or under any circumstances.
>
> Third, when only a few trains or boats can be reached or met, preference be given to local trains, as girls in near-

by towns more frequently come into the cities for work or are led to leave home by advertisements in papers.

Fourth, that we make in the near future Travelers' Aid work a special feature of our Board and urge every single Association to have a Travelers' Aid department.

Fifth, urge that every Association have a director whose sole business it will be to act as Travelers' Aid director.

Sixth, such director, every Aid agent, and all girls known to be about to travel, be provided with a badge, uniform in color, shape and size.

On the second point, those who are to help the traveler at the commencement of her journey, we suggest:

First, that each Association pledge itself to assume a certain district to investigate as to where we can place a voluntary worker.

Second, that we secure helpful literature and disseminate it with careful attention and economy. This literature should comprise:

a. Specific instruction to the volunteer worker; and
b. Specific information to the public; both prepared by a committee of the Board.

This literature could be distributed through the many church societies and home missionary societies.

Third, that there should be large hangers in every depot and steamer and in every available place.

During the Travelers' Aid campaign in connection with the Louisiana Purchase Exposition in 1904, 278,000 leaflets, circulars, placards, and cards were printed and distributed through auxiliaries and individuals from Canada to the Gulf and from ocean to ocean; 7,820 letters were received and answered or sent from headquarters in New York and St. Louis. At the St. Louis headquarters, 2,988 persons were directed to provide homes for lodging. Eight hundred and sixty-six persons from all quarters of the globe were lodged from one to ten days, of whom 397 were entirely alone and 200 were without money.

With such a background for an incentive to large effort, the International Board entered into the formation of an Exposition Travelers' Aid Committee for the Lewis and Clark Centennial Exposition (Portland, Oregon, 1905) in which The American Committeee, the Girls' Friendly Society of America, the National Council of Jewish Women, the International Order of the King's Daughters and Sons, the Women's Auxiliary of the American Bible Society, and the International Sunshine Society, actively cooperated. In Portland also there had been constituted a Travelers' Aid Association of eleven groups of women accustomed to forward civic and religious enterprises.

Mrs. William S. Stewart, of Philadelphia, was chairman of the whole matter, and the Lewis and Clark Exposition, though a smaller fair than that at St. Louis the preceding year, showed an appalling need for the protective work carried on, and proved to the International Board Conference that cooperative Travelers' Aid work is needed in this country, and that every Young Women's Christian Association should share by appointing Travelers' Aid matrons to give protection and information wherever many are traveling by land or water. The 1905 Conference specified this as the department upon which attention should be concentrated.

The International Board also emphasized work at large summer assemblies.

Owing to the importance of Chautauqua Lake, New York, as a gathering place for people alive to every religious and philanthropic work, it was decided to open there each season a room as headquarters, which would be presided over by a hostess conversant with Association progress and methods. This was most happily carried on from 1901 through several summers. In 1902 over 500 guests registered. In 1904 Dr. Anna L. Brown, General Secretary of the International Board, kept open house here while doing preliminary work for the Louisiana Purchase Exposition Travelers' Aid Campaign, and she and others accepted invitations to speak before the Chautauqua Woman's Club, that audience composed of members from every state of this Union, each sorting over from the daily programs those things which she will weave into her next year's web in her own home club. It is an audience invaluable to any such propaganda as that of the Cooperative Travelers' Aid.

Some kinds of Christian duty one performs with faithfulness, some with delight. This seems to have been the spirit animating everyone who had a hand in the unique work at Monteagle. Here in a mountain plateau of Tennessee, the Southern Chautauqua had assembled upon its grounds, buildings for a summer colony of thousands of people from all parts of the South. Headquarters of the International Board were established in a large house where young women resided much as in a city boarding home. There were anniversary days and inspiring meetings. But on the outside of this walled city, the mountain boys and girls were without the advantages which the ladies on the grounds believed could be theirs by a little effort. First a library was started, then a training school of household arts—the Louise Cecile School was opened February, 1905—then a Young Women's Christian Association came into being, directing the local work, and passing on further up the mountains the reading matter which had been first used in their attractive and popular library. It is not strange that the Women's and Young Women's Christian Associations in that whole region found inspiration in their comings together at Monteagle.

But the real history of the International Board and of the Associations through which it touched the life of young womanhood in the great American cities is told better by its periodicals. First the local papers were circulated: *The Earnest Worker,* published in Cleveland from June, 1874, on; *Faith and Works,* the Philadelphia paper which started in September, 1875; *The Christian Worker,* which Utica began to publish the very same month; and *The Gleaner,* of Memphis, dating from 1883; all these contained news of their own and other Associations, with original and selected readings. In April, 1894, there was launched *The International Messenger* as the official publication of the International Board's affiliated Associations. Its twelve large pages were filled with editorials by Mrs. Fanny Cassiday Duncan, whose office of secretary was enlarged to cover this function also, quotations from the last Conference journal, articles of general value, reports from cities and from the various state chairmen, and discussions on Association problems. In succeeding months there were fine historical accounts of flourishing local organizations, and occasionally a symposium upon Summer Homes or other equally attractive themes. For the Conference papers, which once had been found in the Conference Journal, one was now referred to *The Messenger.* For eight years it lived a useful life, and was then succeeded by *The Bulletin,* which condensed the Association news and omitted the general and descriptive reading which had bulked largely in the former organ.

CHAPTER XVI

THE JOINT COMMITTEE PREPARING THE WAY FOR ONE NATIONAL MOVEMENT

ANY chronicle of the first half century span of the life of the Young Women's Christian Associations in this country might well be called Two Score Years and Ten; forty years of sporadic local organisms and separate international groups, from 1866 to 1906; and ten years of one truly national Young Women's Christian Association of the United States of America, from 1906 to 1916.

The person in America who knew girls and women best was Miss Grace H. Dodge of New York City. These friends were at first her own circle in the city, her school mates at Farmington, Connecticut, her neighbors and friends at Greyston, Riverdale. What was a suburb of the city in her girlhood days is now legally within the limits of the city, although the green sweep of lawn at Greyston, fringed by trees and shrubs, is not broken by sight of any human habitation, but seems completed by the shining Hudson River, where the vista is bounded only by the stately Palisades that form the western bank. Her summers at Greyston and her steady deep attachment to the place, led to starting a lending library which found shelf room in her father's greenhouse, and a sewing school which met in her own home until a house was built for the two enterprises which immediately made their way and became part of a large neighborhood association.

Education, cooperation, protection, were the keywords of the work which seemed waiting for her in her other home town, the great city of New York. In January, 1880, she helped form the Kitchen Garden Association, to extend that combination of correct housekeeping instruction and songs and games, which had first been thought out by Miss Emily Huntington, and put into operation in the Wilson Industrial School in 1876. As corresponding secretary Miss Dodge set herself to creating public sentiment for industrial training as an educational factor. After four years the Kitchen Garden Association made way for the Industrial Education Association with a greatly extended scope, including committees on Household Industries, Industrial Art, Mechanical Industries, Outside Organizations, Vacation Schools, Kindergartens, Industries for the Insane, Reformatories, Orphanages and Asylums, Houses and Training for Domestic Science, and Bureau for Teachers. Cooking schools were known, but no foundation existed for industrial training, even Pratt Institute began some two years later. The Association engaged teachers for classes both within and without the building leased for headquarters, at number 9 University Place. These outside classes were not only metropolitan; they assembled in nearby Yonkers, Dobbs Ferry, Hoboken and on Staten Island, in Ogontz Seminary near Philadelphia, and in far off Rochester and Cleveland.

There were not enough adequately trained teachers to meet the demand, and as the Board of Trustees undertook normal classes, they saw that this feature must assume collegiate proportions. Thoughtful educators became interested. Upon the founders was laid a heavy financial burden, the task of securing buildings, accumulating endowment and meeting deficits when endowment funds and students' fees together were insufficient for the annual budget. Miss Dodge as vice-president and treasurer was more than a decider of policies and a disburser of monies put into her hands. She made call after call, telling people what such a teachers' college would mean, why it was necessary, inspiring some with her own vision and getting help for the mission to which she was devoted, often meeting failure, but plodding on with equal stoutness of heart in any case. People began to see the value of academic and graduate instruction in Household Arts, in Physical Education, and various technical subjects. They saw what the study of education from the kindergarten up to university administration was accomplishing for the nation, and gifts began to come more easily. In 1911 she dared to give up the treasury, although she always remained on the board of trustees of Teacher's College.

The ability she showed in the promotion of industrial education could not fail to be coveted for the whole school system of the city. When Mayor Grace appointed women to the Board of Education for the first time, one of the two was Miss Dodge, and she served the full term of three years, January 1, 1888, to 1891. This new commissioner took so seriously her duties as member of committees on the care of school buildings, on sites for new schools, on school furniture, as to cause surprise on the part of those who had not known such keen examination of present conditions and such unerring judgment as to the future. After two years the Board was ready to introduce industrial training as a result of her labors, and the conduct of evening schools was a still further scene of her interest.

Perhaps Miss Dodge's greatest service on the Board was as a member of a committee of eight, appointed to investigate and report what changes ought to be made in the by-laws relating to examinations and marks, also changes desirable in the methods of examinations, course of study, the methods and system of marking both teachers and pupils, the cause and remedy for the excess of pupils who are unable to obtain admission to the colleges, "*also in respect to all other matters in relation to the school system which they may deem proper.*" Earnest, persevering investigation began at once. The committee held seventeen meetings and heard a great mass of testimony from the city superintendent, his assistants, and a number of principals, vice-principals and teachers. Communications were sent to the educational departments of all large and important cities in the United States, asking for full and detailed information as to their respective school systems and the methods of supervising and controlling them. A good share of this correspondence fell upon Miss Dodge. In June the final report was presented in a carefully prepared course of study for both primary and grammar grades. Kindergarten there was none at the time. The committee also reported on an amendment to the by-laws relative to a maximum salary for teachers of all grades.

> It is difficult to characterize Miss Dodge's part in this work, except to say that she was the leading spirit. She had spent the previous summer in England and on the Continent studying the practical application of school systems, consulting the leaders of educational thought and visiting schools, colleges and universities. She brought to the work of preparing a course of study for the city's public schools an exalted sense of what could and should be done. She felt that training young people in industrial education pointed to the solution of some of the outstanding social problems, touched the very roots of our civilization, and affected the prosperity of our nation for future generations. The course of study at that time adopted by the Board of Education contained some of the advanced methods for which she had enthusiastically labored, and more have been added since.

All this educational investigation was later at the service of the mission schools when Miss Dodge was appointed a member of the Educational Commission for the Ecumenical Missionary Conference, which she attended in Edinburgh, Scotland, in 1910. Another service to be mentioned in connection with school matters is the organization of the Girls' Public School Athletic League in 1905.

If her heart was in the educational propaganda, her very heart and soul were in that first-hand contact with girls, which has come to be known as "Girls'

Self-Governing Clubs,'' but which she simply called ''Cooperation.'' One evening she met with a few self-supporting girls in the home of one of them, talking over with them some of the common questions of life. The group grew in membership and rooms for meeting followed; for those who wanted better personal equipment for the years ahead there was a chance to study; they had good times together. Miss Dodge brought in her own friends to teach what they knew and to share in what she was herself enjoying. Up to 1883 when this Irene Club came into being, people had been stirred to do much *for,* but had not thought of doing much *with* the rank and file of self-supporting young women. To her each girl was an individual, even though many worked together or played together in companies. ''How can we cooperate,'' she said, ''before we know how to honor and appreciate those busy women and girls into whose lives we want to bring brightness and cheer. As long as we look upon them as a class whom we are to benefit and uplift, there can be no cooperation. We must learn to know their grand self-sacrificing lives, must make them friends from whom we are to receive more than we can ever give, and then must gain their interest and consent to the cooperative measure hoped for.''

All members were on equal terms, the cash girl earning two dollars per week, the teacher earning ten times that sum, and the so-called girl of leisure, who had received her wages in advance. Business was conducted through strictly Parliamentary methods; committees and a council made easy the execution of the measures voted by the club in the monthly meetings, when three hundred members would sit through an evening of pure business discussion, because it was their own affairs which they themselves were handling.

Besides the business and the classes and the social hours, many inside organizations developed: the Lend-a-Hand, or Resolve Committees, which found ways to comfort unfortunate or friendless people: the Junior Branches, which swarmed the younger fun-loving children and hived them in the rooms on certain evenings in the week with two or three queen bees to keep them out of mischief. Then grew up the "Three P. Circle," with the motto words, "Purity, Perseverance, Pleasantness," from a talk of five club members going home from the club together. These were active workers and cooperating members striving together to develop a more earnest type of womanhood among the girls they knew. And when the older members married, and could not come out at night to the club meetings, the question was asked, "Why not have a Bride, Wife, Mother, Branch and come to the rooms in the afternoons?" The Domestic Circle was the result, and practical talks, lectures and demonstration classes shared the time with the precious social intercourse, while a committee from the main club, of unmarried members out of work, cared for the babies and young children.

Combinations for summer vacations led to the holiday houses; combinations for emergencies led to the Mutual Benefit Fund to provide for sickness and funeral expenses. Combinations to find places for those out of work or to suggest fitting for better positions led to the Alliance Employment Bureau. Miss Dodge was repeatedly asked to tell others about her club work and answer questions, as for example:

Question—"Do you have any trouble with class distinction of one trade with another?"

Answer—"It might be a difficulty elsewhere, but not in New York."

Question—"How do you begin to get acquainted?"

Answer—"Wait for an introduction through some mutual friend. Our club work is not different from any other social life; we meet on feelings of social equality, the same as other friends."

Question—"How intimate are you with your girls?"

Answer—"We are very intimate. They are with my life and I am with theirs."

The club idea made possible the whole oncoming rush of settlements and institutional churches, the industrial, educational and junior departments in both Young Men's and Young Women's Christian Associations. People wanted to get together, wanted to work together. They did not know how until Miss Dodge showed them what could be done in a club where leaders were actively humble and members were honorably ambitious. There would always be outstanding leaders, for equality of rights need not be confused with equality of gifts.

These Irene Club members wanted to hear Miss Dodge talk—always, in any audience, for that matter, the only regret was that soon she would have to stop —and suggested to her topics about which they were thinking and on which they needed her advice. Other clubs wanted to read these words and the little volume "A Bundle of Letters to Busy Girls" was published in 1887 and new editions meet the steady calls for it after nearly thirty years.

When the Honorable Seth Low, a former president of Columbia University, was elected mayor of greater New York, he appointed as his secretary Mr. James Bronson Reynolds, the former student secretary of certain continental universities. To these two academic municipal officers came a rumor in 1902 that some of the employment bureaus licensed by the city were placing immigrant girls and other unprotected young women in immoral resorts. Mr. Reynolds, thinking that the Woman's Municipal League might be able to investigate the conduct of these bureaus, consulted with Miss Dodge as treasurer, but when she learned that absolute secrecy was essential till the inquiry was ended, she herself supplied the required funds, rather than hazard the undertaking by presentation to any organized body for action. On the evidence thus obtained, two managers were sent to prison and about sixty others were legally blocked from this type of business.

Miss Dodge had striven to build up in her club girls that inner wall of protection which every pure minded girl could attain. She had also thought much of how Christian society can build an outer wall of protection around those who are overwhelmed by the forces of iniquity preying upon girls ignorant of moral dangers, and unsuspecting of harm.

She had full respect for the efforts of the local

Women's and Young Women's Christian Association whose agents stood on guard in the docks and stations of a score of cities to greet and guide incoming girls, but she felt that all sporadic actions were only a drop in the bucket; there must be a union of all possible allies, and there must be other than station and follow-up work. Protection must be legal and legislative, it must be international.

This combination was first effected in New York City, for most of her undertakings "began in Jerusalem." A committee composed of Jewish, Roman Catholic and Protestant women began investigation which later led to an incorporated society and a directorate of both men and women, but even at once there was an increased force of Travelers' Aid agents speaking many languages, and a reliable system of reports and records for tracing.

Another part of this same conception of protection was the National Vigilance Committee, later merged into the American Social Hygiene Association. This committee, to whose working she gave the most diligent and scrupulous attention, was organized at her house in 1905. Later it was able to induce the United States government to ratify the White Slave Treaty drafted in Paris in 1902 and already accepted by the leading nations of Europe. Aid was also given in the passage of two national laws to prevent the importation of women from State to State for immoral purposes; state laws to the same end were passed in thirty-one States. These laws enabled the public authorities to overcome the difficulties which had previously existed in prosecuting offenders who had escaped from the State when an offence was committed. Most of the steps in this war for the suppression of commercialized vice bore other people's names, as that of the representative who fathered a bill through the house, for Miss Dodge had an instinct for remaining unknown as the author of any deed, whether it be a benefaction of time, of advice or of money.

All this work of education, cooperation and protection was done with the deepest Christian purpose. Miss Dodge was continually seeking the Kingdom of God and His righteousness, and these many things that made up the days' work and the years' work were means to the coming of that Kingdom. Her personal conceptions of Christianity were as high as her social conceptions. Her morning hour of Bible reading and deliberate prayer, her holy observance of the Lord's day for divine worship and rest and gladness, were the sources of her gigantic achievement. People knew her as a Christian woman, fond of girls—one who was accustomed to work decently and in order with other people. She believed in "freedom guarded by organization." People wondered that she was not identified with the Young Women's Christian Association either nationally or locally. She had been helpful to all. She had read papers at the International Conferences in Cincinnati in 1885, and in Chicago in 1891 when the International Board was formed. She had spoken at the first Northfield Conference. She had opened her house to a parlor conference in 1898, at which Miss Ruth Rouse had presented the Christian opportunities in American colleges and those in foreign lands looking to America, and had brought increased financial support to The American Committee. Her visit to the Baltimore Association in 1887 resulted in a flourishing club which was the nucleus of a branch in the industrial part of the city. She spoke before college girls, presided at meetings, advised with leaders, stood by especial efforts for exposition travelers' aid, contributed lavishly, etc., but was never committed to any board or committee. Said one who knew her well,

> The reason was not hard to find. Her wide vision, clear judgment and broad sympathy could not be satisfied with a divided leadership. The work demanded the largest spirit of love and liberty, and until an organization could be effected which could work unhampered by friction for all the young women of the nation in a definite progressive advance toward the highest and best in all things, she was unwilling to give her time and thought to any lower standard.

She had often said in confidence to those nearest to her in both organizations that if the time should ever come when union was deeply desired on both sides, she stood ready to help.

To Miss Dodge, as a matter of course, the officers of both The American Committee and International Board turned in the spring of 1905 when local city affairs became national complications. In Washington, D. C., young women in business and professional life wished to establish a Young Women's Christian Association with the equipment and program for promoting the spiritual, mental, social and physical welfare of young women that were found in other cities, and asked The American Committee to help them to complete their plans. The Women's Christian Association, which had for thirty-five years maintained a boarding home for women, and carried on other lines of work such as were previously common to many of its sister Associations in the International Board, desired that the new work be undertaken under a title other than Young Women's Christian Association, which was so similar to its own that the public might not be able to make distinctions. But the words Young Women's Christian Association with their universally accepted significance, seemed to the younger body the only title that would indicate the nature and affiliations of their society to the cosmopolitan residents and guests of the capital city, and they felt that the prefix "Young" distinguished it from the other name. Representatives of the proposed new organization had sought the advice of The American Committee when they were assembled in Detroit that April for their tenth Biennial Convention. At the same time members of the International Board's Committee on Relations were in Washington at the request of the Women's Christian Association Board and the State Director for the District of Columbia. A letter from Washington and a telegram from Detroit reached Miss Dodge at the same time. Each asked that she preside at a conference upon the matters involved. In each she saw the desire for such mutual understanding and cooperation as might soon make possible a united Young Women's Christian Association in the United States. She accepted both invitations and asked that representatives meet with her in New York City on May 24.

Miss Dodge received her guests at the Hotel Manhattan and each of the company of fifteen believed as she went in to the meeting place that God, who had been working His purpose out as month succeeded to year, had brought His purpose for the Young Women's Christian Association to the place when its future would be enlarged or thwarted by her individual thought and action that morning. The representatives of the International Board were its president, Mrs. W. S. Buxton of Springfield, Massachusetts, two former presidents, Mrs. R. A. Dorman of New York City and Mrs. W. S. Stewart of Philadelphia, the president and treasurer of the Board of Trustees, Mrs. C. N. Judson of Brooklyn and Mrs. J. T. Whittlesey of Montclair, New Jersey, the State Director for the District of Columbia, Mrs. Frank T. Thurston of Washington, and the former general secretary, Dr. Anna L. Brown of Boston. The American Committee was represented by the president, Mrs. J. S. Griffith, and Mrs. J. J. Tufts, both from headquarters in Chicago, three non-resident members, Miss Helen Miller Gould, of New York City, Mrs. Robert E. Speer of Englewood, New Jersey, and Mrs. Thomas S. Gladding of Montclair, New Jersey, also chairman of the American Department of the World's Young Women's Christian Association, and two members of its staff, Miss Emma Hays and Miss Elizabeth Wilson.

No doubt all had seen Miss Dodge preside over large

meetings, had heard her read papers and give addresses, and many had come to decisions on important puzzling questions in personal conference with her, but no one was prepared for the directness with which the truly vital issue was singled out and the swiftness with which the meeting was brought to its desired haven. Before the opening prayers the chairman read selected Scripture verses:

> "This one thing I do, forgetting those things which are behind, I press toward the mark for the prize of the high calling of God in Christ Jesus."
>
> "He led them forth by the right way."
>
> "The Lord shall guide them continually."
>
> "For this God is our God for ever and ever, and He will be our God even unto death."
>
> "Who teacheth like Him?"
>
> "Be strong and of a good courage, be not afraid, neither be thou dismayed, for the Lord thy God is with thee whithersoever thou goest."
>
> "The joy of the Lord is your strength."

And after it she shared with the assembled friends her vision of the past twenty years, of the hundreds of thousands of young women in the country needing the help that could come when Christian women were banded together and could cover the country as a whole. Each president gave a summary of the position of her own organization as it faced the future, and then each woman present, as they sat in a great circle, answered Miss Dodge's question as to whether the time for union had come. "I most earnestly desire this union." "It has been my deep desire for years." "I have come to-day believing that in God's providence the time has come." "I hope this is the beginning of union." "To my mind union means so much that I do not see how as Christian women we can fail to unite." Thus around the room, then Miss Dodge spoke. "I think we all agree; we want cooperation with union, not cooperation without union. Let us therefore vote now. Those in favor of this sentiment will kindly say 'aye.'" A unanimous vote was taken.

"The end of the exploration is the beginning of the enterprise."

In answering Miss Dodge's second question: "How can we unite," the thought in every one's mind was of previous propositions for union which had failed, because it was impossible to see the end from the beginning, and the beginning had called for more concessions and violation of existing policy than seemed recompensed by the probable achievements of such a united movement. The chief concession was one as to the basis upon which Associations could be admitted. In the International Board where various forms of local organizations made different provisions of membership as regards activity, fees and church connection, there was strong sentiment for liberty of basis in the national charter. All The American Committee Associations held uniformly to an open associate membership, and a voting and office holding active membership of communicants in Protestant Evangelical churches. There were at hand beside these two bases those of the World's Young Women's Christian Association and the International Committee of Young Men's Christian Associations. The latter was called for and read—the well-known statement of their evangelical church position, leaving open the definition of what churches were to be considered evangelical in this connection. As the question reverted to the bases of the two women's movements involved, Miss Dodge continued:

"Now, how can these two be combined?"

The response began as a paradox, it ended as a prophecy sure of fulfillment.

"I have never known how, because every one says they can't be combined. The proposition made in the past has been union on the evangelical basis; that existing bodies may be a part of the whole body without changing their bases, and the new organizations be asked to adopt the evangelical basis." After the first discussion an unofficial and individual vote was recorded as almost unanimous on the resolution thus stated, "That we make the attempt of uniting all present Associations of the International Board and The American Committee on their present bases and all future Associations on the basis of the Young Men's Christian Associations."

Further suggestion as to name, headquarters and convention representation did not call for immediate action. The only other conclusion reached by vote was the recommendation to Washington of a united movement, in which the Women's Christian Association should retain the present status, a Young Women's Christian Association should be affiliated with The American Committee, and that mutual representation, a united finance campaign and a central executive committee should be constituted. That was the first fruit.

People who were told of the Manhattan Conference rejoiced that there was to be "union," but her guests who saw Miss Dodge's face that day knew it was illuminated by something more than the thought of a union of two existent organizations. She saw arising a new creation for young women, of young women, and by young women, in which the spirit of peace and good-will and the joy of the Lord might be felt and through it made outwardly manifest.

Back of the fourteen women who met with Miss Dodge in May, were the Board and Committee which had appointed them, and back of those were the Conference and Convention by which they had themselves been elected. Fortunately the International Conference would be held in Baltimore that very fall, and The American Committee had power to call a special convention competent to act upon all the matters affected by the Manhattan resolution. The sub-committee appointed that day and its chairman, Miss Dodge, spent the summer in constant communication with each other and the field, concluding their labors with recommendations to their legislative bodies, to sanction the points already agreed upon, and to appoint a Joint Committee of fifteen to complete the terms of union. The Baltimore Conference in November, 1905, and the convention which The American Committee called in Chicago early in January of 1906, adopted these resolutions and joined in asking for Miss Dodge as chairman. She associated with her as private secretary Frances Field, general secretary of the State Committee of New York and New Jersey, who prepared the thirty exhibits for the members of the committee and the brochures for the education of the Associations. Such thorough gathering and sifting of evidence bearing upon Relationship to the Churches, on State Work, on the Metropolitan System and many other foundation stones in the Association's structure, had never been known before. Workers in other organizations frankly coveted our opportunity, after forty years of experiment to build fresh from the very ground up. As fast as necessary policies were agreed on by the committee, they were reported to the field so that when the Convention was called for December 5 and 6, 1906, and Associations were asked to make application for charter membership in time to estimate the attendance of their delegates, there was a pretty general understanding of the nature, the privileges and the obligations of the Young Women's Christian Associations of the United States of America.

At the Joint Committee offices there was the greatest excitement as day after day the charter membership applications kept pouring in from East and West, North and South, city and student, large and small Associations. The East had the advantage of transportation, so the blanks from Newark, New Jersey, and Lowell, Massachusetts, were first received. Some one said she felt as members of the Constitutional Convention of 1787 must have felt while waiting for the thirteen original states to ratify the United

States constitution. The returns were equally successful and the credential committee of the Convention was able to announce as charter members 147 city and 469 student Associations. This included all but three of the city Associations of The American Committee and most of their student Associations and almost all of the Associations affiliated with the International Board which carried on work for improving the spiritual, mental, social and physical conditions of young women. Ninety-six of the cities were represented by 338 delegates, and 36 of these student Associations by 54 delegates at the Convention which received the final report of the Joint Committee and inaugurated the new movement.

The South Church (Reformed) at the corner of Madison Avenue and Thirty-eighth Street, New York City, was the scene of the meeting. It was a thinking, praying, working Convention. There was little in the way of entertainment and nothing in the way of spectacle. It made no impression upon the city. Intercession, deliberation and decision were the main features. There were greetings from the two presidents who laid down unselfishly the offices held only until the disbanding of the former national organization, from the general secretaries of the International Committee of Young Men's Christian Associations, Mr. Richard C. Morse, and of the Executive Committee of the Federal Council of the Churches of Christ in America, Reverend E. B. Sanford. There were addresses which threw a search light over the areas to be cultivated by the new national organization. Reverend Charles Stelzle spoke on Christian Cooperation in the Industrial World, Mrs. F. T. Thurston on Christion Cooperation Among Women in Social and Business Life, Mr. Robert E. Speer on The Results of Higher Education Conserved for Christian Leadership, Mrs. Thomas S. Gladding on The Unique Responsibility of the American Associations to the World's Work, Reverend Cleland B. McAfee on The Source of Power in Great Movements, Mr. John R. Mott on Our Summons to a Great Advance. Miss Dodge read the Joint Committee's last report and gave the business to the Convention in the form of resolutions relating to the organization of the body, and instructions as to how the executive board should proceed to accomplish the expressed wishes of the national body. These with slight emendations were adopted. The constitution was presented as giving notice that, after incorporation of the National Board, the next Convention would be competent to adopt it, and until then charter membership rights would be valid. The purpose was stated to be "to unite in one body the Young Women's Christian Associations of the United States, to establish, develop, and unify such Associations; to advance the physical, social, intellectual, moral and spiritual interests of young women; to participate in the work of the World's Young Women's Christian Association."

In the agreement between The International Board and The American Committee, to which constituent Associations had assented in applying for charter membership, it had been stipulated that the new Na-

South Church, New York City,
Where Present National Movement was Formed

tional Board, when organized, should consist of five resident and five non-resident members from the International Board or its constituency; five resident and five non-resident members from The American Committee or its constituency; five members from the American Department of the World's Young Women's Christian Association, and five other persons. The nominating committee, of which Mrs. Margaret E. Sangster was chairman, had looked for women familiar with work already done, but ready to see the new duties taught by new occasions, women who knew girls one by one, as well as by clubs and cabinets and committees, women most of all who felt from the bottom of their hearts that in the twentieth century, as in the first, Jesus Christ must be the center of life and that the Young Women's Christian Associations have come to the Kingdom for such a time as this. The convention elected their nominees. From the constituency of the International Board at headquarters, Mrs. R. A. Dorman, New York City, Mrs. R. C. Jenkinson, Newark, New Jersey, Mrs. Charles N. Judson, Brooklyn, Mrs. William W. Rossiter and Miss Alice Smith, New York City. From the field, Mrs. Dudley P. Allen, Cleveland, Ohio, Mrs. F. L. Durkee, Worcester, Massachusetts, Mrs. Henry Green, Philadelphia, Mrs. J. B. Richardson, Oakland, California, Mrs. B. T. Vincent, Denver, Colorado. From the constituency of The American Committee, Mrs. S. J. Broadwell, Mrs. J. S. Cushman, Miss Helen Miller Gould, Miss Janet McCook, New York City, Mrs. Robert E. Speer, Englewood, New Jersey, Mrs. Henry

M. Boies, Scranton, Pennsylvania, Mrs. L. Wilbur Messer, Chicago, Mrs. Irwin Rew, Evanston, Illinois, Mrs. William F. Slocum, Colorado Springs, Colorado, Mrs. A. McD. Wilson, Atlanta, Georgia. From the American Department of the World's Association, Miss Maude Daeniker, New York City, Mrs. Thomas S. Gladding, Essex Fells, New Jersey, Mrs. David McConaughy and Mrs. John R. Mott, Montclair, New Jersey, Miss A. M. Reynolds, North Haven, Connecticut. The new members were Miss Dodge, Mrs. Stephen Baker, Miss Mary Billings and Mrs. William B. Boulton of New York City and Mrs. E. M. Campbell of Newark.

The Association experience of these board members was as varied as the entire local and supervisory range. Four were presidents in cities. As many more had been pronounced Christian leaders since undergraduate days. Others were on university advisory boards. Several had rare gifts for friendly talks to young women, which had been widely expressed. Several had gathered their friends together for Bible classes, or had led the Bible study of winter evenings, or days in summer conferences. Some had taught in mission schools or had been employed officers. Others had administered large business interests; some had supported financially work which they were not free to do themselves. Many were officers of state committees. Several had visited or resided in mission lands and were familiar with foreign work. Several had taken an active part in the World's Conferences. The record of many covered a half dozen of these points. Mrs. Dorman (Mary Aitken) was a charter member of the Association of New York City and in 1872 it was she who secured for the needlework department a free equipment of Wheeler and Wilson sewing machines for the Young Ladies' Christian Association house at Irving Place and Eighteenth Street, and had since then been president, trustee and held other responsible positions for the International Board. Mrs. Messer had since 1888 belonged to The American Committee for which she had been the first editor of *The Quarterly,* had occupied all the four executive offices, had represented them at two World's Conferences, and was also on the advisory board at the University of Chicago.

There was a verse often repeated in the between hours of the Convention, though not sung as a hymn, nor made a formal motto. It was Arthur's words to Bedivere: "The old order changeth, giving place to new, and God fulfills himself in many ways."

PART III. 1906 TO 1916

THE YOUNG WOMEN'S CHRISTIAN ASSOCIATIONS OF THE UNITED STATES OF AMERICA

CHAPTER XVII

THE PRESENT NATIONAL MOVEMENT

WEDNESDAY and Thursday of that notable December week when the one new movement became an actuality, were grey days drenched with rain; Friday was bitterly cold; but the vagaries of weather did not dishearten the delegates whose votes had instituted the new order of things, nor the twenty-six members of the National Board who made each other's acquaintance at the first board meeting on December 7, nor the one hundred and forty-nine secretaries, superintendents and department directors who remained for a three days' conference after the close of the Convention.

For the business of these board meetings the instructions passed by the Convention were indeed a Magna Charta of the new government; and so comprehensive and far reaching was this document that its contents could be appropriated only little by little. After election of officers—Miss Dodge was made president, and appointment of staff—the former secretaries of The American Committee, International Board and Joint Committee were called, there were set up three immediate lines of communication, through an office department, publication department, and territorial committees. The Joint Committee had tentatively engaged the whole eighth floor of The Montclair, number 541 Lexington Avenue, at the corner of Forty-ninth Street, where its own headquarters had been, and thus it was in their own official home that the new National Board met on December 7 and adopted the policies prefaced by the words,

> As a corporate body we are witnesses of Jesus Christ, and the truest service we can render is to show Him in every detail of work, (and continuing with these paragraphs on the office administration).
>
> That work should be conducted in a business-like, concise way. All details of office work and outside policy thoroughly systematized and yet not so systematized that the loving touch should be omitted.
>
> That relationship with the staff from general secretary to office girl should be that of cooperative spirit, true justice, and a sense that all are working for and with the Board to develop a great work. The office work should be a model for the Associations.
>
> That the spirit of relationship should be generous and fair; that all dealings should breathe this tone. In other words, that from the start it should be felt that this is a Christian movement, and that our basis is being worked out in detail even to the courteous and prompt answering of letters and courteous replies at the telephone. An overworked, under paid staff cannot show the Christian spirit.

During Joint Committee days there had been much correspondence about an official organ. *The Evangel* had made its valedictory address in December, and *The Bulletin,* which had superseded *The International Messenger,* had also said farewell to its old constituency. Both lists of subscribers were turned over to the National Board and on the first of February, 1907, there appeared the salutatory number of *The Associa-*

tion Monthly, official organ of the National Board of the Young Women's Christian Associations of the United States of America. It described itself as a forty-eight page magazine, issued monthly during the year at a subscription price of one dollar. This first copy contained signed articles by Mrs. Robert E. Speer, Rev. J. Douglas Adam, Clara S. Reed, Elizabeth Wilson, Mary F. Sanford, Arthur J. Elliott, Robert E. Speer, Bertha Condé, Eleanor Brownell, Helen Temple Cooke, and communications from writers in the United States and in the fields occupied by foreign secretaries. All was under the editorial direction of Frances E. Field. The keynote was struck in Miss Dodge's first open communication as president:

> As I look at our work there seem to be three or four points that we should remember: First, Cooperation. We need to think of working with our Heavenly Father and his Son Christ, and with his help and power to cooperatively develop the new work. We cannot any of us be in a hurry. We must do the best we can and then be willing to wait, to quietly study all the problems and to see what can be done, to lay foundations that are going to tell many years hence. Then we must all have patience. Cooperative patience means your patience and our patience combined, and with this thought I am sure you will have patience with us and not expect from us too much at once. How far are we ourselves fitted and worthy for the responsibilities which God has put upon us? It is just here that we must all stop and question. We can have in the new movement the greatest of buildings, the greatest number of educational classes, but if we within ourselves are not true spiritually, and have not true fellowship with the friends who come into our buildings, then these great buildings are not worthy for the girls to come into. This would mean no

spirit of patronage, but the loving working with, and not for, the members and girls who are in touch with Association work.

Another topic upon which every bit of available wisdom had been expended was that of division of labor in field supervision. The experience of twenty-two years of State Committees and fifteen years of State Directors within, as well as advice from Young Men's Christian Association leaders without, had been sought and analyzed and weighed. And then like an inspiration there came to both Miss Dodge and Miss Field in their own separate homes and on the same day, an idea which might mean unity without centralization, which would give to every woman in every section of the country a chance to develop those particular interests which they believed most needed emphasis there, yet all in a uniform way, because all would be extensions of a balanced center. In several sections of the country, Associations in the same State belonging to the State Associations of The American Committee and the State Boards of the International Board were charter members of the new national movement. This was true in Missouri, New England, New York and New Jersey, Ohio, etc., and to invitations from these States the National Board representatives first responded, that the break in supervisory relations might be as slight as possible.

The recommendations approved by the convention under which they were working were:

That the National Board shall concentrate upon developing strong state, territorial or field committees composed of women residing in such divisions of territory, and that it shall be the function of the National Board to develop such agencies rather than to do direct local advisory work.

That the relationship of such territorial committees to the National Board be made a subject for study during the next two years, and that the Board shall have liberty to establish tentative relationships, subject to the approval of the next convention.

It was hoped that these sectional committees which would be auxiliary to the National Board would be representative of the local Associations in each district. Each committee would be self perpetuating, submitting its nominations to the National Board for approval. The appointment of secretaries employed by each auxiliary committee would also be subject to the approval of the National Board, which would recognize them as the field workers of the national staff. The annual budget would also be submitted to the National Board for suggestions and approval. Although each territorial committee would be responsible for raising the money in its own district, yet if the financial policies seemed too meager for the necessities of the field, the National Board might be able to help by assigning secretaries to work with the committee in securing a larger budget than the one which was first proposed.

Before the United States membership met in Convention again at St. Paul in 1909, the Associations in twenty-one States had readjusted their immediate supervisory relationships into seven territorial organizations. The six New England States had established headquarters in Worcester, Massachusetts; New

York and New Jersey in New York City; Virginia and the Carolinas in Charlotte, North Carolina; Delaware, Maryland and Pennsylvania in Philadelphia; Ohio and West Virginia in Cincinnati; Missouri and Arkansas in St. Louis; California and Nevada in Los Angeles. The difficulties centered chiefly around securing committee members unafraid of near and heavy financial responsibility, and finding enough strong, well trained and experienced secretaries. Miss Reynolds, the chairman of the Field Work Committee, in presenting this report to the convention, spoke also of the viewpoint of the whole as imperative in the symmetrical development of the different parts of the country.

> This symmetrical development is not a question of the numbers enrolled in Bible classes or sewing classes; but of a controlling spirit and purpose which shall reach out through all the organization and machinery until it works the miracle of a fourfold development in the most insignificant individual girl whose antecedents or environment have dwarfed her life on one side or another. Whether or not the result is brought to pass through the local Association depends upon its leadership, and the territorial committee should be in a position to assist in securing wise and efficient local leaders. Back of the territorial committees stands the National Board as an inspiring and unifying force, working out methods to be used by others in effecting the object of the movement, training both voluntary and professional leaders. The responsibility for the solidarity of the movement rests upon the National Board as a body.

By 1915 all the States of the United States of America had been grouped under eleven committees which were now called Field Committees of the National Board instead of territorial committees. The exceptions were the District of Columbia and Hawaii, which are in direct relation to the National Board, also the colored Associations, which are supervised by specialists in the Department of Method, although a Conference held in Louisville, October, 1915, presaged a more uniform policy.

Theory and policy have always frightened some people; other people have been deaf and blind to all abstract expressions. One might say only the incarnated ideas rouse such people and set them to work. That is the reason that the state secretary and the national secretary, living young women who have visited cities and colleges or whom the members have met at conferences, have stood to people for "state work" and "national work" in scores of Associations. If the situation were severe the presence of the national secretary was implored; plain visitation might be done by the less experienced state secretary, but in an emergency a call was sent for the national secretary. Even in Biblical language the telegram has read, "Come at once, the Philistines be upon us." But the core of the new system is that headquarters secretaries and field secretaries are all employed officers of the National Board, and differ not in degree but in kind.

No one department answers its own questions alone. The Finance Department was to solve the problem of field financial support and its answer was joint finance campaigns. The Secretarial Department was to respond to the plea for suitable employed officers. Its answer was the National Training System. Yet the

Field Work Department did not divest itself of its own most important duty, finding women for auxiliary committees, gaining their cooperation, and then leaving to them the cultivation of the soil. Seed might be sent and implements provided and agricultural experts might come by and inspect and advise, but the farmers themselves were to be responsible for the crops.

All the earlier history had shown that state officers were the pillars which upheld the broad Association structure. One thinks of such chairmen as Mrs. H. M. Boies of Scranton, who created the ideal of what a state chairman could be. Her distinguished husband was one of the first to believe in permanent financial support for a state Association. The State of Pennsylvania had but two chairmen in its eighteen years of history, for when Mrs. L. M. Gates succeeded Mrs. Boies in 1895 she continued until the disbanding of The American Committee in 1906. Mrs. N. B. Bacon was another who stayed by the stuff as the secretaries came and went and the tides of the State Association of Ohio ebbed or flowed. Mrs. F. F. McCrea of Indiana, Mrs. Levi T. Schofield of Ohio, Mrs. C. C. Rainwater of Missouri, Mrs. C. A. Rawson of Iowa, Miss Mary B. Stewart of Michigan, Dr. Ida C. Barnes of Kansas, were all chairmen worthy of the name. A gentleman was waiting in an Association reception room one day until a state committee meeting should release a college friend who had come in town to attend it. As the ladies had assembled one by one and had gone out, several of them before adjournment, he had noted their faces, and finally when he had left the building with his companion, he said, "Why do all your women look so much alike?" It was a laughable query, for that committee, like most of the others, was made up of women of different ages and tastes and environments. Some were faculty members, some wives of business men, some were young alumnæ, some returned missionaries, some were city ministers' wives. What was there in common? There was this —"For we preach not ourselves, but Christ Jesus the Lord, and ourselves your servants for Jesus' sake." There was not much glory, not much sitting on platforms, nor being introduced to admiring audiences, but there was much chance for weighing the results of neglecting opportunities or of making the most of them, for assuming financial burdens without any human assurance of a way to meet them, for intercession when the only possible power able to energize indifferent Associations was the Spirit of God, to whom prayer was made. For such women, barring the difference in the nineteenth and twentieth centuries, the Field Work Department was looking.

In the opinion of certain past grand masters of society organization, the first Convention passed two contradictory resolutions under the head of finance, one, "That the National Board shall adopt a budget of estimated receipts and expenditures, and shall as a corporation be responsible for the payment of bills contracted by it," the other, "That the National Board shall impose no taxes or assessments upon the Associations, but that the Associations shall be invited to make a voluntary subscription to the work of the national organization.'' But these resolutions were the outcome of much study of the processes by which money had been raised for the three great bodies promoting Christian Associations in the United States—The American Committee, the International Board, and the International Committee of Young Men's Christian Associations.

In the first years of The American Committee its income largely consisted of gifts usually proportionate to membership, from student Associations paid through the state treasurers, then as the state budgets had to take into account salary and expenses of the indispensable state secretary for a whole or a part of a year, the proportion of these necessary budgets that was forwarded from state to national Committee grew less. Then, too, as the city Associations enlarged cost of maintenance to keep pace with enlarged work and the student Associations applied most of their revenue to sending delegates to the summer conferences, they sent in less of their local funds to the state, which had already decreased the proportion of state funds sent on to the national treasury. From the first the gifts to the World's Association were individual; an English penny a member was the universal standard, but for America, richer and more accustomed to wholesale missionary enterprises, five cents a member was substituted. This World's Nickel was, as a rule, collected during the World's Week of Prayer, which began on the second Sunday of November.

To augment this fluctuating inside income, members of the Committee supplemented their own subscriptions by asking gifts from their friends and people known to be interested in Christian work, or specifically in the welfare of young women. The treasurers' reports show the status at intervals.

In 1887 the Association subscriptions were 65 per cent. of $689 receipts.

In 1892 the Association subscriptions were 16 per cent. of $7,000 receipts.

In 1897 the Association subscriptions were 4 per cent. of $13,000 receipts.

In 1902 the Association subscriptions were 6 per cent. of $27,000 receipts.

Not yet had the Committee dreamed of an endowment such as colleges possess for each chair of learning, but the missionary board plan seemed feasible—asking individuals for the annual support of a secretaryship, not a secretary, for the work goes on though the worker falls. Mrs. Phoebe Hearst in 1900 offered the first secretaryship. In time a few others were secured and several thousand dollars in legacies were received.

Even though the sum total of the national treasury was small, the plan of voluntary contribution to state and national support was the best possible education for the members at large in the Christian fine art of giving to something which they could not see, and which might not directly benefit them although it might bring them great advantages.

On the program of every state convention there was invariably a finance meeting. It might not be detected on the printed sheet by the delegate who represented her home Association for the first time, but the eye of a seasoned convention goer could pierce through the announcement of an address on "Lengthen thy cords and strengthen thy stakes" and spy the finance meeting lurking underneath. It usually found its place Saturday morning, after the state chairman's report, which closed with recommendations of which the budget was a part, and after the local reports. The leader usually recited the appeals before the state Association for extensive and intensive cultivation and asked the members of the convention to pray for guidance as to what share of the budget needed to accomplish this, each could give or be responsible for securing. As the list of Associations was read, one after another stated the amount that had been previously voted by the Association. Rarely were the personal gifts announced. Only the collectors as they totaled the pledge cards knew of the sacrifice back of a penciled subscription of ten or twenty dollars, the giver of which might have been supposed to do generously if she gave one dollar. In the early days of financing the Association movement, one constantly heard, "How much she would give if she were only able!" Later on more frequent comment was, "How much she might give if she were only interested!" Some of the finance meetings were a revelation of spiritual courage and devotion. Sixty-six delegates of the third Kansas convention in 1888 pledged $1,160; in 1889 seventy delegates at the second Pennsylvania convention subscribed $637, and the next year sixty-five delegates subscribed $1,346. This means an average of from nine to twenty-one dollars each, and few of the pledges were ever repudiated. Most were paid promptly; sometimes a college senior would find that she could not meet the obligation she had assumed until the second year instead of the first year of teaching, a word almost equivalent to earning at that time.

The opportunity for individual members to contribute directly for national work was given at every summer conference, so that although the percentage of Association gifts was small, the percentage of the budget contributed by members of local and state Associations and the members of the national Committee itself was more presentable.

So certain was the Joint Committee that the National Board would need a much larger budget for 1907 than the combination of the largest previous budgets of the International Board and The American Committee, that part of the work of its chairman had been to confer privately with individuals before the Convention. By this means when the National Board organized on December 7 and adopted for the year 1907 a budget of $100,000, the amount was practically underwritten and the whole volunteer and employed force could devote themselves to what is termed "the real work of the Association," as though any one could label one part real and another part spurious, or minimize the Christlike qualities of self-forgetfulness and fearlessness of those who secure money by private appeal.

Aside from the personal subscriptions and those of interested friends, there were also revenue-bringing although not self-supporting departments, and the National Board could reasonably count on part of the necessary income from the Publication, Conference and Secretarial Departments.

Among the first chairmen of standing committees to be appointed was Miss Janet McCook to the position of chairman of the Department of Conventions and Conferences, as the programs and contracts for the season of 1907 must be made. Nothing was attempted the first year beyond eight conferences of the same character as in 1906, the Eastern Student at Silver Bay, the Central Student at Lake Geneva, the Western Student at Cascade, Colorado, the Eastern and Central City at Silver Bay and Geneva, and the general conferences for both student and city members at Capitola, California, at Asheville, North Carolina, and at Seaside, Oregon.

The very year after the International Committee had established its second summer conference at Northfield, Massachusetts, plans were made to open one on the Pacific Coast. But the serious railroad strikes of 1894 interfered. It was not until 1896 that the Mills College grounds near Oakland were used, and so successfully that the conference returned in 1897. Nothing was done in 1898, and this doleful record might have been extended in 1899 but for the tour which Miss Reynolds as World's Secretary was making to the Pacific Coast, and the pluck of the western girls. Twenty-two from the University of

California and four from the University of Nevada went up to Inverness, where their Christian fellowship included cooperative housekeeping as well.

In was in 1900 that Harriet Taylor laid the whole situation before Mrs. Phoebe Hearst, who was interested in girls as girls and had very close relations with those studying at the University of California. She saw how such a conference as Miss Taylor proposed would benefit young women, and grow in strength and numbers until it became permanent, and proved her confidence in the plan by assuming the entire expense of the 1900 Conference, even providing traveling expenses for one student from each college in California, Oregon and Washington. The hotel at Capitola-by-the-Sea was secured and the Conference launched. By 1911 that place was hopelessly outgrown and again Mrs. Hearst came to the rescue. She invited the whole 1912 conference to her own estate at Hacienda and opened negotiations with the Pacific Improvement Company by which the National Board was given an ample site on the Monterey Peninsula a little beyond Pacific Grove. Within forty-two working days roads, piping, electric lines, administration building, ten tent houses and a kitchen were constructed in time for the 1913 Conference of the Young Women's Christian Associations of California, Arizona and Nevada. The grounds were dedicated and christened Asilomar (Retreat by the Sea). In 1915 a beautiful auditorium and a Visitors' Lodge were added to the permanent equipment. The grounds were designed by a woman, and are infinitely homelike with their side walls of sand dunes, their curtains of pine trees, their canopy of California heaven and their outlook of ocean, gray in the fog, blue in the morning sun and purple and gold at sunset time.

By 1915 the eight national conferences had become fifteen and there had been added eight camp councils, under Field Committees, for industrial and high school girls, with less complex programs and more time for vacation resting.

As difficult a problem as any that had presented itself to the Joint Committee was that of professional training for employed officers on local and national and foreign staffs. There were people who believed that the vocation of secretary, like that of nurse, depended upon the nature of the technical education for candidates as well as upon the nature of the candidate. Others honored that view more by the breach than by the observance. Miss Dodge had never questioned in any of the prefatory interviews and correspondence that the national organization must provide for securing and training secretaries and giving advice about filling positions. The chief question was whether the training school—or schools, for that was also debatable—should be directly under the National Board, or under an educational board appointed by the Convention, or under independent corporations, recognized and endorsed by the Convention. Fortunately the leases of the houses in Chicago in which The American Committee carried on its Training Institute would not expire until 1908. This gave the

The Auditorium, Asilomar Conference Grounds, California

National Board time to investigate what sort of training the new movement would require.

What sort of women would be required needed no investigation. That was patent to all. Mr. Theodore Roosevelt might have been delineating the ideal Young Women's Christian Association secretary by the words he used in another connection: "the strongest are needed, those of marked personality, who to tenderness add force and grasp, who show capacity for friendship, who to a fine character unite an intense moral and spiritual enthusiasm."

Both study and experience must be compounded with these personal qualifications. The California State Committee had worked out with Los Angeles, its headquarters Association, a practical course under direction, by which a suitable candidate might help in every phase of the city Association, and be given to understand principles as she went along. This was the key to the practical side before the professional study. It also solved the question of one or more training schools, for each state or territorial Committee could conduct this elementary work at a place not remote from any of the candidates' homes, but the National Board itself could provide the graduate school at its own headquarters, open to secretaries from the preparation centers and to other women who had been successful in the Young Women's Christian Association or similar movements.

Upon this plan, then, the Secretarial Department Committee framed the training system. In the summer of 1908 a catalogue was issued, containing the course of study and requirements for admission; and a large residence, Number Three Gramercy Park, near Fourth Avenue and Twenty-first Street, New York City, was fitted up with the equipment from the Institute in Chicago, which of course was discontinued at the same time. Names of faculty and teachers could not be printed, as the list of instructors was built up slowly even to the moment when class or lecture was due. The construction of the course of study was a veritable labor, as it endeavored to combine Bible and kindred subjects on which Professor Edward I. Bosworth of Oberlin and Professor Ira M. Price of Chicago and other theological professors advised, curriculum staples as tested by the five years of the Chicago Institute, findings of board members and other authorities which came in answer to a questionnaire sent out, and certain fundamentals as to the personal equations involved which were insisted upon by members of the committee—all in a year course.

But on September 23, 1908, the National Training School opened with Caroline B. Dow as dean, and Charlotte H. Adams as resident Bible teacher, and eleven students taking full work. When Miss Dodge gave out the certificates at the first commencement three went to students from outside of the United States: Agnes Kingsmill of Eastbourne, England, Katherine Reid of Glasgow, Scotland, and Charlotte Sutcliffe of Canada.

That same autumn five territorial committees and three state committees conducted training centers on the California plan, and a few of these repeated the course in the winter, with part of their lectures and their Association examinations coming from national headquarters. By 1915 ten of the eleven field committees had maintained training centers.

What of the girls in the meantime? While the National Board was pursuing investigation and reorganization, what was becoming of the girls and young women on whose behalf the Young Women's Christian Association was supposed to exist? These were inquiries steadily and gallantly made and heard from all parts of the country. The Board at times had to remind some of these spokesmen of a general sentiment, that they had sat in the South Church in December of 1906 and glibly voted that the National Board should concentrate upon developing strong supervisory committees throughout the field rather than itself doing direct local work. Miss Dodge's phrase, "cooperative patience," was also used. Even as the founder of the Kingdom of God here upon earth came not to destroy but to fulfill, so this human agency attempting its little share of bringing in the Kingdom of God had to work slowly lest haste should mean destruction of the former things evolved by natural growth before any well-reasoned better new ways were at hand. The girls who might look to the National Board were in two places. They were in every nook and cranny, highway and byway of the United States, and they were in those foreign countries not yet able to administer their own Association work. From the outset the Joint Committee accepted these two parishes and the Convention voted that there should be two coordinate departments, one for Home and one for Foreign work, equal in rank though size and internal development must depend upon what each undertook to do. Later the Home Department was termed the Department of Method, as more adequately expressing the nature of its duties.

It was said at the first annual meeting that,

> The study of the field must be intensive as well as extensive, to know about the needs of girls, the things they do not have, the things they do not want, the things that they are doing, their hard lot or their empty life because of their easy lot, the conditions peculiar to certain sections and certain classes,—these can be brought by scientific study in a form organized for use.
>
> There remains that more difficult process which cannot be accomplished so easily or quickly, but to which all those who work with young women, whether volunteer workers or secretaries, are making a steady contribution, the study of the individual young woman—not so much what she is doing as what she is thinking, what is helping her, what is hurting her, what are the obstacles in the way of her largest life. There is a certain understanding of a young woman that comes only through the opportunity to relate her to every other woman. It is given to us to correlate preparation for service with opportunities for service; to increase the content of the sense of fellowship; to make the claim that we are all members, one of another, something real and vital by actual working; to bind all the activities of our Association life together by such interrelations of foreign and home, student, city and industrial Associations as shall increasingly overcome any tendency to division in our Association life which might result in injuring the dynamic of our movement as a whole.

Interruptions to the work going on with young

women in city and college, in mill, village and factory, had not resulted from the readjustment of supervisory bodies. When the Young Women's Christian Associations of the United States of America met in St. Paul, in April, 1909, and completed their organization by adopting a constitution and approving policies presented by the National Board, there was reported a total membership of 190,795 in the 791 local Associations. And this membership had been well occupied in 1908: 38,290 had been in Bible classes, 2,049 in mission study classes; the students had held religious meetings regularly during the college year, and the other Associations kept up 350 meetings weekly; they had enjoyed 3,912 social occasions, had studied more than 40 educational subjects, had had access to 114,336 books and 2,128 periodicals which they might have read if they had wished to do so; 6,548 had learned to cook, 14,309 had learned to sew, 21,487 had found exercise or amusement or both in 93 gymnasiums, several thousand had helped eat the 5,054,940 meals served in 112 lunchrooms, 4,010 girls at a time or 54,271 for the full year had gone to bed at night under an Association roof; 23,882 had received the address of a safe shelter elsewhere, 17,302 came back to report that they had secured a position through the Employment Bureau; 69,131 journeying by boat or train had had their questions answered and their troubles lightened by the Traveler's Aid; 3,275 employed young women had managed their own 150 clubs, and 3,006 younger girls had begun to learn to do the same in their 49 clubs; and there were 12 secretaries in Calcutta, Bombay, Madras, Lahore, Colombo, Shanghai, Tokyo and Buenos Aires, speeding the day when these figures would be duplicated on other continents.

The city of St. Paul, Minnesota, had organized an Association in 1907, which was the first fruits of the National Board in one respect, since St. Paul was the largest city of its size in the country without a Young Women's Christian Association at that time. Their invitation for the Convention of 1909 was therefore very readily accepted. It was a peculiarly important Convention. People had had time to think as well as to work since New York, December, 1906, and the National Board wanted the benefit of discussion with the field fully as much as its sanction for the proposed order of march for each department. One felt that it was truly a national gathering. Many of the Eastern guests had never gone so far west as Chicago, which they found was only a port of call to the Twin Cities of the Northwest. Some of the visitors from the far South and from California verified the change of latitude by encountering a mild snowstorm.

One result of this thinking was the statement of the purpose of the national organization. Plainly enough had the New York Convention declared its aim of uniting and developing Associations in this country and helping in the World's work. It had even inserted what might be called a "blanket clause," "to advance the physical, social, intellectual, moral and spiritual interests of young women," which might cover expositions or other nation-wide business. But that was only the outer shell of its purpose, some felt; what should be the kernel within? So the old statement was distinguished as "the immediate purpose," and it was capped by these words,

> The ultimate purpose of all its efforts shall be to seek to bring young women to such a knowledge of Jesus Christ as Saviour and Lord, as shall mean for the individual young woman fullness of life and development of character, and shall make the organization as a whole an effective agency in the bringing in of the Kingdom of God among young women.

It will be remembered that charter membership was granted up to the time of this Convention and that admission after this time was upon the terms of active membership—that is, the voting and office holding membership being limited to women who are members of Protestant Evangelical churches. The Joint Committee stood as a unit for an evangelical basis which recognized the Divinity of our Lord Christ, and salvation through Him, together with the inspiration of the Scriptures; also that this basis should be in the form of membership in churches; that is, entrusting the voting power to church members only, rather than requiring a personal test from individual Association members. By such means the Association is placed as an auxiliary of the church and the charge of forming a new creed or denomination is avoided.

How to distinguish these evangelical churches was not, however, so clear, since some felt that the Young Men's Christian Association definition used by The

American Committee was not the most satisfactory that could be devised, and while the Joint Committee retained this definition according to the decision of the first Manhattan Conference, still the chairman was authorized to investigate this matter of some further possible form.

It was known that the first Young Men's Christian Association in the United States, that of Boston in 1851, had been established upon an evangelical church membership basis, as were most of the similar organizations arising after that, but there was some variation, and at the Detroit Convention of 1858 it was resolved

> That as these organizations bear the name of Christian and profess to be engaged directly in the Saviour's service, so it is clearly their duty to maintain the control and management of all their offices in the hands of those who profess to love and publicly avow their faith in Jesus, the Redeemer, as divine, and who testify their faith by becoming and remaining members of churches held to be evangelical, and that such persons and none others should be allowed to vote and hold office.

But a query arose as to what churches were to be regarded as evangelical. Hence the Portland Convention of the Young Men's Christian Association, in 1869, appointed as a committee to frame a definition Dr. Howard Crosby, General O. O. Howard and others, and they drew up in Scripture phraseology a statement aimed rather to signify ecclesiastical bodies which might or might not accept the different clauses, than to enumerate all the essential doctrines of the evangelical or trinitarian faith. This is the wording as adopted, except that the very last clause was added by a later convention:

> And we hold those churches to be evangelical which, maintaining the Holy Scriptures to be the only infallible rule of faith and practice, do believe in the Lord Jesus Christ (the only begotten of the Father, King of kings, and Lord of lords, in whom dwelleth the fullness of the Godhead bodily, and who was made sin for us though knowing no sin, bearing our sins in his own body on the tree) as the only name under heaven given among men whereby we must be saved from everlasting punishment, and unto life eternal.

After that date Associations were entitled to enter the North American brotherhood if holding to this constitutional provision.

The Joint Committee learned that certain people found difficulty in distinguishing between this definition of an evangelical church, and the evangelical basis of church membership. That difficulty would, no doubt, be still greater should the new movement attempt even thirty-seven years later to frame an alternative for the Portland definition. But providentially, at this very time, the evangelical churches of America had come together in the Inter-Church Conference on Federation, and a great convention had been held in New York City in November, 1905. Five hundred official lay and clerical delegates from thirty constituent bodies united in forming the Federal Council of the Churches of Christ in America, "for the prosecution of work that could better be done in union than in separation." Their basic resolution was,

Whereas, in the providence of God, the time appears to have come when it seems fitting more fully to manifest the essential oneness, in our Divine Lord and Saviour Jesus Christ, of the Christian churches of America, and to promote between them the spirit of fellowship, service and cooperation in all Christian work, therefore be it

Resolved, that this conference authorizes the Business Committee to prepare a Plan of Federation which shall recognize the catholic and essential unity of the churches represented in the conference and provide for the cooperation of the denominations in general lines of moral and religious work.

This Plan of Federation listed the denominations entitled to representation, and although an effort was made looking to the admission of non-evangelical churches, only one vote was cast in favor of that position. Bishop Hendrix, the first president, said of this new confession of Christ as Lord and God, "May a positive faith of the Christians in America who believe something have a wholesome effect on those troubled minds who as yet can only see men as trees walking."

One of the main objects seemed peculiarly appropriate in view of the suggestion that the Young Women's Christian Association make use of this recent numeration of evangelical churches, namely, their effort "to secure a larger combined influence for the churches of Christ in all matters affecting the moral and social condition of the people, so as to promote the application of the law of Christ in every relation of human life."

These two methods of defining evangelical churches were brought forward in the proposed constitution in 1906. When the constitution was adopted in 1909 the second was accepted as equally loyal to the deity of Christ our Head, and more truly representative of the churches which in turn represent Him, and the article on membership states that

> By Protestant Evangelical Churches are meant those churches which because of their essential oneness in Jesus Christ as their Divine Lord and Saviour, are entitled to representation in the Federal Council of the Churches of Christ in America, under the action of the Inter-Church Conference held in New York City, November, 1905. The list of churches which have availed themselves of this privilege up to date will be found on record at the office of the National Board.

He saith unto them,
"But who say ye that I am?"
And Simon Peter answered and said,
"Thou art the Christ, the Son of the living God."
"Upon this rock I will build my church."

"But let each man take heed how he buildeth thereon,
For other foundation can no man lay than that which is laid, which is Christ Jesus."

CHAPTER XVIII

THE YOUNG WOMEN OF THE CHRISTIAN ASSOCIATIONS

CHILDREN'S singing games, where each player in the ring crosses her own arms, and with her right hand locks her neighbor's hand on the left, while with her own left hand she grasps her playmate on her right, are always symbolical of a true Young Women's Christian Association. The players stand shoulder to shoulder, facing every other member of the circle, their voices ring out in unison and set time for their actions. All are absorbed in the doing of one thing together, and at any moment the hands can unclasp to make place for a new comer into the game.

The noblest illustration of the American Associations as one part in the great world circle was seen perhaps at the World's Conference of 1910, which met in Berlin. Thirty foreign countries had sent three hundred and forty-nine delegates, and from Germany alone there were eight hundred and forty-five. National consciousness had been lost the first day the Conference assembled in the Lehrervereins Haus, as one saw the number of men present and realized how many continental pastors were heads of parochial branches, as one saw the divers costumes of the different orders of deaconesses and remembered that the deaconess takes up the Young Women's Christian Association as one phase of parish duties, as one saw the mourning garb of the ladies from all sections of the British empire and recalled the death of Edward VII but ten days before. With national consciousness out of the way one had brain space for girl consciousness, that came in an abundant measure through the various sessions. But on Sunday it came in a revelation overwhelming as an avalanche. It must have been a revelation to the entertaining city as well, judged by the account, a column and a half long, found in one of the daily papers next morning.

Zirkus Busch was filled up to the roof with 7,000 people, almost exclusively young women. Berlin had never seen such a picture before.

On their way there the troops of girls in their holiday clothes made a striking appearance.

They gathered in great crowds in front of the huge stone building, each group in charge of a deaconess. As the doors were opened, whole hordes would vanish inside, then the police would bar entrance until these had found their seats, before admitting another mass of humanity.

One asked where did all this throng come from, as they did not look like well known people. You were told that it was the World's Conference of the Evangelical Jungfrauenverein.

The nearby cathedral was opened and immediately filled. Here an overflow service was held.

It was about half an hour after the police closed the doors of Zirkus Busch upon this gigantic gathering of girls that the program began, but the time was occupied in singing some of the beautiful German hymns.

Youth and animation were there in full measure. The aspect was brightened by the brilliant characteristic garb of a group of girls from the Spree River district. One of her majesty's ladies in waiting and a number of society women occupied the royal box.

It was like a swift illumination to see that mammoth chorus of a thousand Berlin members rise "like one man" for the singing; their voices were clear and true, it was a pity one dared not applaud them vigorously. The men's cornet band of the Berlin Foreign Missionary Training School accompanied the congregational singing. All stood to sing,

From far and near with one accord
We rise to praise our common Lord.

After a part song, a Japanese lady, Miss Michi Kawai, appeared on the platform. It was the first time, at least in Germany, that a Christian Japanese woman had been seen on such an occasion. She was clad in her long blue national costume, with wide sleeves and a sash tied at the back, and wore white gloves. She was obliged to use eyeglasses. After making several profound bows, letting her arms hang straight down as she bent low, she came forward and in a clear voice began a most thrilling testimony to Christianity. Her address was in English, translated by Pastor LeSeur.

Brief abstracts of the two addresses by Germans and the greeting by Miss Dodge followed this reporter's account of Miss Kawai's speech. But the indelible impression was made by the people, by the girls, for the older women had stayed away to let the girls in.

The World's Conference report rather took exception to the careless classifying of the audience, and remarks:

It may be an audience of those of whom little is generally known. It was an audience, however, which indeed demonstrated the power of the Association among the working classes, and those who are some of the most indispensable members of society the world over. Also more than one

Michi Kawai,
Secretary of the National Committee of Japan

foreign delegate present that afternoon took fresh courage to return home and emulate the wonderful success of the German Association leaders in reaching large numbers of working women and girls. For working women and girls are everywhere. Everywhere they have much the same needs and the same possibilities.

Miss Dodge had shared this feeling, as she sat high up in the speakers' balcony, and looked down at that garden of girls' faces and hats, then had gazed up at the row after row of galleries, filled with girls, only rarely the black coat of a pastor or the hood of a deaconess with the girls from her church or the bonnet of an elderly woman. "We must do this in America," she said, and the program committee for the 1911 Biennial Convention caught at this idea.

Tomlinson Hall is the popular scene of all the political and similar mass meetings held in Indianapolis, Indiana. Here the spectacular scene of the Third Biennial Convention took place, a gymnasium exhibition planned by Dr. Anna L. Brown of the National Board staff, and executed by Mabelle Ford, physical director, of the Cleveland, Ohio, Association. Whether the one hundred and seventy-five gymnasts of the fourteen competing teams, or the thousands of young women spectators were more enthusiastic over the drills and competitive sports it is hard to say. The audience sang and cheered and sang again. "Yes, I am satisfied," replied Miss Dodge again and again to the friends who had known of her Berlin experience. But that was only half of the demonstration. The Indianapolis press may describe the next part.

> At least five thousand women endeavored to enter Murat Theater Sunday afternoon. About three thousand of them succeeded in getting within the doors. Another thousand filled the banquet hall under the theater, and a third large audience attended another overflow meeting at Roberts Park church. Several hundred women who could not get in the theater returned home.

But a many-sided movement like the Young Women's Christian Association of a republic where more girls are developing life freely than under any other government ever known, could not rest with the emphasis upon only the physical and spiritual sides. For the next Convention, in Richmond, Virginia, in 1913, there was conceived the idea of a processional in which side by side should march the rank and file of Association members, the grave and the gay, the old and the young, the learned, the unlearned and the learning, from the city, the country, from the school and the university, the busy poor and the busy rich, the girls of America and those from beyond seas. This expanded into a pageant, "The Ministering of the Gift," which by song and speech and action, portrayed the study and work and play of all the Associations. Six thousand people were on the benches, five hundred members of student and city Associations on the floor, dressed to represent every element of the diversified membership, and singing, as they walked round and round the great arena and finally disappeared, what has come to be known as "The Hymn of the Lights" and has been adopted into every Association family. The demonstration typified girls by the thousand, no two alike, each with something to bring

Delegates to the Fourth Biennial Convention, Richmond, Virginia, 1913

into and something to take from the Young Women's Christian Association.

The Association is not the building, but the membership. For ages people have been making clear distinctions between these two applications of the words, The Church, and saying "The Church is not the edifice, even a consecrated edifice. It is the congregation that has consecrated that edifice to the worship of God." The Richmond Convention marked the application of that same truth to the Young Women's Christian Association.

But again the true membership does not limit the ministering of the gifts to its membership, and three commissions reported during those sessions on their programs, which might be carried out by every Association in its own community or by individuals in their own lives and in the lives of their friends. The first was on Social Morality from the Christian standpoint, seeking and holding the place of the Association in the present day crusade against the social evil. The second was on Thrift and Efficiency, setting before young women the worth of simple principles of living, desiring and achieving a balanced life. The third was on Character Standards, calling the attention of young women in a concerted and sustained way to the danger of letting down ideals of conduct, appealing to a firmer, surer moral estimate, and offering power to realize it.

Never again could this contrast of human life and interest against material equipment be so striking as in this year 1913, when the whole national membership was being congratulated upon possessing its new national Headquarters. The grounds and building were given by National Board members and a few interested friends, the furnishings and equipment by 245 local Associations. In September the offices moved from 125 East 27th Street, where for four years they had occupied quarters in the building of the International Committee of the Young Men's Christian Association, and the Training School from 3 Gramercy Park, to this splendid eleven story structure at the northwest corner of Lexington Avenue and Fifty-Second Street, New York City. It was dedicated on December 5, 1912, "To the glory of God and the service of young women." As it was the first national woman's building erected in America for sole occupancy of any such movement, it serves as a natural and convenient meeting place for women's church councils and kindred organizations, and encourages a natural and constant cooperation with other movements in which thousands and hundreds of thousands of women are also united.

Another notable structure also bore the name Young Women's Christian Association. It was the building on the grounds of the Panama Pacific International Exposition at San Francisco, California, open from February 20 to December 4, 1915, as a headquarters for the women employed in the Exposition and for visitors. The National Board assumed the undertaking and sent out a representative, Ella Schooley, who was executive of the cooperating committee and staff which carried on the enormous work. The building

135 East 52d Street, Training School

600 Lexington Avenue, Administration Building

of the

National Board of the Young Women's Christian Associations of the United States of America

contained a free information desk, reading and writing pavilions, lavatories for men and women, a women's rest room, a small auditorium containing a motion picture installation and a cafeteria where wholesome food was sold at a moderate price. Social occasions and employment bureau and classes in salesmanship and stenography were maintained. At the Club House on the Amusement Zone in another part of the grounds employees found comfortable couches and baths, opportunity for reading and music, inexpensive food, and sympathetic friends to help in constant emergencies. At the request of the Exposition Management a Day Nursery was attached to the main building. The daily attendance at these three places was numbered by thousands. On Sundays a vesper service was held on the portico of the main building addressed by clergymen from all parts of the United States.

The National Board also cooperated with the Travelers' Aid Society, with the Committee of One Hundred, which conducted an evangelistic campaign in the city of San Francisco, with the local Associations in supplying suitable housing to women guests, and with most of the religious and betterment conventions held in connection with the Exposition.

Not alone to the young women of the Associations was this service offered, but to all old and young men, women and children in need of its particular ministrations which were offered in the name of Him who had compassion on the multitudes.

No other Exposition had seen such a challenge so

adequately accepted, nor had any one undertaking of the National Board so opened the door to further co-operation among young women and the Christian Associations.

CHAPTER XIX

THE STUDENTS

FACING its future, the Student Committee of the National Board recognized in 1909 that the legitimate field of its efforts was the 17,000 women students in state universities, 37,000 in private high schools, 47,000 in denominational or church schools, 68,000 in women's colleges, 17,000 in seminaries and colleges of the second grade, 20,000 in nurses' training schools, 10,850 in independent music schools, 14,000 colored young women who were attending secondary and high schools, and 1,100 young women who were enrolled in the Indian schools. About 450,000 more were registered in public high schools and normal schools. The Association itself had been acknowledged as the academic religious institution in which students might claim as much proprietorship and as much right to self expression as in other student organizations which they controlled.

Since 1909 the advance has been noted by the types of institutions and activities, by the increase in student initiative, and by the American participation in national and international affairs where Christian women undergraduates are needed to round out some strategic attack.

In the state universities there have been in this last period large evangelistic campaigns where field and headquarters secretaries cooperated with leaders of the men's student movement. In the University of Minnesota there was cooperation in calling a religious work director for the two Associations. In 1907 the University of Illinois Young Women's Christian Association called its own religious work director. This Association in 1912 also raised $18,000 to meet a $20,000 gift for a building of its own.

In the church colleges there was also cooperation in evangelistic services with the clergymen connected with the evangelistic movements of the denominations. The college presidents and officers of the church boards of education helped in formulating the part the Young Women's Christian Association could best take in the promotion of Christian education; this seemed to be furnishing a means of expression for the religious life of the women students, helping them to translate their religion—sometimes a form of inherited religion—into practical Christian living both before and after graduation.

In nurses' training schools Bible classes were organized out from some one common center, or a regular student Association was sometimes possible when some keenly interested superintendent or senior student had time to make it a living reality. When the National Board assigned Bertha Condé to the field of professional schools, she concentrated upon the nurses' profession and in 1910 the graduate nurses of New York City formed a Central Club which was one of the charter branches of the Metropolitan Young Women's Christian Association. In May of that year the club opened two houses at 54 East 34th Street, called a general secretary, and continued Bible classes in hospitals for nurses in training as well as among the graduates eligible for membership.

In New York City also an art students' club with a religious aim was begun at the same time that the Joint Committee was laying the foundations of this present national movement, and was affiliated with the Territorial Committee of New York and New Jersey in January, 1907, as a Studio Club. First two rooms were occupied, then two apartments, then in 1912 there was given a splendid house at 35 East 62d Street, where seventy students live and hundreds of non-resident members come for spiritual and social contact.

Boston undertook metropolitan student work in 1911 without a building and though the secretary "rode all unarmed and rode all alone," the results of her errantry are already seen in the established colleges and amid the transient tides of professional students of art, music and drama in that center.

Before the recommendations of the National Board were submitted to the Convention for adoption it had sent a secretary to visit colored student Associations, Mrs. W. A. Hunton, wife of the senior secretary for the colored work of the International Young Men's Christian Association, and in a year the roll of Associations was doubled in schools on government and private foundations in fifteen states. Colored conferences have been held, leaders have received training for secretaryships of colored branches in city Young Women's Christian Associations, and they have had a place in the great intercollegiate gatherings of the decade.

In May, 1914, a negro student convention at Clark University, Atlanta, Georgia, brought together five hundred and twelve colored men and women from eighty-five schools and colleges, and ministers, educators, editors and other leaders, both white and colored, for a five days' deliberation under the chairmanship of Dr. John R. Mott. The stated purposes are being related to the whole membership through the student Associations and will help in gripping the present generation of Negro students with strong spiritual and moral impulses in bringing them face to face with Christian life callings and other places of leadership, in meeting the claims and crisis of Africa, and in bringing Christian thought to bear on present and future cooperation of the races.

The smallest group, but that one for which any organization writing the words United States of America in its charter must feel the keenest responsibility, is the Indian girls who have found their way to the higher schools within or without the reservations. Some of the Indian Associations were many years old before any committee or secretary made a study of the situation and aligned the Association movement with the federal government, the Council of Women for Home Missions, the Indian Rights Association and other helpful agencies. Some had found a big sister in a neighboring University Association, as Haskell Institute, at Lawrence, Kansas, with the University of Kansas; the state secretaries had made other friendly alliances, but after 1909 it was possible to make a long enough, strong enough bond of connection to endeavor to surround Indian members with Association influences even when they had gone back to their homes.

As to student activities, the most pronounced advance in this decade has been in the relation of Association Bible classes to the Sunday school and the relation of curriculum and volunteer classes. The outcome of much consultation with the Intercollegiate Young Men's Christian Association, the Student Volunteer Movement, and the Sunday School Educational Boards of the evangelical churches was framing a comprehensive course of voluntary Christian education to be promoted jointly by the Sunday school and the Association, planned to supplement the academic Bible work, to include the daily quiet hour, and to be based on Bible study one semester of each year, and mission and social study the other. The first text authorized was "Student Standards of Action," by Ethel Cutler of the National Board staff and Harrison Elliott, and was issued in time for the first semester of 1914–1915. Each succeeding semester an additional text has appeared.

The work of relating graduates to some form of community service on a wide scale was begun in 1911, when 859 seniors in colleges stated their willingness to take up the burdens of the old home towns or the new place of work or permanent residence. The first year 512 expressed themselves as ready to help in the church or Sunday school, 55 would join the home missionary societies, 80 the foreign societies of their church, 583 would enter social and philanthropic channels of usefulness, 175 specified the Young Women's Christian Association, 103 expected to help in women's clubs or granges. These recruits were referred to church boards for home and foreign missions, charity organizations, societies, local pastors and Association leaders. The last census (1915) records 1,558 outgoing students ready for work in 940 towns and cities; of which 1,250 recruits would come into church and Sunday school, 135 into the Home and 142 into the Foreign Missionary Societies, 483 into social and philanthropic activities, 460 into Young Women's Christian Associations and 445 into women's clubs and granges.

Even more indicative of the spirit of the new generation is the student initiative. Within the college it is a matter of course. Organizations abound until it requires organized effort to regulate the number of major or minor offices that can be held by one student who constantly achieves, or has thrust upon her, positions which may not lead to emolument, but certainly evidence trust. Field Committee members' duties are so vast, that only a few faculty women can spare time for the visitation, correspondence, and sitting in council that would accurately represent current student life to this larger Association group, and truly interpret that in turn to the undergraduates. Alumnæ soon get out of touch or those who are committee members may not know the adjacent student situation. Summer conferences are inspiring, but they are made for conferring, not legislating. To get around all these difficulties in securing the undergraduates' voice on their own matters, the Ohio and West Virginia Field committee devised and put into practice in 1912 the Annual Members' plan. For each group of three degree-conferring colleges or universities in a field division of the national organization, one upper classman is chosen to be for one year a member of the student department of the Field Committee. She meets at least twice in the year with the department in a formal meeting, and when her term expires is succeeded by next year's "annual member," elected from the next in order of the three colleges in her group.

Student initiative is also carried over into the summer conferences, where the "self government" of college or of dormitory is reproduced in the daily schedule of the conference. All those elements of life on a crowded conference estate which when we enjoy, we call personal, and which when others enjoy them to our discomfort, we call public, come under the student government of a conference. The idea spread further into the city conferences and the girls vacation camps where college girls as councillors led in making rules and became popular in enforcing them.

The conferences have brought the girls of each student generation to think for themselves about their own careers, because representatives from the church mission boards come there yearly seeking recruits for vacant posts in America and all the lands of the globe where Americans are needed.

No Christian movement of the twentieth century dares to stand alone or tries to advance alone. Up to 1912 the Intercollegiate Department of the North American Young Men's Christian Association, composed of men student Associations in the United States and Canada, had courteously included the women's student Associations affiliated with the National Board and the Dominion Council of Canada as the one American student body, incorporated into the World's Student Christian Federation. But in that year a definite working basis and program were established by forming the Council of North American Student Movements, of three members from each of the three above mentioned forces and from the Student Volunteer Movement. One of its first undertakings was a magazine, *The North American Student,* published during the academic year beginning March 1913. Into it was merged *The Intercollegian,* which had in turn absorbed *The Student Volunteer.* The close relations with Women's Foreign and Home Missionary Boards were furthered by the 1913 conference on plans of cooperation when delegates from twenty-four boards participated in a two days' valuable session under the hospitable roof of the national headquarters building.

1913 was truly world extension year. In April the delegates at the Richmond Convention listened to a call, the first that had ever come to the Associations of the United States after nineteen years of affiliation with the World's Young Women's Christian Association, and eighteen years of affiliation with the World's Student Christian Federation, a call to look into our own methods of procedure, in view of the ends we were trying to reach in common with others, but by means not akin to theirs. They then voted to appoint a commission "to consider as a result of the request of the General Committee of the World's Student Christian Federation," "a restatement of the evangelical basis in student Associations in personal terms, in accordance with the method of the Federation," and later elected such a commission. This reported to the National Board its suggestions, which were approved and circulated to the entire field. At the Los Angeles Convention in April, 1915, after a long debate in which class legislation, the ultimate object of student Associations, and emphasis upon church relationships were presented, the first vote approved the following amendment to be definitely accepted or rejected in 1918 at the next Convention.

Any student Young Women's Christian Association may be admitted to membership whose constitution embodies the following provisions: I. The Young Women's Christian Association of ———, affirming the Christian faith in God, the Father; and in Jesus Christ, his only Son, our Lord and Saviour; and in the Holy Spirit, the Revealer of truth and Source of power for life and service; according to the teaching of the Holy Scripture and the witness of the Church, declares its purpose to be:

PURPOSE

1. To lead students to faith in God through Jesus Christ;
2. To lead them into membership and service in the Christian Church;

3. To promote their growth in Christian faith and character, especially through the study of the Bible;
4. To influence them to devote themselves, in united effort with all Christians, to making the will of Christ effective in human society, and to extending the Kingdom of God throughout the world.

II. MEMBERSHIP.

Any woman of the institution may be a member of the Association provided:

1. That she is in sympathy with the purpose of the Association;
2. That she makes the following declaration:
   "It is my purpose to live as a true follower of the Lord Jesus Christ."

III. QUALIFICATIONS FOR LEADERSHIP.

1. All members of the Cabinet (officers and chairmen of standing committees) shall commit themselves to furthering the purpose of the Association.
2. Two-thirds of the Cabinet members shall be members of Churches which are entitled to representation in the Federal Council of the Churches of Christ in America, and only those delegates who are members of such Churches shall be entitled to vote in conventions;
3. Members of the Advisory Board shall meet the qualifications of Cabinet members.

In June of 1913 the Tenth Conference of the World's Student Christian Federation met in the United States, at Lake Mohonk, New York. There were preliminary meetings in Princeton, where a statue by Daniel Chester French was unveiled. This was a bronze figure of heroic size representing "The Student Christian" and commemorating the origin of the Intercollegiate movement there in 1877. There was a garden party at Greyston, Riverdale, a dress parade at West Point, and on the evening of June 2 there were met with one accord in one place three hundred and twenty delegates from forty countries, and under their motto "Ut omnes unum sint" they thought and spoke and prayed together. Full of meaning was this petition framed for Times of Retreat.

> O Lord Jesus Christ, Who didst say to Thine apostles, "Come ye apart into a desert place and rest awhile," for there were many coming and going, grant, we beseech Thee, to Thy servants here gathered together, that they may rest awhile, at this present time, with Thee. May they so seek Thee, when their souls desire to love Thee, that they may both find Thee and be found of Thee. And grant such love and such wisdom to accompany the words which shall be spoken in Thy name, that they may not fall to the ground, but may be helpful in leading us onward through the toils of our pilgrimage to that rest which remaineth to the people of God; where, nevertheless, they rest not day and night from Thy perfect service, Who with the Father and the Holy Spirit livest and reignest ever one God, world without end. Amen.

Women had not met with the Federation in 1897 at Williamstown when once before Americans were the hosts, but forty official women delegates from the United States of America were present at Mohonk, besides many Oriental and other foreign students matriculated in colleges and Christian training schools here. There was no business; each person present was at liberty to appropriate any part of the presentations of student life, thought, and religious opportunity to her own use, and that of the students she served as class mate or faculty member or dean or secretary or in any capacity.

But in December, 1913, a goodly percentage of five

thousand passengers, arriving in Kansas City the morning of December 31 for the Seventh Convention of the Student Volunteer Movement, were young women, although all the inspiring voices from the main platform were those of men. But in the sectional meetings there were scores of women missionaries who knew the life of women and children in the Far East and the Near East and Latin America, and who knew where best the undergraduates who were pondering over the location of their lives, could plant each one her own life, and there were women in the company which sat on the platform Sunday night, that last great night of the feast. They heard read the list of Volunteers who had died during the last quadrennium and joined in singing, "For all the saints who from their labors rest." Some of them spoke briefly of their reasons for offering their lives under the supreme command, and then came down to shake hands with their friends in farewell and receive their congratulations at being able to obey that command.

This Convention, which comes once in a student generation, speaks not only to those whose careers are yet to be settled, and to those who can transfer to a vocation in a foreign country, some occupation begun here, but to the undergraduates who can introduce a vital spiritual atmosphere and a missionary propaganda in their own colleges, to the church and Association leaders who are teaching women to love to give, and to those students from other lands who had not found in our United States the brand of Christianity of which home-loyal missionaries had told them.

CHAPTER XX

THE CITY GIRLS

WHAT is a city? The answer changes with every decade. "Where people live and work," was a close enough definition at first for Association statistics. Then it was any place where people did anything but study, and we had City Associations and College Associations. Then it was any place willing to begin, even if not able to sustain, an independent Association. Geography and politics also help in this identification. One may speak of cities over 500,000 population, between 500,000 and 100,000, between 100,000 and 25,000, and under 25,000. 369 cities over 12,000 were enumerated by the census when the National Board began to chart its field. Young Women's Christian Associations exist in all of these strata. In all of these, some people understand that the Association is "the members—not the building," and some fancy that the building and its privileges, how much can be bought for a dollar membership fee, and what must be shopped for in the various departments, is the real Association.

When *a* building or *the* building is the embodiment of the loyalty and enthusiasm of the members, that glorifies it as nothing else can adorn it, from the swimming pool in the basement to the moving picture installation and soda fountain on the roof. It is also praiseworthy according to its figurative windows and doors. From how many windows do the workers look out upon the community and see all the girls as they move about in all directions? Are there plenty of doors on the four sides for girls to come in—large doors for great assemblies, and little doors for steady, everyday wants?

Some buildings, like those in Brooklyn, in Minneapolis, in Milwaukee, in Rochester, in South Bend, show that some one donor saw that what young women had accomplished in cramped, rented quarters was good, but with a bigger place all their own they could do and have and be better, hence a splendid gift was made. Some buildings, like those in Youngstown, Ohio, or Cedar Rapids, Iowa, and elsewhere, show that the whole community of young women believed in the Association and they often worked quietly for years, and culminated in one final wild whirlwind campaign to make up the required sum.

The campaign which has been most noised abroad was the $4,000,000 campaign which closed on Thanksgiving Eve of 1913, in which $3,000,000 was given for seven Young Women's Christian Association buildings in New York City. One of these was the already completed National Headquarters and six were for various branches of the metropolitan Association effected in 1912 as the first example of genuine metropolitan organization.

New nomenclature has been introduced. In early

Young Women's Christian Association, St. Louis, Mo.
Modern Type of Administration Building

years one often spoke of the Association as the "Home." Almost every feature of certain Associations was for the permanent or transient residents of the home. Then the boarding home was called the "Association" and sometimes it dominated or elbowed out other departments, sometimes it was encroached upon by them. Then separate buildings were erected, and by 1913 the newly christened "Residence" was more generally regarded as simply one effort of the Young Women's Christian Association to solve the young women's housing problem of that city. It was an important department, but still a department. Even with the addition of "The Harriet Judson" in Brooklyn and the "Mary Clark Memorial" Home in Los Angeles, the capacity of all Association residences is only 7,207, though with the ceaseless coming and going, permanent residents and transient guests have numbered 157,380 in a year. But members' initiative is flourishing and nearly every house has effected some sort of inside organization for social and religious expression, growth and enjoyment.

"Members, not building," is the key to much of the recent development. It explains the Stenographers' Association in the Lancaster, Pennsylvania, Association; the Members' Council at Aurora, Illinois; the Onondaga Indian Girls' Club in Syracuse; the Business Women's Club in Augusta, Georgia, where they have erected standards seen only by their results in professional and personal life; in Washington, D. C., where they have erected a Woodland Lodge, goodly to look at and to live in. There are now almost as many club ideas and practices as clubs, all are inventors; clubs of graduates from the business courses and the cooking schools, choral clubs which have competed in song festivals, clubs from every department. Even in the employment bureau of St. Louis over a hundred hotel maids gathered regularly for a Bible class, prayer circle, and Sunday afternoon supper, helped support the Association's foreign secretary, took charge of a monthly service in a sanatorium, and created other ways of reaching and sharing an abundant life. The Hermosa Club, of Los Angeles, set a fine example to other young women in domestic occupations, though their club house on the Pacific Coast has not been rivalled as yet.

Inside the buildings the members have come for classes; at least twenty per cent. join for these privileges. They have taken courses in First Aid to the Injured and received certificates at first signed by President Taft of the American Red Cross Society and Miss Dodge, President of the National Board. They have learned the laws of sex with all their social and moral ramifications. When work in their own trade was slack they have prepared themselves by special study to do work that the Association had discovered was in demand. They have come in the evening because they were earning during the day, and they have come by day to fit themselves to earn, or because father or husband had already earned for them. They came to the gymnasium to exercise their bodies or their spirits, they came winter and summer to the swimming pools to learn to float and

Mary A. Clark Memorial Home,
Los Angeles, California

dive and laugh. They came week days and Sundays into long or short course Bible classes, and for vespers, and for meetings and classes which they planned and conducted for fellowship in soul growth, fellowship with their known friends, and with other young women not of the fold but who could really become one flock and might own one Shepherd.

Outside the building they have been just as truly on their own Young Women's Christian Association premises, as they have frequented the downtown lunch rooms or played on the athletic field or congregated as students of high schools or business colleges or met in temporary quarters rented in the locality that best met their convenience. Some of the members of colored branches worked so splendidly in the great finance campaigns that they can erect their own beautifully appointed headquarters.

The last clause in the recommended city constitution of 1912 makes this all plain by stating the purpose.

> To associate young women in personal loyalty to Jesus Christ as Saviour and Lord; to promote growth in Christian character and service through physical, social, mental and spiritual training, and to become a social force for the extension of the Kingdom of God."

A once popular hymn began,

> Throw out the life line across the dark wave.

Some decades later we realize that the enemies of girls' souls are working when the lights are brightest. So the modern Association steps over its own threshold.

Where cross the crowded ways of life
Where sound the cries of race and clan
Above the noise of selfish strife
We hear Thy voice, O Son of Man.

Some of the most powerful evangelistic messages which the girls of a city ever went to hear were delivered in theatres. The Rochester Association in 1904 paid $458 for an opera house and speakers for four Sunday afternoons. Two thousand girls in Los Angeles represented to that community the abundant life which Christ came to bring, by giving the Pageant, The Ministering of the Gift, in 1914. They have organized Know Your City weeks where by lecture and visitation information was gained and diffused about the status of the city at that very moment. The City Council, Public Health, Child Life, Courts and Jails, Charities, Welfare Work, Industrial Life, Amusements, Housing Conditions, Immigration and kindred conditions and institutions were discussed. They have cooperated with the churches of which they are a standing committee on young women's righteousness, in occasional and protracted religious meetings, they have found teachers for classes and sometimes pupils for the teachers. Groups of members have met in homes to study the Bible, or the unfolding page of the foreign Association story. They have come together Sunday afternoon on a shady lawn for a quiet service or have brought sacred music into a far corner of a city park. Hundreds and thousands of members in the Central and Eastern states have lavished their time and strength as loyal church members during great evangelistic campaigns, and then kept on through the following months and years after the tabernacle was dark and the voice of the evangelist and the sound of the singing were no longer heard in that city, helping into Christian tastes and habits the new followers of their own Lord. They have carried Travelers' Aid work alone or in conjunction with other societies, they have been in league with police departments to conduct to the Association headquarters girls and women who were perishing because they did not know where to find these Isles of Safety, or did not know that there was any such thing as a Young Women's Christian Association to ensure safety. And several cities watching the tide of affairs added to their staffs "police women," as the protective agents were styled.

"You build a great building and then you try to see how much you can do outside it!" Yes—for the weeks of opportunities are not all in the winter, as was once taken for granted. The summer program is often as heavy, though vastly different. From 1910 to 1912 the number of summer camps and cottages increased more than 200 per cent. These are not all owned outright; college dormitories in the suburbs sheltered guests who turned trolleywards every morning; winter homes have been put at the disposal of Southern Associations, even state barracks have been loaned when girl guests from the whole municipality were invited. Neighboring Associations have set up their tents side by side and within the Field Committees' great camps on the lakes or ocean, and among the hills and mountains, city girls have come together for the summer season. "We came, two girls together, for two weeks. We went away knowing two hundred girls and will never stop being acquainted with them."

But the clearest proof of the democracy of the Young Women's Christian Association, some one has said, is the City Summer Conference, and among the 1,502 city delegates at six conferences in 1915, coming from 224 places, there was a record of 83 occupations in which they spent their work days, and 38 church affiliations through which they worshiped on Sunday.

Might one say that the democracy aimed at is of the nature which does not declare "I am as good as she is," but "She is as good as I"?

Eastern City Conference, Silver Bay, New York, 1915

CHAPTER XXI

THE GIRLS IN INDUSTRY

"LET us resolve that in the new body we will work with girls, not for them."

This was the thought of a letter written to the chairman of the Joint Committee in 1906.

An invitation to grown up people to "Come and work with us" is almost as acceptable as an invitation to children to "Come and play with us." And among the 1,199,452 women in manufacturing and mechanical pursuits, the 142,265 saleswomen, the 21,980 telephone and telegraph operators and the 328,935 employees in laundries, there were hundreds of proved leaders already a part of the Young Women's Christian Association. Not the cities alone but the prairie towns with their canning factories, the hillside villages with their water powers, the fruit regions with their packing houses, become industrial centers, and when girls come together in any kind of a center, association is possible and the Young Women's Christian Association may be needed.

It was reported in 1909 that 14,877 young women in the industrial field had some part in the weekly classes and meetings held in mills and factories and business places, while 3,046 were club members in eighty-nine Associations. Fifty-five industrial and extension secretaries were helping in bringing people together and working out plans which needed an outside ally. Besides this general extension of manifold interests from the main administration there were several separate industrial and branch Associations.

Early in 1904 young women in the cotton mill villages of the Piedmont section, South Carolina, were able to open a local Association by the generosity of the mill managers, notably Mr. Thomas F. Parker of the Monaghan Mills, Greenville, who set apart a place for the general activities and a cottage for the general secretary and teacher of household economics. In 1905 the office and factory employees of the Larkin Company of Buffalo evolved an Association with classes and most of the usual all-round features as a branch of the Buffalo Association, and this scheme was adopted in many details in several other manufacturing houses, chiefly in New York and New Jersey.

The next step in working with this great group, one third of all the women over sixteen years of age in gainful occupations at that time, was a resolution adopted at Indianapolis in 1911.

> That in order to make more far-reaching the contact of the Young Women's Christian Association with women in industry, the extension of Association work into factories through noon meetings, classes and informal clubs be continued, and whenever possible in preference to organizing Associations within factory walls, the establishment of rented centers in the industrial sections of cities be advocated and employers be encouraged to contribute to the funds of the central Association which shall employ the secretaries in charge of this work.

And after this came Federation. For nearly a score of years the self-governing club in the factory had been the favorite form of cooperation. In cities where club officers and forewomen from several establishments met to discuss common interests, it was natural to think of making closer contact between the club memberships. Detroit projected the idea of a Federation of Industrial Clubs from the original Grace Whitney Hoff League, begun in 1908. Then Akron and other cities followed. This has developed as an industrial movement which belongs to the girls, accustomed to self government by the management of their own factory clubs, and finds a place in the City Association through membership there taken for granted in the club membership.

It is true that the great summer conferences were democratic and catered to all tastes, but so much was offered, conscientious club leaders followed so exacting a program schedule, that the joyful days failed as vacation. The club girls' daily councils were the heart of their whole conference. This made easy transference to the vacation camps of the Field Committees, and in 1913 the club girls' council was discontinued at Silver Bay and the club members of the Northeastern Associations came together at Altamont, New York, and those of the Delaware, Maryland and Pennsylvania Associations at Camp Nepahwin, Canton, Pennsylvania, for conference on their own work, and quiet hours of Bible study and intimate religious meetings to gain inspiration to do what they saw before them. Other sections continued the idea.

CHAPTER XXII

THE COUNTRY GIRLS

"MEMBERS, not equipment," is equally the active principle of work in the country, but members with the cooperation of a secretary of their own, working toward a higher spiritual and mental and social and physical and economic plane.

In the series of resolutions adopted at the St. Paul Convention in 1909 the unit of organizations for towns of 12,000 and under, and adjoining communities, was fixed as the County Association. At the same time there was more or less discussion of rural development, but in the "Secretaries' Association" Conference which followed in Plymouth Church, Minneapolis, the keenest interest centered in the section for county workers, when Elizabeth McKenzie recounted the bursting into Association life of Woodford County, Illinois.

A girls' club in the little college town of Eureka, Illinois, had found a way to open up clubs, Bible study, and a class in physical education in the college gymnasium taught by the physical director of the Peoria Association. This was the beginning, and on October 17, 1908, girls and women came together in the Presbyterian Church at El Paso and organized a county Young Women's Association. In April there were two hundred and sixty-nine members in seven branches in small towns, ranging up to 2,545 in population. In Roanoke they had furnished rooms, used as a center for the farmers' wives who came to town for shopping, and for their own classes in gymnasium drill, normal Bible study and shirt waist making. Washburn members held their gymnasium class in a board member's home. The El Paso girls turned their Christmas Gift Club into a self-governing evening club which they named "Alta Vista," and took for it the altruistic motto, "Give to the world the best that you have, and the best will come back to you." An alumna of the University of Illinois who had also been graduated through the various degrees of committee, cabinet, and conference of that student Association was chairman of the local committee in Minonk where a Bible class of twenty-two and a sewing class of eight were the stated weekly gatherings of members. There had been nearly five hundred present at the seven social gatherings held during two months in the whole county.

The college girls were also heard from at Minneapolis. Another report came from the University of Michigan, where a group of seniors whose homes were in small communities had formed a club to study what they could do for their home localities after leaving college. In line with this was the account of a class, other than of seniors, in the University of Kansas Association, studying what may be accomplished through the channels of home, church and school in small communities. Each member determined to work out some of the methods during her vacation days and to report progress.

Under these two heads have the women and girls of the small towns and country been developing their Association life, permanent county organization, and summer Eight Week Clubs. "How can I, except some one shall guide me?" is not only the cry of the solitary traveler in the desert between Jerusalem and Gaza, it is the cry of the isolated girls of the country districts of the United States. The Eight Week Clubs which Helen F. Barnes started in Texas and elsewhere stood for eight weeks of learning how during the college year, and eight weeks of passing on in the summer vacation, passing on in that most difficult of all fields for new enterprises, one's own home neighborhood. The girls who came back to college had so much to tell that was new and absorbing and girls who stayed on at home had so much to do and think of that was new and suggestive, that nation-wide expansion was next in order and in the spring of 1913 a detailed plan was sent to all student Associations offering a certificate of Commendation for Community Service to clubs making adequate report of adequate service. These certificates were signed by Miss Dodge and by Miss Jessie Woodrow Wilson of the National Student Committee. The purpose as stated in the outline could almost be pieced together line by line from the reports of the three following seasons.

To bring the girls and young women in smaller communities together during the summer vacation season for the pur-

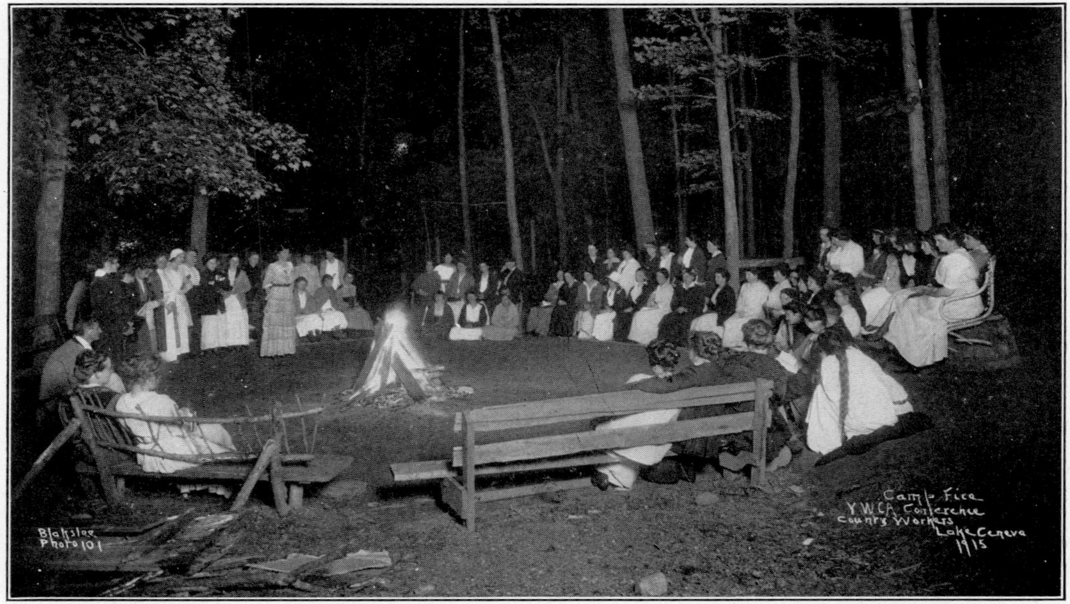

CAMP FIRE, FIRST COUNTY CONFERENCE, CONFERENCE POINT, LAKE GENEVA, WISCONSIN

pose of learning some of those things which mean a happier and more useful life; to unite them for definite service to their home neighborhoods; to learn about the work of the Young Women's Christian Association, and to be of help in bringing its opportunities to other girls in the country and small towns.

The reports for 1915 give figures as follows: 213 Eight Week Clubs with a total membership of 3,658 girls and with leaders representing 98 different colleges.

Any team work soon means a conference. The title of the Central City Conference was changed to Central City and County in 1914, and there were eighty representatives from fourteen counties who enjoyed it but asked for their own conference for 1915. This the National Board arranged at the nearby site, Conference Point, by which name old Camp Collie again comes upon the Young Women's Christian Association scene. Here in 1886 nineteen college girls from eight states had started their National Association, a work so visibly feeble that almost anything might break it down. Yet within eight years it was seen around the world and must be modeled after in India and elsewhere where the World's Committee had oversight. Here in 1915 eighty-three girls from the small towns and open country of twelve counties in seven of these same states, and four others, came together for the first county summer conference, and no one dares predict what they may achieve in that same space of years.

So much for facts. The inspiration comes to many through memorizing the "Helen Gould Bible Verses," as the list of Scripture passages is called, for learning which Mrs. Finley J. Shepard gives every member a copy of the Bible. Although the offer is open to all Association members yet the country girls seem to have more quiet time for committing verses to memory. Inspiration comes to others through the county camps like Camp Chedwell of Chautauqua County. Inspiration comes to all through cooperating with country churches and realizing that while the county Young Women's Christian Associations are a part of a new country life movement, they are also part of an established Christian order centuries old, adapted not alone to "yesterday," but equally well to "to-day and forever."

CHAPTER XXIII

THE YOUNG GIRLS

"LITTLE Girls' Christian Association." This comprehensive title was the name which a company of children in Oakland, California, were pleased to take thirty-five years ago. Their desire to become an auxiliary of the Oakland Young Women's Christian Association was granted, and though their Saturday morning's meetings did not continue for any length of time, nor their charitable exertions in collecting clothes and distributing them to the poor families persist until all the deserving and undeserving of the town had been freshly clad, yet the children were happy, did much good and were overjoyed at the thought of being lawfully connected with an international movement.

More persistent has been the girls' branch in Poughkeepsie, which claimed for many years to be the only definitely organized branch of its kind in the country. On March 30, 1886, girls from ten to sixteen years of age formed a miniature Association and within a year counted one hundred and ten members and a secretary of their own, Bertha Van Vliet. They had raised money towards furnishing a reading room, and a game room. They had also a spacious hall for entertainments and calisthenics, but were not content with this and found time during the three afternoons of each week for cooking and music classes. They chose their own members as leaders of their Monday half hour devotional meetings.

Young girls were in evidence in most of the city Associations, sometimes welcomed as "the women of to-morrow," sometimes unwelcome and sometimes considered a natural detriment because older girls did not like "to find the rooms full of little girls," as the fact was sometimes hospitably stated. They were always allowed in a Saturday morning gymnasium class, however. In the '90's the Association tried to assemble all the junior activities in some form of branch organization on the segregation principle. Even so late as 1909 there were only ten junior department secretaries.

But the girls were to have their day. As the self governing clubs made their way along, young girls kept proving in them their capacity for self-control and cooperation. They showed that they could be on hand and not under foot. In the rooms or building a line between children and girls of Association age was drawn. Then the secretaries began confessing that they needed to know more about girls before they could deal fairly and justly and affectionately by individual girls, and they took the topic of the Adolescent Girl for their Minneapolis Conference in 1909. After that they "stayed not for brake, and they stopped not for stone"; they besieged the National Board for help and they took counsel with the active girls in their own Associations, the high school students and grade girls, the girls who had stopped school to go to work and for other reasons. They put a plank into the platform of the County Association. All the resources of the Association were now opened everywhere.

The National Board through many volunteers and secretaries took part in those days and months of consultation in the Board Room of the National offices and of demonstration at the Studio Club before the arcana of the Camp Fire Girls were first revealed to an eager audience at the annual meeting of the whole Board in 1912.

Many local Associations and one Field Committee followed the example of calling a secretary for the Girls' Department. In four years the membership has increased eighty per cent. and the value of membership even more greatly.

In 1915 two conferences were held for high school girls alone. This was necessitated by the rapidly developing student movement among secondary school girls manifested by clubs, branches and Associations under city, county and older student leadership. In large cities where there are several high schools, unions of these clubs have been effected by the organization of High School Councils, the last word in younger student initiative.

CHAPTER XXIV

THE STRANGERS WITHIN OUR GATES

THE first immigrant girl in whom Americans as a whole have been interested was Priscilla Mullens, whose domestic graces and social readiness as appreciated by John Alden and Captain Miles Standish have been recorded for us by Longfellow. Girls coming over the border from Canada and the English speaking arrivals of the middle of the last century fitted into United States conditions almost imperceptibly; the Germans and Scandinavians of the next generation also went with swift steps straight into domestic occupations in American homes.

When the Young Women's Christian Association folk realized that to the difficulties all strangers in a strange land encountered, these newcomers added the handicap of ignorance of the still stranger speech, they attempted English classes for foreigners in many places. These were usually informal Thursday afternoon affairs. The girls came as regularly as they could, got acquainted with each other and their volunteer teachers, learned to read a little, tried to master the English consonant combinations and ceased the afternoon with a little fancy work and coffee drinking.

The teachers, for the most part, knew little of phonetics or of Grimm's law, but if they were sympathetic the pupils made headway enough to merge into the regular departments of the whole Association. But this took many years and only a few went unswervingly on.

All America began to think more about the foreigners on our shores. Christian prophets like Edward A. Steiner waked up the churches; the Women's Home Missionary Societies began to think of what lay here and over the sea, outside Ellis Island, to which they had largely confined themselves; and the National Board of Young Women's Christian Associations appointed a Committee of Research and Investigation. Then there appeared in December, 1910, an open door on Manhattan Island and a new term in the Association encyclopedia, an "International Institute" of the Young Women's Christian Association. Later this removed to 113 East 34th Street. Girls released to New York City by the port officials were called upon a few days after they arrived by a visitor speaking their own language, explaining to them the ways of working and going about and living in this new part of the world. Invitations to free English classes for other Finns or Italians or Syrians were accepted, then came acquaintance and friends and a grasp of spiritual truth. Trenton, Lawrence, Massachusetts, and Los Angeles adopted the same plan, namely, a branch headquarters accessible for foreign people, an American Immigration secretary, foreign visitors, teachers and director of special activities.

Back of this are efforts to connect American helpfulness to the organizations in the old home lands; and on every side are efforts to relate the new Americans, as soon as may be, to the best institutions and forces in the land they chose or were forced to adopt.

CHAPTER XXV

GIRLS IN OTHER COUNTRIES

ALL the young women upon the globe are not claimed by the United States of America in its membership, but from India, China, Japan, the Argentine and Turkey, they have asked for American leaders, and therefore seem to stand in a closer relation to us than do young women of other nations working independently or with assistance of other secretaries of the World's Young Women's Christian Association.

Before there was any thought of the city Association or national committees or secretaries, missionaries who had once been Association workers had made use of the Association plan of members and officers and committees with the school girls they were teaching. Mrs. Wishard wrote of several such during her early work tours, and *The Evangel* occasionally printed messages from such student groups in Nagasaki (1889), Hang Chow (1890) and Tung Cho (1892). That they were truly indigenous and not a mere projection of the foreigners' American notions may be seen from incidental extracts of this correspondence.

We were in all nineteen members in it, but now there are thirteen—some of them have gone to their homes and some were married, and some have gone to learn other things. One with us is a new member. She was baptized this month on the second Sunday.

We must pray for you in America: we know that is a good work we should do. Zech. iv:6. That is true a good motto, also we have written it on the blackboard. Are there any girls in your Association who have studied the Holy Bible from Genesis to Malachi? Our first class has studied and been examined on every book.

We had such a good letter in English from Nagasaki Japan School Assistant. They told us the Association of theirs was organized May, 1889, and we have answered to them. Miss Guinness wrote the book, "In the Far East." We have seen her. She lives in Honan, China. Last year in the June month she was here and attended our Wednesday evening prayer meeting; such very kind words to exhort us in the 14th chapter of St. John. She is a very lovely lady.

I write this English myself, but I cannot very fast.

Signed by a Chinese teacher.

It has already been seen how India came into contact with America through calling a secretary to Madras in 1894 who became national traveling secretary two years later, which was about twenty years after the first Indian branches had come into existence. Miss Maud Orlebar of England had reached Calcutta early in 1894.

Even when Agnes Hill was succeeded in 1908 by Ethel Hunter of Scotland as national secretary, the American bond was still strong, for Miss Hunter got her technical preparation at the Secretaries' Training Institute in Chicago and was in constant communication with the United States.

It sounds like the most ancient of ancient history to read in the report of the world's conference in 1898:

European and American leaders in China are made much of and their presence is eagerly desired at all the social occurrences. They would confess themselves that they are encouraged to lead very empty and thoughtless lives. I venture to hope that our Young Women's Christian Association with its Bible reading has been of some use to some of them. The only two unmarried girls in the place joined us. . . . And in our day China is opening. The Chinese young woman in her soft and brilliant dress, with her broad brows and her skilful fingers, is about to step upon the world's stage. She has a natural love for going about and seeing what is new. She would travel more now if she could be sure of her inn. The time may soon come when the Young Women's Christian Association home, on native lines, will be added to our missionary agencies, and be to travelers what at present our boarding schools are to students.

Nearly a score of years passed before this hope was realized.

When the honorary secretary of the Canton Branch forwarded this account, there were three other small branches in China, likewise of English speaking ladies, in Shanghai, Foochow and Hong Kong: the latter was the most vigorous and had formed a Chinese branch of forty members.

Foochow was supposed to be the first place where Chinese women students started their own Association by formal adoption of a constitution. This was in the Methodist School and Seminary in December, 1898, through the help of Mr. Fletcher S. Brockman, national secretary of the Young Men's Christian Associations of China. This little band of girls faithfully kept the Morning Watch and found out many ways of showing Christ's spirit in the day schools around and in the hospital.

The China National Committee received Miss Berninger in November, 1903, and after a year which she spent in language study, they were able to reorganize the Shanghai Association and open a house on the Yang tze poo Road, near the cotton mills. The girls and women employed there in western processes of manufacture took very kindly to the western ideas of Christian friendliness as expressed in this branch. Sometimes more than four hundred visitors dropped in to see Miss Berninger during an ordinary week and once during the first sixteen days after her return from vacation she made 1,088 callers welcome. In the autumn of 1905 A. Estella Paddock arrived as the first national secretary.

Miss Reynolds in her oriental tour of 1900 met with the pioneer Association of Japan, that of Yokohama, and with other ladies keen on calling an American secretary for work among the girls of government schools, alumnæ of mission schools and girls in factories. An experienced American secretary replied, but not from the United States. A. Caroline MacDonald, city secretary of the Dominion Council of Canada, offered to go, and the Canadian Association with a generosity amounting to sacrifice, let her go out in 1904 and generously supported her as national secretary of a sister country. Theresa Morrison was the first secretary from this side of the border. She went out in 1903.

Japan is rich in native leaders; Miss Michi Kawai is the Japanese active member of the World's Committee and Miss Ume Tsuda, the leading woman in the Japanese world of education, is president of the Tokyo Association. Both were college students in the United States. Even as far back as 1907, when women from other oriental lands met in Tokyo in the eighth World's Student Christian Federation Conference, they recognized that the national work would not bear the hall marks of Canada or the United States or of any foreign country, but would be distinctly Japanese. Action and reaction are equal.

As calendars go, it was half way between the Paris World's Conference in June, 1906, which discussed with utmost elaboration the lines for demarcation between church missions and missionaries supported by Christian Associations, and the extension of the Young Women's Christian Association into other lands, and the organization of the present national movement with a foreign department on a par with the home work, in December, 1906, that the first American secretary, Emma Jean Batty, took her departure for South America. Like all American secretaries, except those in India, she was confronted by a new language, but the first months were occupied with reorganization of the Buenos Aires Association for English speaking girls, which dated from 1890, and search for a central building. Six tiny rooms, up a flight of seventy-two stairs, were used as a boarding home, where seven regular members of the family hospitably made room for frequent transient guests and more than a score took luncheon daily, and in seasonable weather both English and Spanish speaking girls came in for Bible classes. Exorbitant rents have always made finding a location a serious problem.

From the United States the pioneer Association secretaries went out to Turkey in 1913 as the pioneers had gone to China in 1903 and to South America in 1906. And again like Miss Berninger in Shanghai, Frances Gage had once been a missionary in Turkey in Asia. She had a fine background of language and customs. Anna Welles, appointed to student work in Constantinople at the same time, had been for some years a resident of Paris and an active force in the Student Hostel.

The great war which began in 1914 not only curtailed the usual work in South America and Turkey, but called out the Association forces into necessary relief measures. New opportunities of this kind have also been responded to by the Associations in India.

Ten newly appointed secretaries went out in 1915, two to India, one to Japan, and seven to China. In these three countries the summer conferences have come to be spiritual power stations as in the older Association lands.

The building era has come to Japan and China as to India. Through the combined efforts of the Japan National Committee and the Pacific Coast Field Committee, the greater part of the money needed for the Tokyo Building has been secured and the building was opened in the autumn of 1915.

In Shanghai arrangements have been made with the Southern Methodist Mission for land and buildings which enabled the national and local work to take ad-

Ying Mei Chun Directing Gymnastic Drill in Shanghai, China

vance steps such as the organization of a Physical Training School for Chinese women, which opened October, 1915. For this the Director of Physical Education for Women at the University of Wisconsin, Abby Shaw Mayhew, had gone out in 1912, and Ying Mei Chun had returned in 1913 after thorough professional preparation in the United States. Secretarial residences in Canton and Foochow had also been provided.

Foreign Associations seem much more a part of the American sisterhood than they could otherwise seem even with secretaries going out and returning on furlough, because students from Oriental, Latin American and other foreign countries are studying in colleges, universities, preparatory and professional schools all over the United States. They are members of student Associations and guests at summer conferences as well as at special functions which Mrs. Helen Gould Shepard and other members of the foreign department have arranged.

That summer of 1900, when one picked up the morning paper with reluctance, fearing to see that still more missionaries had been borne down by the fury of the anti-foreign outbreak in China, that summer when Christians, wherever gathered, in church or camp, almost sought to dictate to God for a speedy end to the struggle, brought forth a harvest in the fall of 1914, which would never have been dreamed of in those days of weeping—twelve Chinese girls arrived in the party of students sent to this country by their government for education in different subjects.

And the money to be drawn upon for ten of these bursaries was the indemnity fund granted by China to the United States for those losses in 1900 and returned by our government to the Chinese treasury. In these years the Young Women's Christian Association has so fitted in among things Chinese that it was the China National Committee which was entrusted with administering the examinations and arranging the departures, and the National Board of the United States which received them here at the Training School building, telegraphed about admission to the desired schools, and stood by during the students' inevitable fall shopping. Best of all since the Association is only a department of the church, it was learned that ten of these students had come from mission schools, that all the indemnity students were Christians, and two of them were pastors' daughters.

Still other countries turn their eyes to America when seeking executive officers. In the British American Association established in Paris in 1904, under the inspiration of Mrs. Grace Whitney Evans Hoff, first president of the Detroit Association, the staff has been almost continuously made up of Americans at the main building, long known at No. 5 Rue de Turin, and at the Paris Student Hostel which has been, since 1906, the shadow of a rock in a weary land to women studying under the faculties of the Universities and those others who knew neither where to look for tuition nor abiding place. Through the World's Student Christian Federation certain American secretaries or volunteer workers studying abroad have cooperated with continental women students in university advance steps.

Even before Australasia had any regular national confederation, Adelaide called an American secretary, Esther L. Anderson, who went out in 1907, to be followed in 1911 by Helen F. Barnes as secretary of the National Association formed four years previous.

From all the five countries where the American foreign department has sent out secretaries, students have come to the Training School, and from Canada, France, Russia, South Africa, Finland, Norway, Switzerland, and Great Britain students have come also, for observation and training. They aim not to transplant but to select some of the ideas for grafting into either older or younger Association growths.

In thinking of the World's Association which bands all these lands together, one notices how stages of progress are marked unconsciously by the successive World's Conferences. The first met in London from June 14 to 18, 1898, at the invitation of the World's Executive Committee, it is true, but in a way it was the British Association asking their sisters to visit them, since hospitality was offered in private homes for some days before and after the conference proper; 204 of the registered delegates were from Great Britain, the other 192 came, nineteen from India, fourteen from the United States, thirteen from Sweden, five from Italy, three from Canada, one from Norway—these were the seven regularly affiliated countries—and one or more from each of eleven additional continental and extra European lands; and all the program sessions were in English, although in the business meetings there was much informal translating by the presiding officers, and in the devotional meetings there were prayers in many tongues that helped to make Pentecost and the Whitsuntide season very real. The English ladies realized the diversity of administration with such delicacy that the communion service was not a stated part of the program, but was held the morning after adjournment lest any might fear they had been forced to accept the ritual of an alien state church.

It was in a way a retrospective conference, for few of the 1898 delegates had been in that little group which in 1892 had decided that the time was ripe to effect world federation. Still smaller was the group to which the drafting of the constitution had been referred. And even in those countries (four at the outset, three in the next four years), which had legally adopted the proposed constitution through action of conventions or executive committees, the members at large were not very familiar with the scheme, and much explanation of that action was sought and was graciously and patiently given. Another link with the past was the reception at Exeter Hall tendered by Sir George Williams, the founder of the whole Christian Association movement, upon whom Queen Victoria had conferred knighthood in 1894 when the parent London Young Men's Christian Association celebrated its Jubilee by entertaining the World's Conference at the British capital.

Yet the deliberations were all constructive. It

would hardly seem, looking back to the morning when the constitution was adopted, that any delegates would object to the first Article: "Name, This organization shall be called the World's Young Women's Christian Association," but one delegate rose to protest on the grounds that Christians are to flee from the World, the Flesh and the Devil. But she was fully content when reminded that "God so loved the world that he gave his only begotten Son."

The recommendation of an International Week of Prayer brought most keenly to mind the geographical differences of Northern and Southern hemispheres, which must be observed even when people's hearts are all at one. October was proposed, then November. This was satisfactory except to South India, which would be in the monsoon then. But India's large delegation undertook to bear with this inconvenience and the date, which has never been changed, was agreed upon. The designs for a world's badge were also presented then and every one knows the incident relative to the language of the inscription. Around the circle of the globe the world's motto was to be printed. But in what language? Should it be a separate tongue for every country? That would not be a uniform universal badge. A Scotch mind, trained to philosophical niceties, suggested printing the motto in the original Hebrew of Zechariah iv, 6, and each wondered that she herself had not hit upon so happy a solution.

One cannot forget the social meetings: that at the heart of London, the Mansion House, when the Lord

Mayor and Lady Mayoress received the delegates in pomp and circumstance, and as soon as seats were taken for the program, an honorable attendant lifted the mighty gold chain of office from the mayor's neck and he listened with the others to the remarkable address of Isabella Bird Bishop, Fellow of the Royal Geographical Society, and to the other speakers of the evening; that at the heart of England, when by train and *char-a-bancs* we journeyed to a glorious country estate and then sat under the shade of a century old tree to listen to a Bible reading by one of the hosts; that at the heart of the British Empire, when we were received by royalty in the Dean's Garden at Windsor and stood at divine service in St. George's chapel, and walked through state apartments and listened to a message sent from Victoria, Queen of England and Empress of India.

And now came Stockholm, 1914. Again there was royal recognition. Again there were delightful excursions, but here there were only 325 from the entertaining country in proportion to 463 from twenty-two other countries. Each of the eighteen national Associations was represented, several of them far beyond voting capacity, but the members were welcomed as visiting delegates. The program was as international as the delegations. Sweden generously permitted the use of French, German, and English as the official languages and was content to have only the public addresses interpreted into Swedish. There was a union Communion service on Sunday, and whereas in the immediately preceding conferences the sacra-

Clarissa H. Spencer,
General Secretary of the World's Committee

ment had been offered by clergy of three church bodies, that delegates might receive it each after her own custom, this time all partook together of the communion after the Lutheran order, as administered by clergymen of the Swedish National Church, and all the children of the Heavenly Father were together in their Father's house and at His table. Previous conferences had discussed matters of organization. The Stockholm Conference dwelt, it is true, with adjustments that come from growth and national expansion, but the conference theme reduced the organization to the place of a necessary intermediary. This theme was stated as, "The Unfolding of the True Plan for Woman in God's Purpose for the World." There was appeal made for public service, for Christian women to take their due share of the municipal work of their nations, but the supreme obligation laid upon the women assembled in that conference was the winning of the individual soul for the Kingdom of God. About 800 delegates represented about 670,000 members in all parts of the world. It is a beginning.

One sentence phrased by Dr. A. Johnston Ross stands ever as an explanation of the close relation desired between the girls and women in other lands and the members of the Young Women's Christian Associations of the United States of America.

> It is only when that mystical collectivism of the East, and the individualism of the West, and the strenuous gravity of the North and the tender passion of the South, have all been brought in together to study the mind of Jesus, that we shall be able to understand what God has given us in Him.

CHAPTER XXVI

THE SECRETARIES

"WHY do you say 'secretaries'?" is a question repeatedly asked by people unfamiliar with Association traditions. That was the title used in calling the first person to spend his whole time in Christian Association work and receive a salary for his services.

George Williams and his colleagues could awaken interest in personal Christianity among the young men in their own drapery establishments, they could project plans outside, they could make their Sundays the longest working days of the week, but when by 1845 the Hitchcock-Rogers example had been followed in all parts of London and fourteen business houses had branches, there must be a man free to go about, to execute as well as to devise plans, to look after affairs on week days as well as Sundays.

J. H. Tarlton, a city missionary who had been conducting morning worship for the employes of Hitchcock-Rogers, seemed suitable as this salaried organizing secretary or missionary, and he was asked

> To act as assistant secretary, to attend all general meetings of the Association, to assist in conducting services in houses when they want help; to establish and render as efficient as possible district Associations; to form by com-

municating with Christian young men in the large towns and cities of the Kingdom, branch Associations (it may sometimes be necessary that he should visit young men in illness); and make himself generally useful among the class to which his efforts will be directed, by pointing them to "the Lamb of God which taketh away the sins of the world."

He was evidently a secretary, a unifying force, a chaplain, an organizer, a friend to young men, a general factotum and an evangelist. His sphere was not only London but any part of the United Kingdom. Mr. Williams is said to have supplied most of the ideas and much of the enthusiasm while Mr. Tarlton carried them into effect so he was evidently an administrator also. Little is said about his duties as host, and as the London Association was housed its first five years in a room in a hotel, those were probably so incidental that no one considered them worthy of mention.

But in America the woman secretary was first of all a hostess, even though like Mary Foster in Boston in 1866, the realm over which she presided was only two rented rooms. Many of the employed officers elsewhere in early years were happy to welcome girls to the one room which for utility eclipsed the cottage furniture which Goldsmith says "contrived a double debt to pay," for this one room, bounded on the north by a desk, on the east by a piano, on the south by a gas stove, and on the west by a reading table, was office, employment bureau, audience room, noon rest parlor and library, all in one. When the boarding home was the dominant feature, the superintendent of the home was also manager of the employment bureau and organizer of other departments of work. The records of the Young Ladies' Branch of the Ladies' Christian Association show that Mrs. M. C. Uhler, the clergyman's widow who was their first secretary, received $50 per month. This was a maximum wage for a long period for positions where no living was provided.

Traveling secretaries from 1886 on were evangelists, advisers, correspondents, organizers, too, though curiously enough Nettie Dunn, the pioneer traveling secretary, organized no Associations whatever during her first year of office. Visitation claimed all her time. Most of the state workers' visits were made to colleges and the secretary was paid a small salary and expenses of board, whenever hospitality was not offered.

At the first national convention at Lake Geneva, in 1886, there were no secretaries present, because there was none in the movement at that time. Three years later nine of the seventy-four delegates to the second national convention in Bloomington were secretaries, one national, four state, three local city. They found time for a little conference together before the convention began, for it has always been recognized that the distinction between volunteer and professional work is genuine. The volunteer worker selects the task for which she is naturally fitted, and stays by it as long and does as much or as little as devotion and circumstances and other claims allow. Her service may strike any note of the Association scale. The professional worker is held to a standard, the Association is her ranking claim, and she binds the separate notes into a harmonious chord.

Every national Convention since then and many state meetings have been made the opportunity for formal or informal discussion of the problems for which these women had made themselves responsible in becoming salaried workers in the Young Women's Christian Associations.

After the organization Convention of 1906 there remained for a three days' conference at the Park Avenue Hotel, New York City, one hundred and forty-nine superintendents, secretaries, clerks, and directors of departments, for three days of acquaintance and inspiration. Miss Dodge explained what "Cooperation of the Secretaries in the Development of the New Movement" would mean, and there were other speakers.

The Minneapolis meeting of secretaries following the second national Convention claims to have started the immediate advance in girls' work through the powerful addresses delivered on these topics, The Importance of the Study of Adolescence, How a Girl's Early Belief May Be Developed Through the Student Association into Mature Christian Faith, The Girl in the City High School, in the Private School, in the Small Town High School, The Cooperation of City and Student Associations in Developing and Training Individual Girls, What Has Led the Young Men's Christian Association to Inaugurate Its Present Work for Boys. At this conference also the beginnings of county work were made the basis of a morning program as suggestive as it was absorbing.

How the Young Women's Christian Association Can Meet the Appeal of the Times in Its Secretarial Work was the theme of the Indianapolis Secretaries' Conference of 1911, following the third national Convention, and the theme was treated through commissions on city and student problems which sent out their findings to members in advance, so that discussion could be instant and intelligent. The debate of five years concerning the name of this body was settled in favor of the progressives when the constitution was adopted.

> The name of this Association shall be the Association of Employed Officers of the Young Women's Christian Associations of the United States of America.
>
> The object shall be study and conference concerning the questions that affect the efficiency of the salaried staff of the Young Women's Christian Associations.

Thus this gathering of three hundred members decided to enlarge the terminology so as to describe the whole staff, not only that section known as secretaries. The link between the United States and other countries was seen in the constitution's provision that employed officers trained in America, as well as outgoing workers, could be active members while serving Associations affiliated with the World's Association.

The importance of the technical department was seen by provision for sectional organization when the department directors desiring such a branch constitute one-tenth of the paid up membership. Under this provision the directors of physical education at once formed a department organization.

> O wad some power the giftie gie us
> To see oursel's as ithers see us!
> It wad frae monie a blunder free us,
> and foolish notion!

This was the theme of the Richmond Conference of Employed Officers in 1913, and Church, Social Service and Student criticisms were presented. But the consciousness of helpless ignorance on the questions considered by the Commission on Social Morality had led the Committee to invite Dr. Richard C. Cabot to offer a course of three lectures on The Consecration of Affections. The sessions of the conference are always closed and the verbatim reports are circulated only among members, but the addresses by Dr. Cabot could not be churlishly kept by the five hundred members of the Employed Officers' Association. The National Board printed them in a small book, "The Christian Approach to Social Morality" and in Dr. Cabot's larger book, "What Men Live By," the ideas which set the workers at Richmond to thinking those April days, have now become current throughout the reading world.

Asilomar was the scene of the next conference. A Commission on the Secretary's Efficiency reported on the physical, intellectual, social, professional, spiritual and economic aspects of the question. Una Saunders, executive of the Dominion Council of Canada, gave a series of addresses on The Woman Movement, Mabel Cratty, another series on Women Working Together, and Anna V. Rice two talks on the Religious Trend of the Times. Michi Kawai spoke Sunday morning when the auditorium was dedicated. The beauty, retirement and sense of proprietorship at Asilomar made for a poise of mind suitable for reflection and decision. These recommendations were adopted.

> In the light of what we have heard these last two days, we who are present realize afresh the claims of the Kingdom of God. We recognize that the mere passive acceptance of these claims is not adequate, but that day by day and year by year we must face the issues involved in making the Kingdom of God a reality, and having faced these, determine our course and act.
>
> Our committee would therefore urge: That we here assembled dedicate again our lives to the bringing in of the Kingdom of God, cost what it may, and that we endeavor, through the power and might that come from Bible study, and the knowledge that comes from reading and discussion, and the daily practice of meeting the moral challenge which is never absent from responsibility, to make ourselves fit leaders of women.

That other employed officers aside from secretaries are recognized as practising their professions within the Young Women's Christian Association is evidenced by the system of training of the National Board. As soon as the preparatory Training Centers had been well set up and the second class graduated from the National Training School, a study was made of Association education for physical directors and a six weeks' summer course planned for 1911 in connection with Teachers' College, Columbia University, which put a physical director of both Association and academic experience, Abby Shaw Mayhew, in their

Mabel Cratty,
General Secretary of the National Board

regular summer faculty. To this summer school was transferred from the Field Committees the preparatory work for student secretaries. A Training Center course for secretaries in city colored branches was also introduced, since most of the candidates were teachers and could not make use of the Training Centers conducted during the school year. The plans for 1912 were much the same.

But in 1913 the National Training School had moved into its magnificent new building where more serious academic work could be undertaken in the summer school. An independent faculty was made up of professors and instructors from recognized schools of physical education, who gave both theoretical and practical courses of study. An even larger group of salaried officers were the superintendents and matrons of Association residences and lunchroom and cafeteria directors, hence a short advanced course of four weeks in Household Economics was added to the other three departments in 1914. The season of 1915 followed the same divisions.

In the meantime women who had been on local supervisory staffs from one to twenty-two years, and scores of women tested through other experience, had been enriching their lives through the full academic year of the regular graduate National Training School course. The United States has never usurped international rights, but owing to the commonly accepted business and professional status of women in America and the recognition of salaried employment in the Young Women's Christian Association as a profession ranking with teaching and the newer forms of social service, technical training was more advanced here than in any other country, not even excepting England, where the location of the World's Headquarters would make an international school most convenient.

Because of its graduate character in relation to the preparatory Training Centers the National Training School does not emphasize practical work. Its academic course and the observation of and general participation in Association activities are sufficient to fill a student's time in New York and the vicinity.

The five semesters in Gramercy Park before it was announced that the Training School was to be given a new home, were long enough to teach very forcibly the requirements for a model building. The school must be residential, there must be reception rooms, and offices, library, large and small lecture rooms, seminar room, there must be single rooms for students, accommodation for faculty and administration staff, a common living room, a dining room large enough for the occupants of all bedrooms and for additional guests, and amid all other considerations in construction and equipment, the health and safety of the family must be kept in mind. All this and more, too, was granted in the eleven story headquarters building, in its new quarters at 135 East 52nd Street, New York City, in which the fifth academic year opened September, 1912.

The endowment which every college has learned to expect is yet to be provided. Two small bequests to

Class of 1915, National Training School

The American Committee transferred to the National Board were at once appropriated toward the support of this professional school, and one handsome gift was made to the library by Mr. and Mrs. L. Wilbur Messer of Chicago.

CHAPTER XXVII

A PROPHET AMONG WOMEN

AN institution is distressed by change; it fears disturbance and disintegration. A movement craves change; in this way it will attain to progress and achievement. Miss Dodge had repeatedly said that she would continue as President of the National Board not longer than a ten years' term, but her co-workers refused to listen. Her power of close observation was exceeded only by her power of a long look ahead. Everybody had confidence that the Young Women's Christian Associations of the United States would be moving, and moving in the right direction, so long as she was president. But a higher form of confidence yet was to be revealed by the American Association members; it was faith to continue building on the foundation she had laid.

December of 1914 at headquarters was full of plans for the coming Convention in Los Angeles in 1915, and with preparations for the Panama-Pacific Exposition. Miss Dodge had attended all the Conventions—New York, 1906, St. Paul, 1909, Indianapolis, 1911, Richmond, 1913, and was planning for the California journey, making Association visits en route. She presided at the December board meeting; she met

262 Madison Avenue.
S.W. Corner 39th St.

December 16, 1914

My dear Miss Thoburn:

It is a pleasure to think that we are co-workers and I feel very close to my friends these days. It is near the close of the year, the eighth of our new Association movement. As we are entering into a new year, and the one when we are to have a Convention, I want to write to all of you who are partners with me in our work. We are national and have to consider those who work in the North, South, East and West; the girls in industry, the city girl, the country, the student, and the girls in other countries as well as the strangers within our gates. Will you not write me your view of our organization, and how we can improve it? I know so well the red tapism which we feel hampers us in our work, and how easy it would seem to us to work alone and to have things just as we wish. I have felt this so often, and yet could we grow all over the country as we have grown without organization or red tapism? I would like you to send me constructive criticism - any plan you would prefer to the one we have appointed. I would like the criticism in writing. We may not be able to adopt all the ideas but I would like as your leader to have your views and then I will want to confer with certain personally. As I say, we are co-laborers and you and I should freely talk things over. I am sorry I have other interests so cannot give the National Board all my time. I want 1915 to be a good year of growth and development. With freedom guarded by organization and God's great help, we should do much during the coming year. I hope that a very happy New Year will come to you all and that the spirit of peace and good will may be in our midst as it has been so wonderfully in the past. Please feel me your friend and companion in all the work.

Faithfully yours,

Grace H. Dodge

President.

LETTER SENT BY MISS DODGE TO ALL THE NATIONAL BOARD STAFF

with the staff the next day; she went to Boston for the meeting of the Board of Trustees of Constantinople College, of which she was president. On the 22nd of December she led the Christmas service in the assembly room at Headquarters, reading with her positive glad emphasis, "Peace I leave with you, my peace I give unto you; let not your heart be troubled, neither let it be afraid. He that believeth shall not make haste. Rest and be still." "A wonderful Christmas to you, my friends," was her farewell word. Christmas fell on Friday that year and the next afternoon there was at her home one of the beautiful Christmas parties of Oriental students whom she loved to entertain. But she was unable to come downstairs to greet her guests.

The next morning, Sunday, December 27, she was not, for God took her.

When her hand was lifted, knowledge of the multifold activities of her busy years began to flood in. Such knowledge she had always suppressed and many of the daily papers searched their files almost in vain for printed announcement of her deeds or her benefactions. But friends in every station in life contributed to make up the record which places her as a formative power second to no woman of this period except Florence Nightingale. She was a constructive pioneer in education for practical life. She initiated cooperation in social work; she led in the protection of women, and she introduced a Christian statesmanship that works through college women in all lands for a society in which educated women must take a place unconceived by any previous generation. "Probably no other woman in history has done so much for the direct uplift of young girls—always reaching out for the young girl." Thus spoke a wise Christian woman of four score years when she heard of her death.

The National Board had lost only one other member by death, Mrs. Malcolm D. Whitman, who died in December, 1909. As Janet McCook she was made a charter member of the Board when she was only twenty-four, but she embodied the four-fold ideal as few had ever done, through her beauty and vitality, her mental vigor, her personal charm, and the spiritual vision illuminated by obedience. Her Bible classes of her own friends in her own drawing-room, of the Barnard College Christian Association in her own Alma Mater, of groups of younger girls in New York City, and at Silver Bay Conferences, were renowned. The fruit of these classes was shown when one new phase of Association work after another was started in New York City by people to whom the Young Women's Christian Association was totally unknown or hopelessly unappealing until she revealed its scope and possibilities.

As Mrs. Marshall O. Roberts was first directress of the Ladies' Christian Union, and after her death the title was not used, so the National Board despaired of ever finding any one to fill Miss Dodge's place. They recognized that she had given the presidency a content impossible to demand of any successor, and they divided the duties of the office she had held, creating a new office, Chairman of the Executive Committee, to which committee many business details had always been referred by the Board. In the winter of 1915 they elected two charter members of the board to these positions: Mrs. Robert E. Speer was made President of the National Board, and Mrs. John French, Chairman of the Executive Committee.

CHAPTER XXVIII

MOTTOES AND SPIRIT

IN those earliest days when Miss Robarts was seeking to make the tiny little Association known in order to increase the number of its praying members, and to unite them locally into bands under leaders whom she named their secretaries, she sent out modest leaflets from time to time, undated, although from the context the dates have been somewhat accurately assigned by her co-workers. Perhaps about 1860 there appeared the paper headed

YOUNG WOMEN'S CHRISTIAN ASSOCIATION
PRAYER UNION

Motto: "Not by might, nor by power, but by my spirit, saith the Lord of Hosts."—Zechariah iv, 6.

One sentence read, "The Young Women's Christian Association affords opportunities of work for God within the reach of all, and the Prayer Union binds the workers together, and is the source of all strength and success in the work of the Young Women's Christian Association." Nine suggested means of usefulness were cited, beginning with "Example in conduct, dress, etc., to manifest Christian consistency and separation from the world," and ending, "The encouragement of total abstinence principles."

When the Prayer Union and Institute Branches officially united in 1877, after many individuals had been personally connected with both, it was decided to adopt some uniform nomenclature. They called "members" those who joined the Prayer Union, those who had entered into a living union with Christ by faith, and taken as "The only principle of action the constraining power of His love shed abroad in the heart by the Holy Ghost." Those who could not as yet say that they desired to be absolutely and avowedly on the side of Christ were called Associates. The Prayer Union motto was retained for the "members," and for the Associates Mrs. Pennefather, in 1877, chose the general motto, "By love serve one another" (Galatians v, 13). The Total Abstinence diamond shaped badge was much admired and finally made the general badge, with the general motto upon it. This blue enamel diamond pendant bearing the words, "By love serve," has been worn in every part of the world.

When the Young Women's Christian Association *Quarterly* first appeared in Chicago in 1888, the words, "Not by might nor by power but by my spirit, saith the Lord of Hosts," were printed in the heading of the little eight page paper, and elsewhere there was a note explaining that that was the motto adopted by the Associations affiliated with the National Committee. Consequently, in 1894, when the World's Association was being formed of only four national committees, these two countries might naturally suggest the motto already dear to them as a suitable keynote for the combined movement.

The Honorable Emily Kinnaird, in speaking to a company of British and Americans that year, drew attention to the motto already adopted by both continents and expressed the hope that the Association would ever go forward in the strength and inspiration of such a motto. As is known, the first World's Conference adopted these words upon the official badge, and this text of warning and promised strength has appeared upon official papers ever since.

At the Montreal Conference of the Women's and Young Women's Christian Associations in 1897, a committee on a badge for members and Associations connected with the International Board brought in a design which bore on an enclosed triangle the words, "By love serve," which was accepted as the motto.

Even the people who do not care for badges appreciate the stable fact of which the badge is the outward symbol, and it was with great satisfaction that the members at large learned that the National Board had chosen from the tenth chapter of the Gospel according to John, these words as a part of the official seal.

"I am come that they might have life, and that they might have it more abundantly."

This became also the motto of the entire national organization.

The previous mottoes referred to the Christian woman undertaking something for her Lord and Master. They spoke of human deficiency and divine power, of human love poured out in divine service.

The new motto speaks of Christ's own thought for the girls at the beginning of life, relates Him to them and them to Him, and opens to them a future exceeding abundant, above all that they could ask or think.

In the decades ahead, as in the five decades already compassed, Jesus Christ, the same, yesterday, and forever, can be recognized as the central figure of the Young Women's Christian Association.

CHRIST IS THE END, FOR CHRIST WAS THE BEGINNING,
CHRIST THE BEGINNING FOR THE END IS CHRIST.

APPENDIX

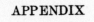

CHRONOLOGY

1844. June 6. London Young Men's Christian Association organized.

1851. December 9. Boston, Mass., Young Men's Christian Association organized.

1855. English Prayer Union formed.

English Institute Branch formed by enlarging scope of Nurses' Home.

1858. January. Students' Christian Association organized in the University of Michigan (not co-educational).

October 12. Young Men's Christian Association of the University of Virginia organized.

Young Women's Christian Improvement Association started in the Home in London.

November 24. Ladies' Christian Association organized in New York City.

1859. Agitation for Young Women's Christian Association in Boston.

1860. June 1. Boarding Home opened in Amity Place, New York City, by Ladies' Christian Association.

Meetings held in New York factories by Ladies' Christian Association.

1861. Pall Mall Institute opened in London.

1866. March 3. Boston Young Women's Christian Association organized (name first taken in America).

May. Rooms opened in Chauncey Street, Boston.

Mary Foster became secretary of the Boston Association.

Thursday evening prayer meeting in rooms of Boston Association.

Singing taught in Boston Association.

Name of Ladies' Christian Association changed to Ladies' Christian Union of New York City.

1867. April 23. Providence Women's Christian Association organized.

June. Hartford organized Women's Christian Association.

July 23. Providence Association opened combination Home.

Pittsburgh Women's Christian Association organized.

Astronomy and physiology taught in Boston Association.

1868. February 19. Beach Street property occupied by Boston Association.

Dining room of Boston boarding home conducted on restaurant plan.

Penmanship and bookkeeping taught in Boston Association.

March. Providence Association reorganized on protective lines.

June. Cincinnati Women's Christian Association organized.

November 10. Cleveland Women's Christian Association organized.

December. St. Louis Women's Christian Association organized.

1869. Botany taught in Boston Association.

1870. February 10. Young Ladies' Branch of the Ladies' Christian Union of New York City organized by Mrs. Roberts (later Young Women's Christian Association of City of New York).

Women's Christian Association of Dayton, Ohio, organized.

Women's Christian Association of Utica organized.

Women's Christian Association of Washington organized.

Women's Christian Association of Buffalo organized.

November, Women's Christian Association of Philadelphia organized.

1871. February. Women's Christian Association of Germantown, Pa., organized.

June 22. Women's Christian Association of Newark, N. J., organized.

October 9–10. National Conference of Women's Christian Association held at Hartford, Connecticut.

Women's Christian Association of Springfield, Mass., organized.

1872. February. Class in machine sewing conducted by New York City Association.

Ella Doheny commenced Sunday afternoon Bible Class in New York City Association.

Philadelphia Association opened restaurant for women.

Hartford dedicated first building erected for such purposes.

November 12. Young women's meetings for prayer began at Normal, Illinois.

1873. January 19. Young Ladies' Christian Association of Normal, Illinois, organized by Normal School students.

1874. Boston Association occupied Warrenton Street building.

Sea Rest, at Asbury Park, N. J., opened as summer home of the Philadelphia Association.

History taught in Boston Association.

Telegraphy taught in Philadelphia Association.

1875. C. V. Drinkwater became Superintendent in Boston.

October 12–15. Women's Christian Association Conference became international.

November 4. Young Ladies' Christian Association of Northwestern College (later Young Women's Christian Association) organized.

Exposition of Authors held in St. Louis.

1876. October 17. Young Women's Christian Association organized in Southern Illinois Normal University, Carbondale.

October 21. Young Women's Christian Association of Olivet College, Michigan, organized.

1877. Union of Prayer Union and Institute Branches in London.

Princeton University Young Men's Christian Association led in Intercollegiate Movement.

October 30. Young Women's Christian Association of Lenox College, Hopkinton, Iowa, organized.

Calisthenics taught in the Boston Association by one of the boarders in Warrenton Street Home.

1878. Providence Association conducted summer home on Conanicut Island.

Kensington and Crewel classes held by New York City Association.

1879. Domestic Training School, Boston.

Ladies' Cooking Classes, Boston.

1880. Public School Cooking Class in Boston Association.

Phonography, typewriting, photo negative, photo coloring and painting on china classes in New York City Association.

Young Ladies' Society of Co-workers organized in Doane College, Crete, Nebraska. (1883 changed to Young Women's Christian Association.)

1881. February 20. L. D. Wishard spoke to the Young Ladies' Christian Association at Normal.

April 23. New Constitution adopted by the Young Ladies' Christian Association of Normal.

September 11. Name of Young Ladies' Christian Association of Normal changed to Young Women's Christian Association.

October. Committee on Young Women's Christian Association work in colleges and seminaries appointed by the Sixth International Conference of Women's Christian Associations.

St. Louis Association offered a public course of cooking lessons by Juliet Corson.

Technical design and free hand enlarging taught in New York City Association.

Little Girls' Christian Association in Oakland, California.

1882. Boston Association sent class to Miss Allen's gymnasium.

Household Training School opened by St. Louis Association.

1883. Course of Emergency Lectures instituted by Boston.

Baltimore opened rooms adapted for noon lunch as prominent feature.

1884. Young Women's Christian Association of Pleasant Valley township, Johnson County, Iowa, organized.

February 7–11. First State Young Women's Christian

Association organized at Albion, Michigan convention.

February 14–17. State Young Women's Christian Association of Ohio organized.

November 15. Iowa State Young Women's Christian Association organized.

December 8. Berkeley Street Building, Boston, dedicated. It contained the first Young Women's Christian Association gymnasium in America.

United Central Council formed in Great Britain.

1885. Kalamazoo, Michigan, Young Women's Christian Association organized.

Great Fair held by New York City Association.

Travelers' Aid placards posted in London.

Delegation from State Associations attended International Conference of the Women's Christian Associations at Cincinnati.

1886. Lawrence, Kansas, Young Women's Christian Association organized.

March 30. Poughkeepsie Girls' Branch organized.

"Noon Hour Rest" conducted by Poughkeepsie Association.

July. Student Volunteer Movement for Foreign Missions originated.

August 6–12. National Association of the Young Women's Christian Associations of the United States formed at Lake Geneva, Wisconsin.

Mrs. John V. Farwell, Jr., elected president of the National Committee of Young Women's Christian Associations.

December. Nettie Dunn became general secretary of the National Committee of Young Women's Christian Associations.

1887. February. Bertha Van Vliet became secretary of the Poughkeepsie Girls' Branch.

Ypsilanti, Michigan, Young Women's Christian Association organized.

Topeka, Kansas, Young Women's Christian Association organized.

Exhibit of class work in millinery and dressmaking held in Philadelphia.

Self-Governing Club organized by Miss Dodge in the Baltimore Association.

Calisthenics taught in New York City, Philadelphia, and Poughkeepsie.

Hope Narey became gymnasium instructor in Boston—'88, physical director.

July. Mary E. Blodgett became Travelers' Aid in Boston.

October. Ida L. Schell became state secretary of Iowa.

December. Nellie Knox became state secretary of Ohio.

1888. St. Joseph, Missouri, Young Women's Christian Association organized.

Scranton, Penn., Young Women's Christian Association organized.

Brinton Hall, Philadelphia, given for headquarters to the Women's Medical College Association.

Physical education in Worcester, Scranton, Coldwater, Michigan, and Newburgh, N. Y.

Current Events class held in Worcester.

Advanced classes in cutting and fitting held by New York City Association.

Boston Association opened School of Domestic Science.

Young Women's Christian Association Quarterly published by the National Committee of Young Women's Christian Associations.

1889. Constitution of the "National" Association of Young Women's Christian Associations changed to "International" to admit Associations in the British Provinces.

First national gathering of secretaries at Bloomington.

Young Women's Christian Association Quarterly changed to the Evangel.

Branch Association opened by Baltimore.

1890. Kansas City, Missouri, Young Women's Christian Association organized.

Mary S. Dunn became general secretary and physical director in Kansas City.

Toledo, Ohio, Young Women's Christian Association organized.

Trained attendants' class opened in Brooklyn.

1891. March. The Cafeteria system introduced into the Kansas City, Missouri, Association.

Close Hall occupied by the joint Associations of the University of Iowa, Iowa City.

Minneapolis Young Women's Christian Association organized.

The International Conference reorganized into the International Board of Women's Christian Associations, in 1893 The International Board of Women's and Young Women's Christian Associations.

Mrs. C. R. Springer elected president of the International Board.

Summer Bible and Training School held at Bay View, Michigan.

1892. Preliminary meeting of World's Young Women's Christian Association in London.

Summer Conference removed from Bay View, Michigan, to Lake Geneva, Wisconsin.

Abby S. Mayhew became physical director in Minneapolis.

Busy Girls' Half Hour established by Dayton in the National Cash Register works.

1893. Northfield Summer Conference established.

Exhibits at the World's Columbian Exposition by both National bodies.

1894. April. Initial number of the "International Messenger" appeared.

Organization of World's Young Women's Christian Association.

Annie M. Reynolds became general secretary of the World's Young Women's Christian Association.

Agnes Gale Hill called to Madras, India.

Toledo Association raised support for Foreign Secretary.

Harlem Association Clubs, "Birthday Building," "Literary" and "Annex Choral," organized.

1895. World's Student Christian Federation formed.

Industrial extension begun in Milwaukee. Maude Wolff, secretary.

Mary Armstrong became general secretary at the University of Wisconsin.

Colgate Chrysanthemum Club formed in Harlem Association.

1896. Summer Cottage on Genesee Lake, Wisconsin, given to the Milwaukee Association.

1897. Boston Association offered courses for Young Women's Christian Association secretaries.

December 31, 1897, to January 2, 1898. Fillmore County, Minnesota, Convention.

1898. First County Association organized.

March. Dodge County (Minnesota) Young Women's Christian Association organized.

First World's Conference fixed World's Week of Prayer in November and adopted motto and badge.

Charlotte H. Adams became Religious Work director in Pittsburgh.

1899. International Committee of Young Women's Christian Associations became The American Committee of Young Women's Christian Associations, releasing Canada.

American department of the World's Committee created.

Dr. Anna L. Brown became Religious Work director in Boston.

1900. Neva Chappell called to Minneapolis as extension secretary.

Support of a national secretaryship assumed by one donor.

1901. Headquarters opened by International Board at the Chautauqua, N. Y. Assembly Grounds.

Milwaukee included a model housekeeping apartment in its new building.

1902. Division of Student and City Conferences at Silver Bay.

1903. The Bulletin replaced the International Messenger as official organ of the "International Board."

Headquarters opened by the International Board at the Southern Chautauqua, Mont Eagle, Tenn.

Martha Berninger appointed first secretary to China.

Theresa Morrison appointed first secretary to Japan.

1904. Secretaries' Training Institute opened in Chicago.
Monaghan Mills Association opened in Greenville, S. C.
Louisiana Purchase Exposition Travelers' Aid work instigated by International Board.

1905. May 24. The Manhattan Conference considered union of the two National bodies.
Woman's Department of the World's Student Christian Federation formed.
Exposition Travelers' Aid Committee formed for Lewis and Clark Exposition at Portland.
Swimming taught in pool in Buffalo and Montgomery.
November 2–7. The 18th Biennial Conference of the International Board voted for union, Baltimore.

1906. January 2–4. A special Convention of The American Committee Associations, Chicago, voted in favor of union.
Emma J. Batty appointed first secretary to South America.
December 5–6. First Convention of the Young Women's Christian Associations of the United States of America, New York City.
December 7. Miss Grace H. Dodge elected President of the National Board.

1907. February. Initial number of The Association Monthly appeared.
The Studio Club of New York City opened rooms.

1908. September 23. National Training School opened at No. 3 Gramercy Park.
October 17. Woodford County, Ill., Association organized.
First Federation of Industrial Clubs formed in Detroit.

1909. National organization completed at Second Biennial Convention, St. Paul.
Organization of the Employed Officers Association.
Employed Officers Association considered "Adolescence" as theme of their Minneapolis Conference.

1910. Central Club for Nurses established in New York City.
International Institute opened in New York City.

1911. Boston Metropolitan Student work undertaken.
April. Third Biennial Convention held in Indianapolis.

1912. Annual members elected by Ohio and West Virginia Field Committee.

Camp Fire Girls' movement developed.

Council of North American Student Movements formed.

National Headquarters in New York City erected.

New York City Metropolitan organization effected.

September. The National Training School opened its fifth year in its new building, 135 East 52nd Street, New York City.

1913. March. Initial number of the North American Student appeared.

April. Fourth Biennial Convention held in Richmond.

Certificate offered for Eight Week Clubs.

June. Tenth Conference of the World's Student Christian Federation met at Lake Mohonk, N. Y.

Industrial Club Councils held at Altamont and Camp Nepahwin.

Asilomar Conference Grounds opened.

Frances C. Gage and Anna Welles appointed first secretaries in Turkey.

Campaign for $3,000,000 for Young Women's Christian Association buildings in New York City.

1914. December 27. Miss Grace H. Dodge, deceased.

1915. February 3. Mrs. Robert E. Speer elected President of the National Board.

Headquarters and Club House erected by the National Board on the Panama-Pacific International Exposition ground at San Francisco.

May. Fifth Biennial Convention held in Los Angeles.

First County Summer Conference, Conference Point, Lake Geneva.

SOURCES AND GLOSSARY

Chapter I

Abbott, Edith. History of the Employment of Women in the American Cotton Mills. Journal of Political Economy, Vol. XVI, pp. 602–21; Vol. XVII, pp. 19–35.

Child, Lydia Maria. Brief History of the Condition of Women in Various Ages and Nations. C. S. Francis Co., New York. 1849.

Fairchild, James H. Oberlin, the Colony and the College. E. J. Goodrich, Oberlin. 1883.

Larcom, Lucy. A New England Girlhood. Houghton Mifflin & Co., Boston. 1889.

Nearing, Scott, and N. M. S. Nearing. Woman and Social Progress. MacMillan & Co., New York. 1912.

Penny, Virginia. The Employment of Women. (No publisher.) Boston. 1863.

Taylor, James Monroe. Before Vassar Opened. Houghton Mifflin & Co., Boston. 1914.

Chapter II

Braithwaite, Robert. Life and Letters of Rev. William Pennefather. Robert Carter & Co., New York. 1878.

Williams, J. E. Hodder. The Life of Sir George Williams. A. C. Armstrong Co., New York. 1906.

Martin, Sir Theodore. The Life of H. R. H. the Prince Consort. Smith, Elder & Co., London. 1878.

Moor, Lucy M. Girls of Yesterday and To-day. S. W. Partridge & Co., London. 1911.

Stock, Eugene. History of the Church Missionary Society, London. 1899.

Facsimile of title page of first report

The First Report of the
Young Men's
Christian Association
for the
Improvement of the Spiritual Condition
of Young Men Engaged in the
Drapery and other Trades
by the
Introduction of Religious Services
into
Houses of Business
Instituted in London
June 6, 1844.

Association Men. Vol. XXXIII, Number 10 (July, 1908), pp. 457–459.

Go Forward (1905). Historical papers by Mrs. M. M. Gordon, Lucy M. Moor, Jessie Coombs, etc.

Sisters. Illustrated pamphlet of the British Jubilee, 1905.

Prayer Union circular letters (No. 2 quoted above).

No. 2. "To the Members of the Young Women's Christian Association."

No. 3. "Young Women's Christian Association Prayer Union."

No. 4. "Sketch of the Young Women's Christian Association" (signed) E. R.

"Young Women's Christian Association" (signed) Miss L. M. Moor.

"Letter to Y. W. C. A. Provincial Workers." November 12, 1884 (signed) Lucy M. Moor.

F. R. Havergal.

Other hymn writers connected with the British Associations were Emily Steele Elliott, who wrote, "Thou Didst Leave Thy Throne and Thy Kingly Crown"; Katherine Hankey, author of "Tell Me the Old, Old Story" and "I Love to Tell the Story"; and Mrs. Horatius Bonar, who wrote "Fade, Fade, Each Earthly Joy."

CHAPTER III

Cook, Sir Edward. The Life of Florence Nightingale. Macmillan & Co., London. 1913.

Fraser, Donald. Mary Jane Kinnaird. James Nisbet & Co., London. 1890.

Hill, Georgiana. English Life from Mediæval to Modern Times. R. R. Bensley & Son, London. 1896.

Hodder, Edwin. The Life and Work of the Seventh Earl of Shaftesbury. Cassell & Co., London. 1886.

Nightingale, Florence. Notes on Nursing. D. Appleton & Co., New York. 1860.

January, 1856—Circular (signed) A. Kinnaird (2).

June, 1856—Circular (signed) A. Kinnaird.

Undated—A. Kinnaird; name heads page as treasurer.

1856—Announcement of Home.

1858 (?) Announcement of Young Women's Christian Improvement Association.

May, 1860—Circular letter to members of Y. W. C. I. A. (signed) M. J. Kinnaird.

July, 1861—Announcement and circular of United Association for the Christian and Domestic Improvement of Young Women. President, the Earl of Shaftesbury.

1861—A Brief Sketch of the origin, aim and mode of conducting the Young Women's Christian Association and West London Home for Young Women engaged in houses of business.

1871—Pamphlet, "The Christian Association for Young Women."

Later than 1877—Pamphlet, "Y. W. C. A. and Institute Union."

London Times—August 15, 1911, Biographical article on Florence Nightingale.

Go Forward—July, 1901, p. 164.

Report of the North London Home, 51 Upper Charlotte St., for 1856, including Rules and Treasurer's statements.

Same for 1857.

First Report of United Association for Christian and Domestic Improvement of Young Women, 1862.

London Young Women's Institute Union and Christian Association. Report for year 1877.

Speech of the Earl of Shaftesbury (from 1881 report).
Annual reports of later dates containing historical references.

Chapter IV

Girls of Yesterday and To-day.
Money—Townsend. The Story of the Girls' Friendly Society. Wells, Gardner, Darton & Co., London. 1913.
"Y. W. C. A. Sketches." Illustrated pamphlet prepared for Queen Victoria's Diamond Jubilee, 1897.
Pamphlet—Ten Years' Record of the World's Y. W. C. A. , 1901. Annie M. Reynolds.

Chapter V

Thompson, Joseph P. The Royalty of Faith—A meditation on the life of Mrs. Marshall O. Roberts. No Publisher. 1875.
Reports of the Ladies' Christian Union. 1859–1915.
New York Christian Advocate—Nos. 46 to 141, cited September 9, 1858.
International Conference reports—1871 *et seq.*
Report of Ninth International Conference, 1887—page 109.
This antedates the first otherwise known record. The London Y. W. C. A. report for 1885 mentions regular visits begun April, 1885, in laundries in the west of London.
The London report for 1888, however, speaks of a special Institute in South Belgravia, when the Y. W. C. A. began separate work among factory hands in 1872.

Chapter VI

Morse, Richard C. History of the North American Young Men's Christian Associations. Association Press, New York. 1913.
Putnam, James Jackson. Memoirs of Dr. James Jackson. Houghton & Mifflin, Boston. 1905. The Congregational Building was formerly the residence of Judge Jackson.
The Watchman and Reflector. October 9, 1861.
The Watchman and Reflector. January 15, 1852.
Reports of International Conferences. 1871–1905.
The International Messenger. 1894–1902.

Boston reports from 1867–1915. Several of these, e.g. 25th and 40th, contain historical material.
Announcements, circulars, prospectuses, etc.
Letter from Wm. H. Cobb. Congregational Library. Historical statement, C. V. Drinkwater.

Chapter VII

Journal of the International W. C. A. Conference, 1871–1891.
History pamphlet by Mrs. M. S. Lamson.
Annual reports. Hartford, St. Louis, Cincinnati, New York City, etc., etc.
Historical sketches in pamphlet or newspaper form.
Occasional copies of Faith and Works.

Chapter VIII

Reports of the International Committee of Y. W. C. A.'s, 1886–1891.
Reports of State Associations, 1884 *et seq.*
The Y. W. C. A. Quarterly, 1888–1889. The Evangel, 1889–1891.
Reports, Circulars, etc.
Historical material of local Associations.
Model constitutions, 1, 2, 3 editions.
Our Young Women, 1894, Toledo, Ohio, page 8.

Chapter IX

Bevier and Usher. The Home Economics Movement. Whitcomb and Barrows, Boston. 1906.
Journals of the International Conferences, 1891–1905.
Annual Reports of The American Committee, 1891–1906.
The International Messenger, 1894–1902.
The Bulletin, 1903–1905.
The Evangel, 1891–1906.
State Convention Reports, 1891–1906.
Reports of local Associations and various printed matter.
Articles on Household Arts in Education, Physical Education, etc., in the Encyclopedia of Education.
Campbell, Helen. "Certain Forms of Women's Work for Women." The Century Magazine, June, 1889.

Chapters X and XI

History of the North American Young Men's Christian Associations.

Williams, Wolcott B. A History of Olivet College. No publisher. Olivet, Mich. 1901.

Leonard, Delavan L. The History of Carleton College. Fleming H. Revell, Chicago. 1904.

Typewritten Minutes of the Y. W. C. A. of Normal, Ill., from 1872 to 1884. Also historical papers of various dates.

Reports of The American Committee, 1886–1906.

Journal of the International W. C. A. Conference, 1881–1891.

Year Books of the International Committee Y. M. C. A.

Y. W. C. A. State Committee Reports, 1884–1906.

The College Bulletin of the International Committee, Y. M. C. A.

The Y. W. C. A. Quarterly, 1888–1889, The Evangel, 1889–1906.

World's Conference Reports, 1898 to 1906.

Report of Ecumenical Missionary Conference. New York, 1900. Volume I, page 47.

Chapter XII

The Evangel, June, 1898.

State Y. W. C. A. Reports, especially Iowa.

Journal of the International Conferences of the W. C. A.

Annual Reports, International Committee Y. W. C. A's., 1886–1891.

Iowa State Notes, Y. M. C. A., 1887–1889.

Historical Sketch of Johnson County Association.

Report of State Committee Y. M. C. A. of Iowa, 1886.

Typewritten volumes of Memorabilia, by Robert Weidensall.

Chapter XIII

Journals of International Conferences of the W. C. A., 1871–1891.

Chapter XIV

Annual Reports, 1886–1906.

Y. W. C. A. Quarterly, 1888–1889. The Evangel, 1889–1906.

Typewritten history of the National Organization in India. Hon. E. Kinnaird and A. G. Hill.

Girls of Yesterday and To-day.
History of the North American Y. M. C. A.
Resolutions from State Associations to W. C. A. Conference.
Proposition carried by the Committee to Cincinnati, 1885.
Report of same committee to the State Committees.
Circular calling the Lake Geneva Convention.
Autograph list of delegates at Lake Geneva, 1886.
Pencil list of Associations in 1886.
Circulars of the National Committee, International and American Committees.
Publication list of The International Committee, 1894.
Pamphlets on Secretarial Training, Basis, Summer Conferences, etc.
World's Committee Circulars.
Historical pamphlets of the University of Michigan.
Alumni Bulletins of the University of Virginia, Jan., 1909, October, 1910.
Students fall campaign Handbooks.
Letters from original Associations, etc., etc.
Typewritten volumes of memorabilia of Robert Weidensall.
State Committee constitutions, circulars, etc.
The Lawrentian, May, 1884. Student publication, Lawrence University.
Circular and constitution sent out by Mrs. Miller and Mr. Wishard.
Student Volunteer Movement leaflets.

Chapter XV

Journal of the International Board Conferences, 1891–1905.
The International Messenger, 1894–1902.
The Bulletin, 1903–1906.
Brief Handbook. The International Board, 1891.
The Philosophy of W. C. A. and Y. W. C. A.
A Message from the fourteenth Biennial Conference.
Covenant between the International Board and Local Associations.
Statistical card. Convention programs.
and other pamphlets.

Papers read at Conferences.
Exposition Travelers' Aid Committee circulars and reports.
Travelers' Directory, 1898.
State Board circulars and programs.

Chapter XVI

The Bulletin, 1905–1906.
The Evangel, 1905–1906.
The Association Monthly, February and March, 1915.
Journal of International Board Conference, November, 1905.
Report of Special Convention of The American Committee, January, 1906.
Report of first Convention of the Y. W. C. A.'s of the U. S. of America.
Report of Manhattan Conferences and circular letter from first committee.
Circular letters from Miss Dodge.
Joint Committee Leaflets, 1 to 8 with supplements.
Joint Committee Exhibits.
Agreement and Application Form for Charter Membership.
Replies to questionnaires.
Papers bearing upon terms of union.
Material relating to Inter Church Conferences on Federation, definition of "Evangelical," etc.

Chapters XVII to XXVIII Inclusive

The Association Monthly, 1907–1915.
The North American Student, 1913–1915.
Reports, recommendations and year-books, 1908–1915.
Reports of National Conventions, 1906–1915.
Reports of World's Conferences, 1898–1914.
Joint Committee leaflets.

OTHER SOURCES WILL BE CITED IN PLACE

"As a corporate body," Association Monthly, Feb., 1907, p. 45.
"As I look," Association Monthly, Feb., 1907, p. 42.
"That the National Board shall concentrate," Final Report of the Joint Committee, Leaflet No. 8, p. 6.
"The symmetrical development," Rep. and Rec. of the National Board to the second Biennial Convention, p. 52.

"That the National Board shall adopt," First Convention Report, p. 15.

Table of receipts. Annual treasurer's reports of The American Committee.

Convention subscriptions, Kansas and Penn. State convention reports.

"The strongest are needed," Introduction to "The Claims and Opportunities of the Christian Ministry." Y. M. C. A. Press, N. Y. 1911.

"Intensive as well as extensive," Mabel Cratty, Association Monthly, Jan., 1908, p. 568.

"The ultimate purpose," Second Convention Report, p. 107.

Evangelical Church basis. History of the North American Young Men's Christian Association, pp. 91, *et seq.*, and Leaflet No. 4.

Federal Council, Joint Committee Leaflet No. 5.

"Der Reichsbote," May 23, 1910.

"It may be an audience," page 43, Fourth World's Conference Report.

"At least 5000," quoted in Association Monthly, June, 1911, p. 200.

See article by Jessie Woodrow Wilson, "What Girls can do for Girls in Good Housekeeping," April, 1913.

"Times of Retreat," from Manual of Prayers prepared for Mohonk Conference.

See report of Mohonk Conference, Association Monthly, July, 1913.

See "Students and the World Wide Expansion." Report of Student Volunteer Convention of 1913.

Garden City Report under title, "Social Needs and the Colleges."

See pamphlet given each guest at the "Harriet Judson."

"Let us resolve," Mrs. Warren Buxton, Joint Committee, Exhibit XIV.

"Not the cities alone," see Wage Earning Women. (The Macmillan Company, 1910.) Report of Dr. Annie M. MacLean, director of sociological investigation undertaken by the National Board in 1907.

Woodford County, see minutes of sectional conference in Report of Secretaries Association to be had only of members of the Association.

Camp Fire Girls, Association Monthly, March, 1912, p. 43.
"European and American," first World's Conference Report, p. 114.
Mrs. Wishard, The Evangel, December, 1890, p. 7.
The Evangel, January, 1891, p. 9, also January, 1893, p. 7.
"We were in all," Evangel, September, 1891.
"A Scotch mind," Ten Years Record, p. 15.
Dr. Johnston Ross in The Universality of Jesus Christ. The Evangel, September, 1906, p. 25.
J. H. Tarleton—George Williams, p. 133.
Grace H. Dodge, article in The World To-day, October, 1910. Association Monthly and Supplement, January, 1915, March, 1915.
Janet McCook Whitman—see Association Monthly, January, 1910, p. 1.
English Mottoes—Girls of Yesterday and To-day, pp. 70–73.
Hon. E. Kinnaird. The Evangel, July, 1894, p. 13.

ASSOCIATIONS COMPRISING THE YOUNG WOMEN'S CHRISTIAN ASSOCIATIONS OF THE UNITED STATES OF AMERICA, JANUARY 1, 1916

Stars indicate charter membership—December 5, 1906.

* Previous affiliation with The American Committee.

**Previous affiliation with the International Board.

(Charter Associations coming in between 1906 and 1909 not indicated.)

CITY ASSOCIATIONS

Alabama
- Alabama City
- Birmingham*
- Mobile*
- Montgomery*

Arizona
- Bisbee
- Phoenix

Arkansas
- Fort Smith
- Little Rock

California
- Fresno*
- Long Beach*
- Los Angeles*
- Oakland**
- Pasadena
- Redlands
- Riverside*
- Sacramento*
- San Bernardino
- San Diego
- San Francisco**
- San José

Colorado
- Colorado Springs**
- Denver**
- Denver, Rest and Recreation Rooms
- Denver, Scandinavian

Connecticut
- Bridgeport*
- Meriden
- New Britain
- New Haven**
- New London

Delaware
- Wilmington

District of Columbia
- Washington, Colored
- Washington** (W. C. A.)
- Washington*

Florida
- Jacksonville
- Tampa

Georgia
- Athens*

Atlanta*
Augusta
Savannah*

HAWAII
Honolulu*

IDAHO
Boise

ILLINOIS
Aurora*
Bloomington
Chicago* (Assn. House)
Danville
Decatur*
East St. Louis
Elgin*
Peoria*
Quincy*
Rockford*
Springfield

INDIANA
Elkhart
Evansville
Fort Wayne*
Indianapolis*
Marion
South Bend*
Terre Haute*

IOWA
Boone
Burlington*
Cedar Rapids*
Clinton
Council Bluffs
Des Moines*
Dubuque*
Fort Dodge
Keokuk*
Marshalltown
Mason City
Muscatine*
Ottumwa*
Sioux City*
Waterloo

KANSAS
Kansas City* (Center)
Leavenworth
Topeka*
Wichita*

KENTUCKY
Louisville

LOUISIANA
New Orleans

MAINE
Bangor
Bar Harbor*
Lewiston**
Portland*

MARYLAND
Baltimore**

MASSACHUSETTS
Boston
Haverhill
Holyoke*
Lawrence*
Lowell*
New Bedford
Springfield**
Worcester**

MICHIGAN
Ann Arbor*
Battle Creek*
Bay City*
Detroit*
Flint
Grand Rapids*
Jackson*
Kalamazoo*
Lansing*
Muskegon
Owosso
Saginaw*

St. Joseph
Traverse City

MINNESOTA
Duluth*
Minneapolis*
St. Paul
Winona

MISSISSIPPI
Laurel

MISSOURI
Joplin**
Kansas City*
St. Joseph*
St. Louis** (W. C. A.)
St. Louis
Springfield

MONTANA
Billings
Great Falls
Missoula

NEBRASKA
Lincoln*
Omaha*

NEW HAMPSHIRE
Nashua*

NEW JERSEY
Camden
Jersey City*
Newark**
Newton*
Passaic*
Paterson*
Phillipsburg
Plainfield
The Oranges
Trenton*

NEW MEXICO
Albuquerque

NEW YORK
Albany
Batavia
Binghamton*
Brooklyn**
Buffalo*
Cohoes*
Elmira
Gloversville*
Jamestown*
Lockport
Newburgh*
New York City
Central Branch**
Harlem Branch*
Bronx Branch
Colored Women's Branch
International Institute
French Branch**
Recreation Center
West Side Branch**
Poughkeepsie*
Rochester*
Schenectady*
Syracuse**
The Tonawandas
Utica**
Yonkers*

NORTH CAROLINA
Asheville
Charlotte*
Greensboro*
Wilmington
Winston-Salem

NORTH DAKOTA
Fargo
Grand Forks*

OHIO
Akron*
Canton
Cincinnati**
Cleveland**
Columbus**

Dayton**
East Liverpool
Elyria
Hamilton**
Lancaster
Newark
Portsmouth
Springfield**
Steubenville
Toledo*
Youngstown*

OKLAHOMA
Oklahoma City
Tulsa

OREGON
Portland*
Salem

PENNSYLVANIA
Allentown**
Altoona*
Chester
Coatesville
Easton
Erie**
Germantown
Harrisburg*
Hazleton
Hershey
Johnstown
Lancaster*
McKeesport
Meadville
New Castle
Norristown
Philadelphia**
Pittsburg*
Pittsburg, East Liberty**
Pottstown
Reading*
Scranton*
Sunbury
Warren
Washington
Wilkes-Barre*
Williamsport*
Wilmerding
York*

RHODE ISLAND
Pawtucket & Central Falls
Providence**

SOUTH CAROLINA
Charleston*

TENNESSEE
Chattanooga*
Knoxville**
Nashville*

TEXAS
Austin
Beaumont
Dallas
El Paso
Fort Worth
Galveston
Houston
San Antonio

UTAH
Salt Lake City

VIRGINIA
Lynchburg
Norfolk**
Richmond**
Roanoke

WASHINGTON
Bellingham
Everett
North Yakima
Seattle*
Spokane*
Tacoma*

WEST VIRGINIA
Charleston
Wheeling*

WISCONSIN
- La Crosse*
- Madison
- Milwaukee*
- Racine*

COUNTY ASSOCIATIONS AND HEADQUARTERS

ILLINOIS
- Lake County
  - Highland Park
  - Lake Forest
- Woodford County
  - Minonk

IOWA
- Cherokee County
  - Cherokee
- Page County
  - Clarinda
  - Shenandoah

KANSAS
- Montgomery County
  - Independence

MINNESOTA
- Goodhue County
  - Red Wing
- Mower County
  - Austin

NEBRASKA
- Hall County
  - Grand Island

NEW JERSEY
- Lakewood and Ocean County
  - Lakewood

NEW YORK
- Chautauqua County
  - Fredonia
- Greene County
  - Tannersville

OHIO
- Greene County
  - Xenia

TEXAS
- Coryell County
  - Gatesville

WISCONSIN
- Dodge County
  - Beaver Dam

STUDENT ASSOCIATIONS

ALABAMA
- Agricultural and Mechanical College .... Normal
- Alabama Central Female College .... Tuscaloosa
- Alabama Girls' Technical Institute .... Montevallo*
- Alabama Normal College for Girls .... Livingston*
- Alabama Synodical College for Women .... Talladega
- Athens College .... Athens*
- Downing Industrial School .... Brewton
- Eighth District Agricultural School .... Athens
- First District Agricultural College .... Jackson*
- Judson College .... Marion
- Lomax-Hannon High and Industrial School ... Greenville
- Loulie Compton Seminary .... Birmingham*

Marion Seminary .... Marion*
Miles Memorial College .... Birmingham
Ninth District Agricultural School .... Blountsville
Seventh District Agricultural School .... Albertville
State Normal School .... Florence
State Normal School .... Jacksonville*
State Normal School .... Montgomery
State Normal College .... Troy
Talladega College .... Talladega
Tuskegee Normal and Industrial Inst. .... Tuskegee
University of Alabama .... Tuscaloosa*
Women's College of Alabama .... Montgomery

ARKANSAS

Arkansas Baptist College .... Little Rock
Arkansas Conference College .... Siloam Springs
Central College .... Conway
Crescent College and Conservatory for Women..........
.... Eureka Springs
Galloway College .... Searcy
Henderson Brown College .... Arkadelphia*
Philander Smith College .... Little Rock
Second District Agricultural School .... Russellville
State Agricultural College .... Monticello
State Normal School .... Conway
University of Arkansas .... Fayetteville*

CALIFORNIA

College of Pacific .... San José
College of Physicians and Surgeons .... Los Angeles
Leland Stanford Jr. University .... Stanford University*
Mills College .... Mills College*
Occidental College .... Eagle Rock*
Pomona College .... Claremont
Sherman Institute .... Riverside
State Normal School .... Chico*
State Normal School .... Los Angeles*
State Normal School .... San Diego
State Normal School .... San José
University of California .... Berkeley*
University of Redlands .... Redlands
University of So. Cal. .... Los Angeles*
Whittier College .... Whittier*

COLORADO

Boulder Preparatory School ....Boulder
Colorado College ....Colorado Springs*
Colorado Woman's College ....Montclair
State Agricultural College ....Fort Collins*
State Teachers' College ....Greeley*
State High School ....Greeley
University of Colorado ....Boulder*
University of Denver ....University Park*

DELAWARE

Woman's College ....Newark

DISTRICT OF COLUMBIA

Gallaudet College ....Washington
Howard University ....Washington

FLORIDA

Baptist Academy ....Jacksonville
Florida Agricultural and Mechanical College..Tallahassee
Florida State College for Women ....Tallahassee*
John B. Stetson University ....Deland*
Rollins College ....Winter Park*

GEORGIA

Agnes Scott College ....Decatur*
Andrew College ....Cuthbert*
Atlanta University ....Atlanta
Brenau College ....Gainesville*
Cox College ....College Park*
Georgia Normal and Industrial College ....Milledgeville*
Haines Institute ....Augusta
La Grange College ....La Grange*
Lucy Cobb Institute ....Athens*
Martha Berry School ....Mt. Berry
Paine College ....Augusta
Piedmont College ....Demorest
Second District Agricultural School ....Tifton
Shorter College ....Rome*
South Georgia College ....McRae
South Georgia State Normal ....Valdosta
Spelman Seminary ....Atlanta
State Normal School ....Athens*
Vashti Industrial School ....Thomasville
Wesleyan College ....Macon*

IDAHO

Academy of Idaho .... Pocatello
College of Idaho .... Caldwell
Idaho Industrial Institute .... Weiser
State Normal School .... Albion
University of Idaho .... Moscow*

ILLINOIS

Bradley Polytechnic Institute .... Peoria*
Carthage College .... Carthage*
Eastern Illinois State Normal School .... Charleston
Eureka College .... Eureka*
Ferry Hall .... Lake Forest*
Frances Shimer School for Girls .... Mt. Carroll
Geneseo Collegiate Institute .... Geneseo
Grand Prairie Seminary .... Onarga*
Hedding College .... Abingdon*
Illinois College .... Jacksonville*
Illinois Women's College .... Jacksonville*
Illinois Wesleyan University .... Bloomington*
James Milliken University .... Decatur*
Jennings Seminary .... Aurora*
Knox College .... Galesburg*
Lake Forest College .... Lake Forest*
Lincoln College .... Lincoln*
McKendree College .... Lebanon*
Medical Women Students' Christian League ..... Chicago
Monmouth College .... Monmouth*
Northwestern College .... Naperville*
Northwestern University .... Evanston*
Shurtleff College .... Upper Alton*
Southern Collegiate Institute .... Albion*
Southern Illinois State Normal University .. Carbondale*
State Normal School .... De Kalb
State Normal University .... Normal*
University of Chicago .... Chicago*
School for Nurses of the Presbyterian Hospital .. Chicago
University of Illinois .... Champaign*
Western Illinois State Normal School .... Macomb*
Wheaton College .... Wheaton*
William and Vashti College .... Aledo

Women Students' Christian League of the Physical Culture School and College of Physcultopathy ..Chicago

INDIANA

Butler College ....Irvington*
Central Normal College ....Danville*
De Pauw University ....Greencastle*
Earlham College ....Richmond*
Franklin College ....Franklin*
Hanover College ....Hanover*
Indiana Central University ....Indianapolis
Indiana University ....Bloomington*
Moores Hill College ....Moores Hill*
Oakland College ....Oakland City*
Purdue University ....West Lafayette
Spiceland Academy ....Spiceland
State Normal School ....Terre Haute*
Teachers' College ....Indianapolis
Union Christian College ....Merom*
Valparaiso University ....Valparaiso*
Winona College ....Winona Lake

IOWA

Amity High School ....College Springs*
Buena Vista College ....Storm Lake*
Central College ....Pella*
Coe College ....Cedar Rapids*
Cornell College ....Mt. Vernon*
Des Moines College ....Des Moines*
Drake University ....Des Moines*
Ellsworth College ....Iowa Falls*
Epworth Seminary ....Epworth*
Grinnell College ....Grinnell*
High School ....Grinnell
High School ....Indianola*
High School ....Iowa City
High School ....Knoxville
High School ....Nevada
High School ....Toledo*
Highland Park College ....Des Moines
Iowa State College ....Ames*
Iowa State Teachers' College ....Cedar Falls*

Iowa Wesleyan University .... Mt. Pleasant*
Leander Clark College .... Toledo*
Lenox College .... Hopkinton*
Morningside College .... Sioux City*
Parsons College .... Fairfield*
Penn College .... Oskaloosa*
Simpson College .... Indianola*
State University of Iowa .... Iowa City*
Tabor College .... Tabor*
Upper Iowa University .... Fayette*
Western Union College .... Le Mars*

KANSAS

Atchison County High School .... Effingham
Baker University .... Baldwin*
Bethany College .... Lindsborg*
Chase County High School .... Cottonwood Falls
Cherokee County High School .... Columbus*
Clay County High School .... Clay Centre*
College of Emporia .... Emporia*
Cooper College .... Sterling*
Decatur County High School .... Oberlin
Dickinson County High School .... Chapman*
Enterprise Normal Academy .... Enterprise
Fairmount College .... Wichita*
Friends University .... Wichita*
Haskell Institute .... Lawrence*
High School .... Arkansas City
High School .... Atchison
High School .... Cheney
High School .... El Dorado
High School .... Lawrence
High School .... Lyons
High School .... Minneapolis
High School .... Newton
High School .... Salina
High School .... Stafford
Highland University .... Highland*
Kansas City University .... Kansas City*
Kansas State Agricultural College .... Manhattan*
Kansas State University .... Lawrence*
Kansas Wesleyan University .... Salina*

Kingman County High School .... Kingman
La Bette County High School .... Altamont*
McPherson College .... McPherson*
Montgomery County High School .... Independence*
Norton County High School .... Norton*
Ottawa University .... Ottawa*
Pratt County High School .... Pratt
Reno County High School .... Nickerson*
Southwestern College .... Winfield*
State Manual Training Normal School .... Pittsburg
State Normal School .... Emporia*
Sumner County High School .... Wellington*
Topeka Educational and Industrial Institute ..... Topeka
Washburn Academy .... Topeka
Washburn College .... Topeka*
Western University .... Kansas City

KENTUCKY

Berea College .... Berea*
Georgetown College .... Georgetown
Hamilton College .... Lexington
Kentucky College for Women .... Danville*
Kentucky Female Orphan School .... Midway*
Kentucky State University .... Lexington*
Lincoln Institute .... Simpsonville
Logan College .... Russellville
Millersburg Female College .... Millersburg
Science Hill School .... Shelbyville
State Normal School .... Richmond
State University .... Louisville
Sue Bennett Memorial School .... London*
Transylvania University .... Lexington*

LOUISIANA

H. Sophie Newcomb Memorial College ..... New Orleans*
Louisiana Industrial Institute .... Ruston
Louisiana State University .... Baton Rouge
Mansfield Female College .... Mansfield
Silliman Institute .... Clinton
State Normal School .... Natchitoches

MAINE

Bates College .... Lewiston*
Coburn Classical Institute .... Waterville*

Colby College .... Waterville*
East Maine Conference Seminary .... Bucksport
Eastern State Normal School .... Castine
Gould's Academy .... Bethel
Hebron Academy .... Hebron*
Higgins Classical Institute .... Charleston
Maine Central Institute .... Pittsfield
Maine Wesleyan Seminary .... Kent's Hill*
Oak Grove Seminary .... Vassalboro
Parsonfield Seminary .... Kezar Falls
Ricker Classical Institute .... Houlton*
University of Maine .... Orono

MARYLAND

Girls' Latin School .... Baltimore*
Maryland College .... Lutherville*
Goucher College .... Baltimore*
Hood College .... Frederick*
National Park Seminary .... Forest Glen
Western Maryland College .... Westminster*

MASSACHUSETTS

Boston University, College of Liberal Arts ...... Boston*
Cushing Academy .... Ashburnham*
Emerson College of Oratory .... Boston*
Mt. Holyoke College .... South Hadley*
Mount Ida School for Girls .... Newton
Newton Hospital Training School ... Newton Lower Falls
Northfield Seminary .... East Northfield*
Simmons College .... Boston
Wellesley College .... Wellesley
Weston School for Girls .... Weston

MICHIGAN

Adrian College .... Adrian*
Albion College .... Albion*
Alma College .... Alma*
Central State Normal School .... Mt. Pleasant
Ferris Institute .... Big Rapids
High School .... Ypsilanti
Hillsdale College .... Hillsdale*
Hope College .... Holland*
Kalamazoo College .... Kalamazoo*
Michigan Agricultural College .... East Lansing*

Olivet College .... Olivet*
State Normal College .... Ypsilanti*
University of Michigan .... Ann Arbor*
Western State Normal School .... Kalamazoo

MINNESOTA

Albert Lea College .... Albert Lea*
Carleton College .... Northfield*
College of Agriculture .... St. Paul
Hamline University .... St. Paul*
Macalester College .... St. Paul*
Northwest School of Agriculture .... Crookston
Pillsbury Academy .... Owatonna*
St. Paul's College .... St. Paul Park*
School of Agriculture .... St. Paul*
State Normal School .... Mankato*
State Normal School .... Moorhead
State Normal School .... Winona
University of Minnesota .... Minneapolis*
West Central School of Agriculture .... Morris
Windom Institute .... Montevideo*

MISSISSIPPI

Agricultural and Mechanical College .... Alcorn
Agricultural High School .... Oakland
Belhaven Collegiate Industrial Institute .... Jackson
Grenada College .... Grenada
Industrial Institute and College .... Columbus*
Jackson College .... Jackson
Mississippi Normal College .... Hattiesburg
Mississippi Synodical College .... Holly Springs*
Pearl River County Agricultural High School .. Poplarville
Rust College .... Holly Springs
Southern Christian Institute .... Edwards
Tougaloo University .... Tougaloo
University of Mississippi .... University*
Utica Institute .... Utica
Whitworth College .... Brookhaven*
Woman's College .... Meridian

MISSOURI

American School of Osteopathy .... Kirksville*
Carleton College .... Farmington
Central College .... Fayette

Central College .... Lexington*
Central Wesleyan College .... Warrenton*
Christian College .... Columbia
Cottey College .... Nevada*
Drury College .... Springfield*
Forest Park University .... St. Louis
George R. Smith College .... Sedalia
Hardin College .... Mexico*
High School .... Kirksville*
Howard Payne College .... Fayette*
Iberia Academy .... Iberia*
Kidder Institute .... Kidder*
Lexington College .... Lexington*
Lincoln Institute .... Jefferson City
Lindenwood College .... St. Charles*
Missouri Valley College .... Marshall*
Missouri Wesleyan College .... Cameron*
Northwest State Normal School .... Maryville*
Park College .... Parkville*
Scarritt Morrisville College .... Morrisville
South West Baptist College .... Bolivar
Southeastern State Normal School ...... Cape Girardeau*
State Normal School .... Kirksville*
State Normal School .... Springfield*
State Normal School .... Warrensburg*
Stephens College .... Columbia*
Synodical College .... Fulton*
Tarkio College .... Tarkio*
University of Missouri .... Columbia*
Washington University .... St. Louis
William Woods College .... Fulton*

MONTANA

Montana Wesleyan University .... Helena*
State Agricultural College .... Bozeman*
State Normal School .... Dillon
University of Montana .... Missoula*

NEBRASKA

Bellevue College .... Bellevue*
Cotner University .... Lincoln*
Doane College .... Crete*
Franklin Academy .... Franklin*

Fremont Normal School ....Fremont*
Grand Island College ....Grand Island*
Hastings College ....Hastings*
High School ....Franklin
High School ....Seward
Nebraska Central College ....Central City*
Nebraska Wesleyan University ....University Place*
Santee Normal Training School ....Santee
School of Agriculture ....Lincoln
State Normal School ....Chadron
State Normal School ....Kearney*
State Normal School ....Peru*
State Normal School ....Wayne
Teachers' College High School ....Lincoln
University of Nebraska ....Lincoln*
University of Omaha ....Omaha
York College ....York*

NEVADA
Carson Indian School ....Stewart
State University ....Reno*

NEW HAMPSHIRE
Colby Academy ....New London
New Hampshire College ....Durham
Sanborn Seminary ....Kingston*
State Normal School ....Plymouth
Tilton Seminary ....Tilton*

NEW JERSEY
Centenary Collegiate Institute ....Hackettstown*
State Normal School ....Trenton*

NEW MEXICO
College of Agriculture and Mechanic Arts ..State College
Indian School ....Albuquerque
University of New Mexico ....Albuquerque

NEW YORK
Adelphi Academy ....Brooklyn*
Alfred University ....Alfred*
Barnard College ....New York City*
The Castle, Miss Mason's School ....Tarrytown
Cazenovia Seminary ....Cazenovia*
Cornell University ....Ithaca*
Elmira College ....Elmira*

Genesee Wesleyan Seminary .... Lima*
Horace Mann School .... New York City
Hunter College .... New York City
Keuka College and Institute .... Keuka
Mechanics Institute .... Rochester
Central Club for Nurses .... New York City
Studio Club .... New York City
St. Lawrence University .... Canton
State College for Teachers .... Albany*
State Normal School .... Fredonia*
State Normal School .... New Paltz*
State School of Agriculture .... Alfred
Syracuse University .... Syracuse*
Teachers' College, Columbia University ... New York City
University of Rochester .... Rochester*

North Carolina

Bennett College .... Greensboro
Brevard Institute .... Brevard*
Carolina College .... Maxton
Davenport College .... Lenoir*
East Carolina Teachers' Training School ..... Greenville
Elizabeth College .... Charlotte*
Elon College .... Elon*
Greensboro College for Women .... Greensboro*
Guilford College .... Guilford*
Joseph K. Bricks School .... Bricks
Lincoln Academy .... King's Mountain
Linwood College .... Gastonia*
Littleton College .... Littleton
Louisburg College for Women .... Louisburg*
Meredith College .... Raleigh*
Morrison Industrial School .... Franklin
National Religious Training School .... Durham
Normal and Collegiate Institute .... Asheville*
Normal and Collegiate Institute .... Albemarle
Oxford College .... Oxford*
Peace Institute .... Raleigh*
Queens College .... Charlotte*
Salem College .... Winston-Salem
Shaw University .... Raleigh
Southern Presbyterian College .... Red Springs*

State Normal College .... Greensboro*
State School for the Blind .... Raleigh*
Statesville Female College .... Statesville

NORTH DAKOTA

Fargo College .... Fargo*
Jamestown College .... Jamestown
New Rockford Collegiate Institute .... New Rockford
State Agricultural College .... Fargo*
State Normal Industrial School .... Ellendale*
State Normal School .... Mayville*
State Normal School .... Minot
State Normal School .... Valley City*
University of North Dakota .... University*

OHIO

Ashland College .... Ashland*
Baldwin-Wallace College .... Berea
Bluffton College .... Bluffton
Bonebrake Theological Seminary .... Dayton
Cedarville College .... Cedarville
Cincinnati Conservatory of Music .... Cincinnati
College of Wooster .... Wooster*
Defiance College .... Defiance*
Denison University .... Granville*
Findlay College .... Findlay*
Franklin College .... New Athens*
Glendale College .... Glendale*
Heidelberg University .... Tiffin*
Hiram College .... Hiram*
Lake Erie College .... Painesville*
Lebanon University .... Lebanon*
Marietta College .... Marietta*
Miami University .... Oxford*
Mount Union Scio College .... Alliance*
Municipal University of Akron .... Akron
Muskingum College .... New Concord*
Oberlin College .... Oberlin*
Ohio Northern University .... Ada*
Ohio Soldiers and Sailors' Orphans' Home .... Xenia
Ohio State University .... Columbus*
Ohio University .... Athens*
Ohio Wesleyan University .... Delaware*

Otterbein University ....Westerville*
Oxford College ....Oxford*
Savannah Academy ....Savannah*
State Normal School ....Kent
University of Cincinnati ....Cincinnati*
Western College ....Oxford*
Western Reserve University ....Cleveland*
Wilberforce University ....Wilberforce*
Wilmington College ....Wilmington*
Wittenberg College ....Springfield*

OKLAHOMA

Agricultural and Mechanical College ....Stillwater*
Agricultural and Normal University ....Langston
Bacone College ....Bacone*
Central State Normal College ....Edmond*
East Central State Normal School ....Ada
Eufaula Boarding School ....Eufaula
Henry Kendall College ....Tulsa
High School ....Tulsa
Indian School ....Chilocco
Kingfisher College ....Kingfisher
Methodist University of Oklahoma ....Guthrie*
Northwestern Normal School ....Alva*
Oklahoma College for Women ....Chickasha
Oklahoma Institute of Technology ....Tonkawa*
Oklahoma Presbyterian College ....Durant
Phillips University ....Enid
Southwestern Normal School ....Weatherford*
Tuskahoma Female Seminary ....Tuskahoma
University of Oklahoma ....Norman*
Wheelock Academy ....Millerton

OREGON

Albany College ....Albany*
High School ....Dallas
High School ....Eugene
McMinnville College ....McMinnville
Oregon Agricultural College ....Corvallis*
Pacific College ....Newberg*
Pacific University ....Forest Grove*
Philomath College ....Philomath*
Salem Indian Training School ....Chemawa

State Normal School .... Monmouth
University of Oregon .... Eugene*
Willamette University .... Salem*

PENNSYLVANIA

Albright College .... Myerstown*
Allegheny College .... Meadville*
Beaver College .... Beaver*
Beechwood College .... Jenkintown
Birmingham School for Girls .... Birmingham*
Bucknell University .... Lewisburg*
Central State Normal School .... Lock Haven*
Cumberland Valley State Normal .... Shippensburg*
Darlington Seminary .... West Chester*
Dickinson College .... Carlisle*
Dilworth Hall .... Pittsburg
Friends' School .... Germantown
Geneva College .... Beaver Falls
Grove City College .... Grove City*
Indian School .... Carlisle
Irving College .... Mechanicsburg*
Juniata College .... Huntingdon
Keystone State Normal School .... Kutztown*
Lebanon Valley College .... Annville*
Moravian Seminary and College for Women —. Bethlehem
Penn Hall .... Chambersburg
Pennsylvania College for Women .... Pittsburgh*
Pennsylvania Museum and School of Industrial Art......
.... Philadelphia
Perkiomen Seminary .... Pennsberg*
Philadelphia College of Osteopathy .... Philadelphia
Shippen School .... Lancaster
Southwestern State Normal School .... California*
State College .... State College
State Normal School .... Bloomsburg*
State Normal School .... Clarion*
State Normal School .... East Stroudsburg
State Normal School .... Edinboro*
State Normal School .... Indiana*
State Normal School .... Mansfield*
State Normal School .... Millersville*
State Normal School .... West Chester*

Stevens School .... Germantown
Susquehanna University .... Selins Grove
Swarthmore College .... Swarthmore
University of Pittsburgh .... Pittsburgh
Ursinus College .... Collegeville
Walnut Lane School .... Germantown
Washington Seminary .... Washington
Waynesburg College .... Waynesburg*
Westminster College .... New Wilmington*
Williamsport Dickinson Seminary .... Williamsport*
Wilson College .... Chambersburg*
Women's Medical College of Pennsylvania ..... Philadelphia*
Wyoming Seminary .... Kingston*

RHODE ISLAND

East Greenwich Academy .... East Greenwich

SOUTH CAROLINA

Allen University .... Columbia
Anderson College .... Anderson
Benedict College .... Columbia
Chicora College .... Greenville
Claflin University .... Orangeburg
Clifford Seminary .... Union
Coker College for Women .... Hartsville
College for Women .... Columbia
Columbia College .... Columbia*
Confederate Home College .... Charleston*
Converse College .... Spartanburg*
Erskine College .... Due West*
Greenville Female College .... Greenville*
Lander College .... Greenwood*
Limestone College .... Gaffney*
Penn. Normal and Agricultural School .... St. Helena Island
Sterling Industrial College .... Greenville
Winthrop Normal and Industrial College ...... Rock Hill*
Woman's College .... Due West*

SOUTH DAKOTA

Dakota Wesleyan University .... Mitchell*
High School .... Mitchell*
Hope School .... Springfield
Huron College .... Huron*
Indian School .... Rapid City

Northern Normal and Industrial School ......Aberdeen*
Redfield College ....Redfield
Riggs Institute ....Flandreau
Sioux Falls College ....Sioux Falls
State Agricultural College ....Brookings*
State Normal School ....Spearfish
State Normal School ....Springfield*
University of South Dakota ....Vermillion*
Yankton College ....Yankton*

TENNESSEE

Agricultural and Industrial State Normal School... .... Nashville
Buford College ....Nashville
Carson and Newman College ....Jefferson City*
Centenary College ....Cleveland
Cumberland University ....Lebanon*
East Tennessee Normal School ....Johnson City
Fisk University ....Nashville
Grandview Normal Institute ....Grandview
Knoxville College ....Knoxville
Lane College ....Jackson
Lincoln County High School ....Fayetteville
Lincoln Memorial University ....Hurrogate
McFerrin School ....Martin
Martin College ....Pulaski
Maryville College ....Maryville*
Middle Tennessee Normal ....Murfreesboro
Morristown Normal College ....Morristown
Radnor College ....Nashville
Roger Williams University ....Nashville
Tusculum College ....Tusculum*
University of Chattanooga ....Chattanooga*
University of Tennessee ....Knoxville*
Ward-Belmont College ....Nashville*
West Tennessee State Normal School ....Memphis

TEXAS

Baylor University ....Waco
Bishop College ....Marshall
Clarendon College ....Clarendon
College of Industrial Arts ....Denton*
Coronal Institute ....San Marcos*

Daniel Baker College ....Brownwood*
Houston College ....Houston
Howard Payne College ....Brownwood*
North Texas College ....Sherman
North Texas State Normal School ....Denton
Phillips University ....Tyler
Prairie View Normal and Industrial College..Prairie View
Rice Institute ....Houston
Sam Houston Normal Institute ....Huntsville*
Simmons College ....Abilene
Southwest Texas State Normal School .....San Marcos*
Southwestern University ....Georgetown
State School for the Blind ....Austin*
Texas Christian University ....Fort Worth*
Texas Fairmont Seminary ....Weatherford
Texas Presbyterian College ....Milford
Texas Woman's College ....Fort Worth
Tillotson College ....Austin
Trinity University ....Waxahachie*
University of Texas ....Austin*
West Texas State Normal School ....Canyon

VERMONT

Burr and Burton Seminary ....Manchester
Middlebury College ....Middlebury*
Montpelier Seminary ....Montpelier
Troy Conference Academy ....Poultney*
University of Vermont ....Burlington*

VIRGINIA

Blackstone Female Institute ....Blackstone*
Eastern College ....Manassas*
Hollins College ....Hollins*
Martha Washington College ....Abingdon
Mary Baldwin Seminary ....Staunton*
Miller Manual Labor School ....Miller School*
Normal and Industrial Institute ....Ettricks
Oak Park Institute ....Oak Park
Randolph-Macon Institute ....Danville
Randolph-Macon Woman's College ....Lynchburg*
Roanoke Institute ....Danville
Shenandoah Collegiate Institute ....Dayton
Southern Seminary ....Buena Vista*

State Normal School ....East Radford
State Normal School ....Farmville*
State Normal School ....Fredericksburg
State Normal and Industrial School ......Harrisonburg
Stonewall Jackson Institute ....Abingdon*
Sullins College ....Bristol*
Sweet Briar College ....Sweet Briar
Virginia College ....Roanoke*
Virginia Intermont College ....Bristol*
Virginia School for the Deaf and Blind ....Staunton
Westhampton College ....Richmond
Williamsburg Institute ....Williamsburg
Woman's College ....Richmond*

WASHINGTON

Cushman Indian School ....Tacoma
State Normal School ....Bellingham*
State Normal School ....Cheney*
State Normal School ....Ellensburg
University of Puget Sound ....Tacoma*
University of Washington ....Seattle*
Washington State College ....Pullman*
Whitman College ....Walla Walla*
Whitworth College ....Spokane*

WEST VIRGINIA

Bethany College ....Bethany*
Broaddus Institute ....Philippi
Concord State Normal School ....Athens*
High School ....Fairmont
Keyser Preparatory School ....Keyser*
Lewisburg Seminary ....Lewisburg*
Marshall College ....Huntington*
Morris Harvey College ....Barboursville
Salem College ....Salem
Shepherd College ....Shepherdstown*
State Normal School ....Fairmont
State Normal School ....Glenville
State Normal School ....West Liberty
West Virginia Collegiate Institute ....Institute
West Virginia University ....Morgantown*
West Virginia Wesleyan College ....Buckhannon*

WISCONSIN
- Beloit College .... Beloit*
- Carroll College .... Waukesha*
- Indian School .... Tomah
- Indian School .... Wittenberg
- Lawrence College .... Appleton*
- Milton College .... Milton
- Milwaukee-Downer College .... Milwaukee*
- Northland College .... Ashland
- Ripon College .... Ripon*
- State Normal School .... La Crosse
- State Normal School .... Milwaukee
- State Normal School .... Oshkosh
- State Normal School .... Platteville*
- State Normal School .... River Falls*
- State Normal School .... Stevens Point*
- State Normal School .... Superior
- State Normal School .... Whitewater*
- Stout Institute .... Menomonie
- University of Wisconsin .... Madison*
- Wayland Academy .... Beaver Dam*

WYOMING
- University of Wyoming .... Laramie*

PORTO RICO
- Presbyterian Hospital .... San Juan

NATIONAL BOARD

Of the Young Women's Christian Associations of the United States of America

600 Lexington Avenue
New York City

Telephone, 6000 Plaza   Cable Address, Outpost, New York

OFFICERS

Mrs. Robert E. Speer, *President*
Mrs. John French, *Chairman Executive Committee*
Mrs. James S. Cushman, *First Vice-President*
Mrs. William W. Rossiter, *Second Vice-President*
Mrs. Thomas S. Gladding, *Secretary*
Mrs. Samuel J. Broadwell, *Treasurer*

Miss Annie M. Reynolds, *Chairman Department of Field Work*
*Miss Elizabeth W. Dodge, *Chairman Department Conventions and Conferences*
Miss Annie M. Reynolds, *Chairman Secretarial Department*
Mrs. W. W. Rockwell, *Chairman Publication Department*
Mrs. Dave Hennen Morris, *Chairman Finance Department*
Mrs. G. K. Swinburne, *Chairman Office Department*
Mrs. Charlton Wallace, *Chairman Department of Method*
Mrs. James M. Speers, *Chairman Town and Country Committee*
Mrs. Charles N. Judson, *Chairman City Committee*
Miss Gertrude E. MacArthur, *Vice-Chairman City Committee*
Miss Clara Stillman Reed, *Chairman Student Committee*
Mrs. Augustus B. Wadsworth, *Chairman Foreign Department*
Mrs. Samuel Murtland, *Chairman Buildings Committee*

---

*Mrs. Elizabeth P. Allan
*Mrs. E. B. Burwell
Mrs. Edward S. Campbell
Miss Maude Daeniker
Mrs. Henry P. Davison
Mrs. R. A. Dorman
Miss Leila S. Frissell
*Mrs. John M. Hanna
*Mrs. J. H. Hoskins
Mrs. Clarence M. Hyde
Mrs. Francis de Lacy Hyde
Mrs. R. C. Jenkinson
Mrs. Seabury Cone Mastick
Mrs. Frederick Mead
Mrs. John R. Mott
*Mrs. Warren Olney, Jr.
*Mrs. R. H. Passmore
Mrs. Francis B. Sayre
Mrs. Finley J. Shepard
*Miss Helen M. A. Taylor
*Mrs. George Vaux, Jr.
*Mrs. William Shaw Ward

AUXILIARY MEMBERS

Mrs. Lemuel Bolton Bangs
Mrs. F. S. Bennett
Mrs. Robert L. Dickinson
Mrs. William Francis Dominick
Mrs. Charles H. Ferry
Miss Anna C. McClintock
Miss Florence M. Marshall
Miss Margaret Mead
Mrs. James Pedersen
Mrs. Arthur G. Stone
Mrs. Warren H. Wilson

* Field representatives.

FIELD COMMITTEES

Mrs. C. C. Bullock, *Chairman;* Mrs. Irwin Rew, *Treasurer,* Central

Mrs. George Vaux, Jr., *Chairman;* Mrs. Wm. L. McLean, *Treasurer,* Delaware, Maryland and Pennsylvania

Mrs. Charles P. Noyes, *Chairman;* Mrs. W. O. Winston, *Treasurer,* North Central

Miss Elizabeth Dodge, *Chairman;* Mrs. Stanley Rumbough, *Treasurer,* Northeastern

Mrs. E. B. Burwell, *Chairman;* Mrs. Charles Denny, *Treasurer,* Northwestern

Miss Helen M. A. Taylor, *Chairman;* Mrs. F. D. Phinney, *Treasurer,* Ohio and West Virginia

Mrs. Warren Olney, Jr., *Chairman;* Mrs. A. Crawford Greene, *Treasurer,* Pacific Coast

Mrs. Elizabeth Preston Allan, *Chairman;* Mrs. Joseph C. Patton, *Treasurer,* South Atlantic

Mrs. D. S. Brown, *Chairman;* Mrs. C. C. Rainwater, *Treasurer,* South Central

Mrs. John M. Hanna, *Chairman;* Mrs. W. D. Felder, *Treasurer,* Southwestern

Mrs. William Shaw Ward, *Chairman;* Mrs. C. A. Graham, *Treasurer,* West Central

SECRETARIAL STAFF
NATIONAL BOARD OF THE YOUNG WOMEN'S CHRISTIAN ASSOCIATIONS

Headquarters Secretaries

Mabel Cratty, *General Secretary*
Isabel Norton, *Secretary to the General Secretary*
Rebecca F. McKillip, *Social Secretary*

Henrietta Roelofs, *Special Worker*
Helen A. Ballard, *Publicity Secretary*
Mrs. Isabella H. Santee, *Buildings Manager*

SECRETARIAL DEPARTMENT

Elizabeth Wilson, *Executive*
Edith N. Stanton, *Director Bureau of Reference*
Nellie Starr Stevens, *Office*
Caroline B. Dow, *Dean of Training System*
Elizabeth L. Dean, *Assistant to the Dean*
Mary Scott, *Registrar*
Grace Quackenbush, *Bursar*

FINANCE DEPARTMENT

Harriet Taylor, *Acting Executive*
Ella Schooley, *Finance Secretary*
Helen Sanger, *Office Executive*
Jessie MacKinlay, *Cashier and Bursar*

DEPARTMENT OF CONVENTIONS AND CONFERENCES

Mabel Cratty, *Acting Executive*
Louise W. Brooks, *Student*
Bertha W. Seely, *Office*

PUBLICATION DEPARTMENT

Mary Louise Allen, *Executive*
Helen Thoburn, *Editorial Secretary*
Rhoda E. McCulloch, *Editorial Secretary*
A. Estella Paddock, *Editorial Secretary*
Margaret Cook, *Business Manager*

OFFICE DEPARTMENT

Margaret F. MacKinlay, *Executive*
(Office Secretaries listed under departments)

FOREIGN DEPARTMENT

Clarissa H. Spencer, *Acting Executive*
Susan M. Clute, *Office Executive*

DEPARTMENT OF FIELD WORK

Helen A. Davis, *Executive*
Katharine Scott, *Office Executive*

DEPARTMENT OF METHOD

Louise Holmquist, *Executive*
Elizabeth Boies, *Office Executive*
Bertha Condé, *Senior Student Secretary*
Mabel T. Everett, *Student Office Executive*
Mary S. Sims, *City Office Executive*
Leslie Blanchard, *State Universities*
Eva D. Bowles, *Colored Work, Cities*
Mrs. Harry M. Bremer, *Immigration Work*
Anna L. Brown, *Physical Education and Hygiene*
Oolooah Burner, *Church Schools*

Margaret Burton, *Missionary Interests*
Eliza R. Butler, *Secondary Schools*
Ethel Cutler, *Religious Work, Student and Country*
Edith M. Dabb, *Indian Schools*
Jessie Field, *Town and Country*
Blanche Geary, *Economic Work*
Gertrude E. Griffith, *Girls' Work*
Josephine V. Pinyon, *Colored Schools*
Anna V. Rice, *Religious Work, City*
Anna Seaburg, *Large Towns*
Florence Simms, *Industrial Work*
Helen L. Thomas, *Education*

FIELD SECRETARIES

PACIFIC COAST

(Arizona, California, Nevada.)
319 Russ Building,
San Francisco, Cal.

Lillian E. Janes, *Executive*
Alice Moore, *Girls' Work*
Sarah Oddie, *County*
Mary I. Bentley, *Student*
Helen Topping, *Special Worker*
Kathleen I. Bartholomew, *Office*

DELAWARE, MARYLAND AND PENNSYLVANIA

630 Witherspoon Building,
Philadelphia, Pa.

Mary Johns Hopper, *Executive*
Lucy P. Carner, *Assistant Executive*
Caroline Jones, *Special Worker*
Anna Owers, *Industrial—Extension*
Anna G. Seesholtz, *Student*
Caroline Foresman, *County*
Marjorie M. Persons, *Office*

NORTH CENTRAL

(Iowa, Minnesota, Nebraska, North and South Dakota.)
412 Flour Exchange,
Minneapolis, Minn.

Mrs. Emma F. Byers, *Executive*
——————, *City*
Clara I. Taylor, *Industrial—Extension*
Margaret O'Connell, *County*
Adelia Dodge, *Student*
Josephine Lynch, *Student*
Edith Helmer, *Student*
Harriet A. Cunningham, *Office*

SOUTHWESTERN

(New Mexico, Oklahoma, Texas.)
512 Sumpter Bldg.,
Dallas, Tex.

Mabel K. Stafford, *Executive*
Mildred Corbett, *City*
Marguerite Stuart, *Student*
Helen S. Whiting, *Office*

NORTHWESTERN

(Idaho, Montana, Oregon, Washington.)
Fifth Ave. and Seneca St.,
Seattle, Wash.

Jane Scott, *Executive*
Grace Maxwell, *City*
Eleanor Hopkins, *Student*
Van S. Lindsley, *Office*

WEST CENTRAL

(Colorado, Kansas, Utah, Wyoming.)
321 McClintock Bldg.,
Denver, Colo.

Marcia O. Dunham, *Executive*
M. Frances Cross, *City*
Lucy Y. Riggs, *Student*
Katharine Halsey, *Student*
Ethel Adams, *Office*

SOUTH ATLANTIC

(Florida, Georgia, North and South Carolina, Virginia.)
512 Commercial Bank Bldg.,
Charlotte, N. C.

Amy Smith, *Executive*
Ada Starkweather, *City and Industrial*
Mabel E. Stone, *Student*
Willie Young, *Student*
Carrie McLean, *Office*

CENTRAL

(Illinois, Indiana, Michigan, Wisconsin.)
58 East Washington St.,
Chicago, Ill.

Ida V. Jontz, *Executive*
Elva Sly, *City*
Gertrude Gogin, *Industrial—Extension*
Maud Trego, *County*
Mary Corbett, *Student*
Eleanor Richardson, *Student*
Elcy McCausey, *Office*

SOUTH CENTRAL

(Alabama, Arkansas, Kentucky, Louisiana, Mississippi, Missouri, Tennessee.)
1411 Locust St.,
St. Louis, Mo.

Elizabeth MacFarland, *Executive*
Charlotte Davis, *City*
Ina Scherrebeck, *Student*
Frances Y. Smith, *Student*
Sara Foster, *Office*

OHIO AND WEST VIRGINIA

1211 First National Bank Building,
Cincinnati, Ohio

Elizabeth Hughes, *Executive*
Harriet Harrison, *City*
Constance MacCorkle, *Industrial—Extension*
Mabel H. Ward, *Student*
Margaret Brown Moore, *Office*

NORTHEASTERN

(New England, New Jersey, New York.)
600 Lexington Ave.,
New York City

Pauline Sage, *Executive*
Lena M. Farrar, *City*
Mary A. Dingman, *Industrial—Extension*

Anna M. Pyott, *Industrial—Extension*
Anna M. Clark, *County*
Margaret Flenniken, *Student*
Helen Farquhar, *Student*
Lucy T. Bartlett, *Office Executive*

American Secretaries on Foreign Field

INDIA

Florence Bodley Lang,
Myra Withers,
170 Hornby Road, Bombay
Martha C. Whealdon,
Wellington Lines, Bombay
Beatrice Cron,
Mary E. Rutherford,
134 Corporation Street, Calcutta
Florence Denison,
Y. W. C. A., Lahore
Lela Guitner (*on leave of absence*)
Martha Downey,
Margery Melcher,
Poonamallee Road, Madras, N. C.
Laura Radford,
Singapore, Straits Settlement

CHINA

Abby Shaw Mayhew,
Grace L. Coppock,
Freeda Boss,
Ruth Paxson,
Box 713 American P. O., Shanghai
Harriet L. Boutelle,
Jessie K. Angell,
Jean Paxton,
cr. Y. W. C. A., Canton
Helen Bond Crane,
Helen Harshaw,
Ponasang, Foochow
Theresa Severin,
Lilly K. Haass,
Harriet M. Smith,
Catharine Vance,
cr. Y. W. C. A., Peking
Jane S. Ward,
Henrietta Thomson,
Edith Sawyer,
10 West End Lane, Shanghai
Katharine King,
Edith May Wells,
cr. Y. W. C. A., Tientsin

JAPAN

Ruth Emerson,
Ruth Ragan,
12 Tamachi Sanchome, Ushigome, Tokyo
Margaret Matthew,
Mary Page,
41 Sanbancho Kojimachi-Ku, Tokyo
Mary C. Baker,
51 Main St., Yokohama

SOUTH AMERICA

Irene Sheppard,
Persis M. Breed,
Elisa Cortez,
Calle San Martin 243 Buenos Aires, Argentina

TURKEY

Frances C. Gage,
cr. Constantinople College, Constantinople

INDEX

A

Adam, Rev. John Douglas, 235
Adams, Annie L. (Baird), 72
Adams, Charlotte H., 73, 105, 250
Adolescent Girl, The, 298
Albion College, Michigan, 128, 132
Alcott, Louisa May, 5
Allen, Mrs. Dudley P., 227
Allen, Lou (Gregory), 96
Alliance Employment Bureau, 213
Altamont, 291
Althouse, Carrie, 122
Alumnæ in state conventions, 131
  in religious and social service, 273
American department of the World's Y. W. C. A., 188
American Committee, 183–195
American Tract House, 24, 103
Ames, Iowa, 95
Amity Place, N. Y. City, 25
Anderson, Esther L., 190, 311
Ann Arbor, Michigan, 123
Annual Members, 275
Appleton, Wisconsin, 122
Argentina, The, 303
Arkansas, 238
Armstrong, Mary, 152
Asbury Park, 78
Asheville, 246
Asilomar, 247, 321
Associated Charities, 56
Association House, 70
Association Idea, 8
  See also Purpose of Association
"Association Monthly, The," 234
Atlanta Conference, 272
Augusta, Georgia, Y. W. C. A., 283
Aurora Y. W. C. A., 70, 283
Australasia, 311

B

Bacon, Mrs. N. B., 240
Bainbridge, Mrs. W. S., 192
Baker, Mrs. Stephen, 228
Balfour, Lady Frances, 102
Baltimore Y. W. C. A., 83, 87, 104, 217
Bangs, Dr. Nathan, 22
Barnes, Helen F., 157, 190, 294, 311
Barnes, Dr. Ida C., 240
Barnet, England, 9
Barrows, Anna, 46
Basis of Active Membership, 221–222
Bates, Eula (Lee), 72, 133
Batty, Emma Jean, 307
Bay View Assembly, 175
Bay View Cottage, 172
Beach, Rev. Harlan P., 180

Beech, M., 121
Benfey, Ida (Judd), 177
Bennett, Estelle, 152
Berlin, Germany, 260
Bernadotte, Prince, 147
Berninger, Martha (Mrs. Thomas Kydd), 189, 306, 308
Bevier Bell (Isabel), 131
Bible Classes, 34, 46, 67–71, 141
Bible Reading, 69
Billings, Mary (Mrs. John French), 228
Birmingham, England, 20
Bishop, Isabella Bird, 314
Blodgett, Mary E., 44, 45
Bloomington, Illinois, 114, 128, 132, 173
Boarding Homes, 34, 76–78
Boarding Places, 32
Boies, Col. H. M., 240
Boies, Mrs. Henry M., 228, 240
Bonar, Mrs. Horatius, 10
Boston Y. W. C. A., 29–49, 65, 80, 90, 91, 95, 96, 100, 102, 159
Bosworth, Professor Edward I., 250
Boulton, Mrs. William B., 228
Boyd, Mrs. Lucretia, 29
Bradford, Mrs. L. P., 133
Bradley, James A., 78
Branches—not departments, 11
Bridges, Frances (Mrs. George H. Atkinson), 190
Brinton Hall, 151
Bristol, England, 20
British American Association, *see* Paris, France
Broadus, Dr. John A., 123
Broadway Tabernacle, 22
Broadwell, Mrs. S. J., 227
Brockman, Fletcher S., 305
Brooklyn Y. W. C. A., 70, 98, 101, 282, 283
Brown, Dr. Anna L., 73, 203, 219, 263
Brown, Ida E. (Mrs. James Cary), 116
Brown, Lida (Mrs. William P. McMurry), 115, 116
Browne, Mrs. P. D., 163
Brownell, Eleanor, 235
Bryant, W. C., 85
Buckley, Dr. James M., 177
Buffalo W. C. A., 55, 159
 Y. W. C. A., 101, 290
Buenos Aires, Argentine, 307
Buildings, 105–107, 151, 270, 281, 282, 308
"Bulletin, The," 205, 234
"Bundle of Letters to Busy Girls, A," 214
Burnham, Mary, 120
Business Women's Club, 283
Busy Girls' Half Hour, 104
Buxton, Mrs. W. S., 219

C

Cabot, Dr. Richard C., 321
Cafeteria, 84
Calcutta, India, 183, 304
California, 238
Calisthenics, *see* Physical Education
Cambridge Band, 144
Cameron, Minnie (Mrs. J. V. Hartness), 120
Campbell, Mrs. E. M., 228
Campbell, Helen, 105
Camp Collie, 171, 172, 295
Camp Nepahwin, 291
Canada, 175, 183, 311
Canton (English Branch), 305
Camp Fire Girls, 299

Camps, *see* under Conference Department and Summer Homes
Capitola, 246
Carbondale, Illinois, Y. W. C. A. of the S. I. N. U., 121
Carleton College, Minnesota, 59, 156
Cascade, 246
Cassiday, Jennie, 79
Cedar Rapids, Iowa, 129, 132, 282
"Century Magazine," 105
Chappell, Neva A., 105
Charlotte, N. C., 238
Charter members, 225, 255
Chauncey Street, Boston, 33
Chautauqua, 96, 171, 202, 296
Chicago, 171–173, 196–199
Chicago Y. W. C. A., 102, 160, 197
China, 303, 306, 308
Chinese Indemnity Students, *see* Foreign Students in America
Christian Endeavor Society, 59, 132, 155
Christian Improvement Association, 17
Christian Women's Education Union of Scotland, 126
"Christian Worker, The," 204
Chun, Ying Mei, 308
Church, *see* Basis of Active Membership and Federal Council
Church of the Puritans, 22
Cincinnati, 238
Cincinnati W. C. A., 53, 56, 95, 97, 159
City Associations (after 1906), 281–288
Civil War, 6, 91
Cleveland W. C. A., 53, 54, 56
Close Hall, 151
Club Organizations, 86, 87
Coe College, Iowa, 129
Coeducational Colleges, 108–114, 124–133
Coldwater, Michigan, Y. W. C. A., 100
College Associations, *see* Student Y. W. C. A.'s
Colored Associations, 271, 239
  City, 285
  Conferences, 271
  Student, 271
Commercial Studies, 91
Commissions
  Character Standards, 265
  Domestic Service, 76
  Restatement of Student Basis, 276–278
  Social Morality, 265
  Thrift and Efficiency, 265
Committee on Schools and Colleges, 126, 170
Communion of the Lord's Supper, 314
Condé, Bertha, 190, 235, 270
Conference Department
  Before 1906, *see* Summer Conferences
  Camps, 291, 296
  City, 288
  County, 295
  Student, 246
Conferences of the International Board
  1891—196–198, 216
  1893—198–200
  1903—200
  1905—202, 223
Conferences of the W. C. A., 159–166
  1871, 1873—125
  1875—169

Conferences of the W. C. A. —*Continued.*
1877—169, 197
1881—125, 167
1883—128, 167
1885—168–171, 216
1887—170
Conferences of the W. S. C. F.
1895, Vadstena Castle, 147
1897, Williamstown, 279
1905, Zeist, 148
1913, Lake Mohonk, 278, 279
Conferences of the World's Y. W. C. A.
1898, London, 311–314
1906, Paris, 307
1910, Berlin, 260–263
1914, Stockholm, 314
Constantinople College, 327
Constitution
Boston, 32
City, 23, 32
International Conference, 162
Student, 115, 127
World's Y. W. C. A., 313
Y. W. C. A.'s of U. S. of A., 254–259
See also Basis of Active Membership
Conventions of National Association—later The American Committee
1886—171–173
1889—173
1891—175
1893—62
1899—183, 188
1901—188
1903—189, 194
1905—218
1906, special, 223
Conventions, State, 130–133, 242–244
Conventions, Y. M. C. A., 119, 128, 256, 257
Conventions of the Y. W. C. A.'s of the U. S. of A.
1906, New York City, 225–227
1909, St. Paul, 237, 254–259
1911, Indianapolis, 263
1913, Richmond, 264, 265, 276
1915, Los Angeles, 277
Cooke, Helen Temple, 235
Cooking Classes, *see* Domestic Science
Cooper, Hon. Peter, 94
"Cooperative patience," 235, 251
Cornell College, Iowa, 128
Corson, Juliet, 96, 97, 165
Country Associations, 132, 153–158, 292–296
County Organization, 156–158, 292–296
Cratty, Mabel, 193, 321
Crete, Nebraska, 121
Crimean War, 9
Crosby, Dr. Howard, 256
Cross, Frances, 193
Cunningham, Miss, 120
Cushman, Mrs. J. S., 227
Cutler, Ethel, 273

D

Daeniker, Maud, 228
Dashwood, G. L., 165
Davis, Mrs. John, 53, 159
Day Nursery and Kindergarten Society, 56
Day of Prayer for Colleges, 111
Dayton, Ohio, W. C. A., 55, 104
Decker, Debbie, 121
Delegation to Cincinnati, 168

Delaware, 238
Delsarte, 99
Democracy, 86, 288
Denominational Colleges, 108–114
Department of Method, 252
Depauw University, Indiana, 129
de Perrot, Mlle. Anna, 163
Detroit Y. W. C. A., 70, 291
Dick, Jean, 72
Dick, Nellie (Adams), 72
District of Columbia, 218, 239
Doane College, Nebraska—Young Ladies' Society of Co-workers, 121
Dodge County, Minnesota, 157
Dodge, Grace H., 87, 149, 165, 192, 206–251, 262, 263; 284, 319, 326–328
Dodge, William Earl, Jr., 124
Doheny, Ella, 67
Domestic Art, 46, 93–95
Domestic Circle, 212
Domestic Economy, 46, 95
Domestic Science, 41, 46, 96–98
Domestic Service, 41–44, 75–76
Dorcas Societies, 5
Dorman, Mrs. R. A. (Mary Aitken), 219, 227, 229
Dow, Caroline B., 250
Downey, Anna, 168
Drinkwater, Charlotte V., 37–47
Drummond, Professor Henry, 147, 165
Dryer, Emma, 176
Duncan, Mrs. John C. (Fanny Cassiday), 204
Dunn, Helen (Mrs. L. M. Gates), 58
Dunn, Mary S., 100, 177, 190
Dunn, Nettie (Mrs. Walter J. Clark), 60, 174–176, 318
Durant, Mrs. Henry F., 32, 45, 50
Durkee, Mrs. F. L., 227
Dyer, Rev. Heman, 24

E

"Earnest Worker, The," 204
Ecumenical Missionary Conference
  New York, 1900, 148
  Edinburgh, 1910, 210
Educational Classes, 33, 36, 87–98
Eight Week Clubs, 294
Elliott, Arthur J., 235
Elliott, Harrison, 273
Elliott, J. H., 176
Ellis Island, 301
El Paso, Illinois, 293
Emergency Lectures, 43
Employed Officers, 318
  Chaplain, 67
  County secretary, 292
  Extension secretary, 105, 194
  Foreign secretary, 63, 146
  Girls' secretary, 297
  General secretary, 317
  Lunchroom director, 323
  Matron, 323
  National secretary
    headquarters, 233
    field, 237
  Physical director, 100, 322
  Religious work director, 72, 270
  Secretary of colored branches, 272
  State secretary, 133–137
  Student secretary, 152
  Superintendent, 16

Employed Officers—*Continued.*
Traveling secretary, 133–137, 318
World's Secretary, 182, 193
Employed Officers' Conference
1909—319
1911—320
1913—321
1915—321
See also Secretaries' Conferences, 1889, 292, 318
Employment Bureau, 41, 73–76
Eureka, Illinois, 292
"Evangel, The," 135, 189, 234, 303
Evangelical Alliance, 112
Evangelical Basis
See Basis of Active Membership, Commission on Restatement of Student Basis, Constitutions, Federal Council of Churches
Evangelical Churches, 222, 255–259, 273
Evangelistic Campaigns, 130, 141, 270, 287
Ewing, Mrs. Emma P., 46
Exeter Hall, 102, 312
Expositions in U. S. A.
1876—95
1893—189, 198, 199
1901—200
1904—200, 201, 203
1905—200
1915—266–268
abroad, 1851—92
abroad, 1900—200

F

"Faith and Works," 204
Farmington, 206
Farwell, Mrs. John V., Jr., 173
Federal Council of Churches, 257–259
Federation of Clubs, 291
Female Cent Societies, 6
Field, Frances, 224, 235, 236
Field Work Department, 236–241
Fifty-second Street, N. Y. City, 266
Fillmore County, Minnesota, 156, 157
Finance, 85, 242–245, 282
After 1906, *see also* Finance Department
Finance Department, 241–246
Finland, 311
Finney, Rev. Charles G., 5, 7
First Aid to the Injured, 43, 284
Fisher, Martha S. (Mrs. E. E. Stacy), 57
Foochow (English Branch), 305
Methodist School and Seminary, 305
Ford, Mabelle, 263
Foreign Department, 252, 309
Foreign Students in America, 279, 309, 310
Foreign Work, 183–189
After 1906, *see* Foreign Department
Forman, John N., 145
Foster, Mary, 33, 317
France, 311
French, Daniel Chester, 278
French, Mrs. John (Mary Billings), 329
Fries, Dr. Karl, 148

G

Gage, Frances C., 308
Galesburg, Illinois, 129
Gates, Mrs. L. M. (Helen Dunn), 58, 240
Germantown, Pa., W. C. A., 55, 95, 104
Girl's Department, 87, 297
Girls' Friendly Society, 19
Girls' Public School Athletic League, 210
Gladding, Mrs. Thomas S. (Effie K. Price), 219, 226
Glasgow, Scotland, 20
"Gleaner, The," 204
Gordon, Mrs. A. D., 191
Gospel Meeting, 68
Gould, Helen Miller (Mrs. Finley J. Shepard), 219, 227, 295
Grace, Mayor, 208
Grace Whitney Hoff League, 291
Gramercy Park, 250, 266, 324
Gray, Rev. James M., 46
Great Britain, 21, 182, 311
Green, Mrs. Henry, 227
Greencastle, Indiana, 129, 132
Greenville and Tusculum College, Tennessee, 129
Gregg, Lucinda, 47
Griffith, Mrs. J. S., 219
Grinnell, Iowa, 129
Guinness, Geraldine (Mrs. Howard Taylor), 304
Guinness, Lucy, 145
Gymnasium, *see* Physical Education

H

Hall, Thirsa F., 174
Hammond, E. P., 115
Hang Chow, China, 303
Hanover College, Indiana, 124
"Harland, Marion," *see* Terhune
Harlem Y. W. C. A., 70
"Harriet Judson, The," 283
Harrison, President Benjamin, 149
Hartford, Conn., 37, 50, 125, 159, 160
Haskell Institute, 273
Havergal, Frances Ridley, 11, 163
Hawaii, 239
Hays, Emma, 190, 219
Hearst, Mrs. Phoebe, 243–247
Hendrix, Bishop E. E., 258
Henrotin, Mrs. Charles, 198
Hermosa Club, 284
Hill, Agnes Gale, 62, 185–187, 304
Hill, Mary B., 186, 187
Hillsdale College, Michigan, 58, 128
Hitchcock & Rogers, 7, 8, 316
Hoff, Mrs. John Jacob (Grace Whitney Evans), 310
Holland, J. G., 85
Holmes, O. W., 85
Hong Kong (English Branch), 305
Hooker, Mrs. Isabella Beecher, 51
Hoopskirt Factory, 24, 103
Hopkinton, Iowa, 121
Hospital, 34
Household Arts, *see* Domestic Economy
Howard, General O. O., 256
Hunt, Rosamund (Gordon), 120
Hunter, Ethel (Mrs. Charles deJ. Luxmoore), 304

Hunton, Mrs. W. A. (Addie Waite), 271
Hunting, Bernice, 72
Huntington, Emily, 46, 207
Hymn of the Lights, 264

I

Illinois, 72, 132
Illinois Industrial University—later University of Illinois, 96
Illinois State Normal University, 114–119, also *see* Normal
Illinois Wesleyan University, 128
Immigrants, 300–302
India, 183–188, 303, 304, 308
Indian Associations, 272
Indiana, 132
Indianapolis, 263
Industrial Education Association, 207
Industrial Extension, 24, 103–105, 289–291
Institute, 17, 194, 195, 248
See also Secretarial Training
"Intercollegian, The," 276
Intercollegiate Y. M. C. A., 122–124
Intercollegiate Y. W. C. A., 119, 134, 147
International Board, 196–205
International Committee of the Y. W. C. A.—later The American Committee, 173–183
International Institute, 301
"International Messenger, The," 204, 234
Invitation Committee, 69
Iowa, 132, 154, 155
Iowa Agricultural College, 95
Iowa College (later Grinnell College), 129
Iowa Wesleyan College, 128
Irene Club, 211–213

J

Japan, 303, 306, 308
Jenkinson, Mrs. R. C., 227
Johnson County, Iowa, 153, 154
Joint Committee, The, 223–227
Judson, Mrs. C. N., 219, 227

K

Kalamazoo, Michigan, Y. W. C. A., 58, 155, 105
Kalamazoo College, Michigan, 128
Kansas, 72, 133, 155, 244
Kansas Agricultural College, 95
Kansas City, Mo., 280
Kansas City Y. W. C. A., 62, 84, 102
Kawai, Michi, 262, 306, 322
Kingsmill, Agnes, 250
Kinnaird, The Hon. Arthur (later Lord K.), 15–17
Lord (son of founder), 165
The Hon. Emily, 15, 165, 183–184
The Hon. Gertrude, 165, 183
Mary Jane (Lady), 15–20
Kirkland School, 84
Kitchen Garden Association, 207
Knight, Naomi (Mrs. O. M. Easterday), 135, 168, 172
Know Your City Week, 286

Knowles, Mary (Mrs. Walter Lindsay), 80
Knox College, Illinois, 129
Knox, Nellie (Mrs. F. E. Miller), 133
Kyle Margaret (Mrs. E. E. Barber), 190

L

Ladies' Christian Association, *see* New York
Ladies' Christian Union, *see* New York
Ladies' Prayer Meeting, 22, 50, 66
Lake Geneva, 171, 178, 246
Lake Mohonk, 278, 279
Lamson, Mrs. Edwin, 30, 38, 126, 160
Lahore, India, 189
Lancaster, Mass., Industrial School, 38
Lancaster, Penn., Y. W. C. A., 283
Larcom, Lucy, 4, 5
Larkin Y. W. C. A., 290
Lasell Seminary, Mass., 96
Lawrence, Kas., Y. W. C. A., 58
Lawrence, Mass., Y. W. C. A., 301
Lawrence University, 122, 129
Lenox College, Iowa, 121
LeSeur, Pastor, 262
Lewis, Dr. Dio, 99
Lewis, Flora (Gallup), 120
Lexington Avenue, N. Y., 266
Library, 87–89
Lincoln, Mrs. D. A. (Mary J. Bailey), 46, 96
Lindsey, Walter, 80
Literary Societies, 113–114, 139
Little Girls' Christian Association, 297
Liverpool, England, 20
London, 7–21, 30, 101, 160
Longfellow, Henry W., 34
Los Angeles, 238, 283, 301
Louise Cecile School, 204
Louisville, Ky., W. C. A., 79
  Intercollegiate Y. M. C. A., 124
  Conference on Colored Associations, 239
Low, Hon. Seth, 214
Lowell, Maria White, 5
Lowell, Mass., 4, 159
Lowell, Mass., Y. W. C. A., 224
Lucknow College, 148
Lyon, Mary, 5

MAC

MacDonald, A. Caroline, 306
MacDougal, Evelyn, 176

MC

McAfee, Rev. Cleland B., 226
McAlpin, Mrs. D. H., 85
McCollins, Mrs., 164
McConaughy, David, 181, 186, 187
McConaughy, Mrs. David, 187, 228
McCook, Janet (Mrs. Malcolm D. Whitman), 227, 246, 328
McCormick, Mrs. Cyrus H., Sr., 195
McCrea, Mrs. F. F., 240
McDougal, Mrs. John, 125
McKenzie, Elizabeth, 292

M

Madras, India, 184–186
Manchester, England, 20

Manhattan Conference, The, 219–223
Mansion House, London, 313
"Margaret Louisa, The," 82
Mary Clark Memorial Home, The, 283
Maryland, 238
Mayhew, Abby S., 61, 100, 309, 322
Members' Council, 283
Membership, 64, 138, 265
Merom Christian College, Indiana, 128
Messer, L. Wilbur, 71, 325
Messer, Mrs. L. Wilbur, 228, 229, 325
Metropolitan Organizations, 271, 282
Michigan, 72, 132, 155
Mildmay, 9
Miller, H. Thane, 54, 55, 125, 160
Miller, Mrs. H. Thane (Emma P. Smith), 119, 125–129, 167
Mills College, 246
Mill Villages, 290
Milwaukee Y. W. C. A., 104, 105, 282
Minneapolis W. C. A., 58–60
  Y. W. C. A., 58–61, 105, 282
Minnesota, 133, 157
Minonk, Illinois, 293
Mission Board Representatives, 276
Missionary Meetings, 71
Missionary Societies, 6
Missouri, 236, 238
Monaghan Mills Y. W. C. A., 290
Montclair, The, 234
Monteagle, 203
Montgomery, Ala., Y. W. C. A., 101
Montreal, Canada, 31, 126, 163
Moody, D. L., 51, 52, 143, 191
Moor, Lucy M., 12
Morning Watch, 140, 178, 305
Morrison, Theresa, 306
Morse, Rebecca F., 72, 87, 181, 188, 189
Morse, Richard C., 85, 225
Mosher, Dr. Eliza, 98
Mott, John R., 71, 143, 145, 147, 226, 272
Mott, Mrs. John R., 228
Mottoes
  Associates, 331
  International Board, 332
  National Committee of Y. W. C. A.'s, 331
  Prayer Union, 330
  World's, 331
  Y. W. C. A. of U. S. A., 332
Mt. Auburn Institute, 125
Mt. Hermon, 142–145, 191
Mt. Holyoke Seminary, 5
Muller, daughter of George M., 11
Mullens, Priscilla, 300

N

Nagasaki, Japan, 303
Naperville, Illinois, 120
Narey, Hope, 100
National Association, later The American Committee, 142, 171–173
National Board, 226–259, 277
National Cash Register factory, 104
National Headquarters, 266, 282
National Training School, 249, 250, 323–325

National Vigilance Committee, later American Social Hygiene Association, 215
Nebraska, 122, 133
Negro Student Conference, *see* Colored Associations
Nevada, 238
Newark, N. J., W. C. A., 55, 224
Newburgh, N. Y., Y. W. C. A., 100, 107
Newell, Alice (Mrs. Lloyd Davis), 189
New England Pastors, 34
New England States, 236
New Haven Y. W. C. A., 90, 97
New Jersey, 236
New York City, 238
New York City Board of Education, 208
New York City, Ladies' Christian Association, 23–25, 103
Ladies' Christian Union, 25, 50
Young Ladies' Branch (later Y. W. C. A.), 55, 67, 74, 85, 91, 92, 100, 105
New York Cooking School, 96
Nightingale, Florence, 14, 327
New York State, 236
Noon Rest, 83
Normal, Illinois, 114–119, 124
Normal Schools, 108
"North American Student, The," 276
North American Student Council, 276
North Carolina, 238
Normal University, *see* Illinois State Normal University
Northfield Conference, 191, 246
North London Home, 16, 65
Northwestern College, Illinois, Y. L. C. A., 120, 168
Norway, 21, 182, 311
Nurses' Central Club, 270

O

Oakland, California, Y. W. C. A., 297
Ober, C. K., 71
Oberlin Collegiate Institute, 5
Occupations, 35, 75, 91
Office Department, 234
Ogontz School, 84, 208
Ohio, 132, 155, 236, 238
Olivet College, Michigan, Y. W. C. A., 120
Omaha Y. W. C. A., 70
Onondaga Indian Club, 283
Orlebar, Maude, 304
Orrock, Rev. J. M., 47
Oskaloosa, Iowa, 129
Otis, Dr. Edward O., 43
Otterbein University, Ohio, 128, 151
Oxford Movement, 7

P

Pacific Grove, 247
Paddock, A. Estella, 193, 306
Pageant, Ministering of the Gift, 264
Palmer, Mrs. Potter, 198
Panama Pacific International Exposition, 266
Parker, Thomas F., 290
Parloa, Maria, 42, 96

Paris, France,
British American Association, 310
Student Hostel, 308, 310
World's Conference, 307
Parsons College, Iowa, 128
Patriotic Fund, 9
Paxson, Ruth, 190
Pearl Street Church, Hartford, 50, 159
Penn College, Iowa, 129
Pennefather, Catherine (Mrs. William), 9–12, 20, 163
Pennefather, William, 9
Pennsylvania, 238, 244
Pentecost, Dr. George F., 183
Peoria, Illinois, Y. W. C. A., 292
Personal Evangelism, 136, 141
Personal Work, 136, 141
Philadelphia, 238
Philadelphian Society, Princeton, 124
Philadelphia, W. C. A., 55, 74, 78, 82, 91, 100, 159
Philistines, 239
Phillips, Ann Greene, 5
Phillips, Philip, 51
Phillips, T. W., 175
Physical Director, 44
Physical Education, 43, 98–101, 308
Pitkin, Horace Tracy, 145
Pittsburgh, W. C. A., 52
Y. W. C. A., 105
Pleasant Valley, Johnson County, Iowa, 153, 154
Policies of National Board, 234–259
Portland Definition, 256, 257
Poughkeepsie Y. W. C. A., 83, 97, 100, 297
Prayer for Times of Retreat, 279
Prayer Meetings—*see* religious meetings
Prayer Union, 10, 19, 20
Preston, Minn., 156, 157
Price, Effie Kelly (Mrs. Thomas S. Gladding), 189, 191
Price, Prof. Ira M., 250
Princeton University, Philadelphian Society, 124
Y. M. C. A., 124
"The Student Christian," 278
Protective Agents, 287
Providence, R. I., W. C. A., 51, 79, 159
Publication Department, 234
Purpose of Y. W. C. A.'s, 198, 255, 285

Q

Quarterly—*see* Y. W. C. A. Quarterly

R

Rainwater, Mrs. C. C., 240
Rawson, Mrs. C. A., 240
Red Cross Society, 284
Reed, Clara S., 235
Reid, Katharine, 250
Religious Meetings, 34, 66–70, 140, 286
Religious Work, 47
Residence, the Association, 283
Restaurant, 36, 80–84
Revival of 1857–58, 6, 22, 123
Rew, Mrs. Irwin (Katherine S. Jones), 194, 228
Reynolds, Annie M., 182, 188, 193, 228, 238, 246, 306
Reynolds, James Bronson, 147, 183, 214

Rice, Anna V., 322
Richards, Belle (Bunker), 72
Richards, Mrs. Ellen H., 45
Richardson, Mrs. J. B., 227
Riverdale, 206, 278
Roanoke, Illinois, 293
Robarts, Emma, 9–12, 19, 330
Roberts, Mrs. Marshall O., 22–25, 50, 328
Rochester Y. W. C. A., 282, 286
Rome, Italy, 163, 164
Rooms for Student Associations, 151
Roosevelt, Theodore, 249
Ross, Dr. A. Johnston, 315
Rossiter, Mrs. W. W., 227
Rouse, Ruth, 149, 188, 216
Russia, 311

S

Salt Lake City, 163
Sanders, Frank K., 180
Sanford, Rev. E. B., 225
Sanford, Mary F. (Mrs. William G. Morison), 235
San Francisco Y. W. C. A., 102
Sangster, Mrs. Margaret E., 177, 227
Saunders, Una, 321
Schell, Ida, 133, 168, 172
Schofield, Mrs. Levi T., 240
Schooley, Ella, 266
Scranton, Pa., Y. W. C. A., 58, 60, 100, 104
Seaside, 246
Secretarial Department, 248–251
Secretarial Training, 47, 193–195
  After 1906—*see* National Training School
Secretarial Training—*Continued.*
  Secretarial Department
  Summer School
  Training Centers
Self Governing Clubs, 87, 210–214, 284
Self Government
  Conferences, 275
  Residences, 283
Sewing Classes—*see* Domestic Art
Sewing Machines, 6, 77, 93–95
Shaftesbury, Seventh Earl of, 14, 18, 20, 101
Shanghai, China — Chinese Association, 188, 306, 308
  English Branch, 305
Shepard, Mrs. Elliott F., 82
Shepard, Mrs. Finley J. (Helen Miller Gould), 296
Sheppard, Lizzie, 121
Sherman, Jennie, 72, 133
Silver Bay, 192, 246
Silver, Emma, 72
Simms, Florence, 190
Singh, Lilavati, 148
Slocum, Mrs. William F., 228
Smith, Alice, 227
Smith, Mrs. Charles B., 50
Smith, Mrs. Hannah Whitall, 161
Smith, Mary Isabel, 105
Social Features, 84–86, 139
Social Service, 150, 273
South Africa, 311
South America, 307, 308
South Bend, Indiana, Y. W. C. A., 282
South Carolina, 238
South Church, New York City, 225

Speer, Robert E., 145, 226, 235
Speer, Mrs. Robert E., 219, 227, 235, 329
Spencer, Clarissa H., 145, 193
Springer, Mrs. C. R., 196
Springfield, Mass., W. C. A., 55, 95
Starkweather, Ella, 120
State Associations, 130–133, 168, 170
State Executive Committees, 130–133, 236–241
State Student Conferences (co-educational), 130–133
State Universities, 108, *also* under separate names
Statistics—1909, 253
  Alumnæ social service, 274
  Boston residents, 35
  Eight Week Clubs, 295
  Industrial, 289
  St. Joseph, Missouri, 57
  Student bodies, 269
Steiner, Edward A., 301
Stelzle, Rev. Charles, 226
Stenographers' Association, 283
Stewart, Emma V. (Mrs. I. E. Brown), 116
Stewart, Mary B., 240
Stewart, Mrs. William S., 202, 219
Stiles Hall, 151
St. Joseph, Mo., Y. W. C. A., 57
St. Louis, Mo., 125, 238
St. Louis W. C. A., 54, 56, 76, 85, 95, 97, 102
Stockholm, Sweden, 314
Stokes, James, 186–187
Stowe, Harriet Beecher, 5
Strangford, Viscountess, 15
St. Paul, Minnesota, 133, 254
Studd, J. E. K., 145
Student Initiative, 274–275
"Student Volunteer, The," 146, 276
Student Volunteer Movement, 142–146, 185, 276, 280
Studio Club, 271, 299
Student Y. W. C. A.'s, 108–152
Students' Christian Association, 122, 123
Students' Handbook, 140
Sullivan, Captain Thomas, 30
Summer Conferences, 147, 175–180, 190–193. After 1906 *see* Conference Department
Summer Homes, 78–80, 283, 287
Summer School, 322–323
Sutcliffe, Charlotte, 250
Sweden, 21, 182, 311
Swift, John T., 181
Swimming, 101
Switzerland, 311
Syracuse, Y. W. C. A., 283

T

Taft, President, 284
Tarlton, J. H., 316
Tarr, Corabel (Mrs. William Boyd), 174, 181, 189
Taylor, Harriet, 190, 247
Teachers' College, 208
Terhune, Mrs. E. P. ("Marion Harland"), 74, 164, 177
Territorial Committees—*see* Field Work Department
Terry, Prof. M. S., 176
"Three P. Circle," 212
Thurston, Mrs. Frank T., 219, 226
Tokyo, Japan, Y. W. C. A., 308

Toledo, Ohio, Y. W. C. A., 62
Topeka, Kansas, 129
  Y. W. C. A., 58
Topics, 116, 130, 159, 161, 220, 319
Tractarian pamphlets, 7
Trained Attendants, 98
Training School. *See* National Training School for Domestic Service, 44, 95
Training Centers, 249–251, 324
Travelers' Aid, 44, 101–103, 200–202, 215, 267
Trenton, N. J., Y. W. C. A., 301
Tritton, Mrs. J. Herbert, 21
Trumbull, H. Clay, 51
Tsuda, Umé, 306
Tufts, Mrs. J. J., 219
Tung Cho, China, 180, 303
Turkey, 303, 308
Twenty-seventh Street, New York City, 266

U

Uhler, Mrs. M. C., 318
Union Internationale des Amies de la Jeune Fille, 163
Union of Previous National Bodies, 220–223
United Association, 18
United Central Council, 21
United States, 21, 182
University of California, 151, 247
  Illinois, 129, 146, 186, 270, 293
  Iowa, 151, 154
  Kansas, 273, 293
  Michigan S. C. A., 123
    Y. W. C. A., 293
  Minnesota, 152, 270
Universities—*Continued.*
  Nebraska, 129
  Nevada, 247
  Virginia Y. M. C. A., 123
  Wisconsin, 129, 152
Urbana, Illinois, 96
Utica W. C. A., 55

V

Vacation Lodge—*see* Summer Homes
Vadstena Castle, 147
Van Vliet, Bertha, 297
Vesper Tea, 70
Victoria, Queen, 312, 314
Vincent, Mrs. B. T., 227
Virginia, 238
Voluntary Christian Education, 273
Volunteer Workers, 318

W

Washburn, Illinois, 293
Washburn College, Kansas, 129
Washington, D. C., W. C. A., 55, 159, 217, 222
Washington, D. C., Y. W. C. A., 217, 222, 283
Webb, Mrs., 42
Week of Prayer, 242, 313
Weidensall, Robert, 124, 156, 157
Welles, Anna (Mrs. J. Wylie Brown), 308
Wellesley College, 44, 46
Wells, Mrs. Shepard, 78
Western Secretarial Institute, 171, 178
Westerville, Ohio, 128, 132
West Point, 278
West Virginia, 238
Whirlwind Campaign, 282
White Slave Treaty, 215

Whitewater, Wisconsin, 132
Whitman, Mrs. Malcom D. (Janet McCook), 328
Whittelsey, Mrs. J. T., 219
Wilder, Grace, 143
Wilder, Robert P., 143
Williams, Sir George, 7, 8, 312, 316
Wilson, Mrs. A. McD., 228
Wilson, Annis, 122
Wilson, Elizabeth, 174, 189, 195, 219, 235
Wilson, Jessie Woodrow (Mrs. Francis B. Sayre), 294
Wilson Industrial School, 207
Wisconsin, 132
Wishard, Luther D., 119, 124–129, 147, 180
Wishard, Mrs. L. D. (Eva Fancher), 180, 303
Witbeck, Ida (Mrs. Charles DeGarmo), 116
Wolff, Maude, 105
Wood, Anna, 44
Woodford County, Illinois, 290
Wooster University, Ohio, 129
Woman's Medical College, 151
Woman's Municipal League, The, 214
Woman's Work, 3–6
Women's Christian Association, 125–126
Women's Colleges, 126, 138
Women's Exchange, 56
Women's Missionary Societies, 6, 121
Worcester, Mass., 237
Worcester Y. W. C. A., 97, 100, 101
Workers' Training Class, 71, 141
World's Badge, 313
"World's Nickel," 242
World's Student Christian Federation, 147–150, 277, 310
World's Y. W. C. A., 21, 181–183, 277

X–Y

Yokohama, Japan, 306
York, Pa., Y. W. C. A., 89
Young Ladies' Christian Association, 9, 115, 125, 150
Young Men's Christian Association, 8, 22, 30, 50, 52, 53, 58, 99, 101, 115, 121, 122, 123, 124, 134, 147, 153, 157, 173, 213, 221, 255, 273, 312, *et passim*
Youngstown, Ohio, Y. W. C. A., 282
Young Women's Christian Association
(use of name), 11, 16, 18
Y. W. C. A. Quarterly, 135, 189, 220
Ypsilanti, Michigan, Y. W. C. A., 58

Z

Zirkus, Busch, 261
Zone Club House, 267